Michael Esfeld (Ed.)
John Heil
Symposium on his Ontological Point of View

METAPHYSICAL RESEARCH

Herausgegeben von / Edited by

Uwe Meixner • Johanna Seibt
Barry Smith • Daniel von Wachter

Band 6 / Volume 6

Michael Esfeld (Ed.)

John Heil

Symposium on his
Ontological Point of View

ontos
verlag

Frankfurt I Paris I Ebikon I Lancaster I New Brunswick

Bibliographic information published by Die Deutsche Bibliothek
Die Deutsche Bibliothek lists this publication in the Deutsche Nationalbibliographie;
detailed bibliographic data is available in the Internet at http://dnb.ddb.de

Printed with the financial support of the Centre romand Logic, History and Philosophy of Science

North and South America by
Transaction Books
Rutgers University
Piscataway, NJ 08854-8042
trans@transactionpub.com

United Kingdom, Eire, Iceland, Turkey, Malta, Portugal by
Gazelle Books Services Limited
White Cross Mills
Hightown
LANCASTER, LA1 4XS
sales@gazellebooks.co.uk

Livraison pour la France et la Belgique:
Librairie Philosophique J.Vrin
6, place de la Sorbonne; F-75005 PARIS
Tel. +33 (0)1 43 54 03 47; Fax +33 (0)1 43 54 48 18
www.vrin.fr

©2006 ontos verlag
P.O. Box 15 41, D-63133 Heusenstamm
www.ontosverlag.com

ISBN 3-938793-27-9

2006

No part of this book may be reproduced, stored in retrieval systems or transmitted
in any form or by any means, electronic, mechanical, photocopying, microfilming, recording or otherwise
without written permission from the Publisher, with the exception of any material supplied specifically for the
purpose of being entered and executed on a computer system, for exclusive use of the purchaser of the work

Printed on acid-free paper
FSC-certified (Forest Stewardship Council)

Printed in Germany
by buch bücher **dd ag**

Table of contents

Acknowledgements		9
Introduction		11
1	John Heil. On being ontologically serious	15
2	Simon Friederich & Giovanni Tuzet. Inflating truthmakers. A critique of the primitive notion of truthmaking in Heil's ontological picture	29
	John Heil. Commentary	43
3	Jens Harbecke. Levels of being being there?	47
	John Heil. Commentary	71
4	Vera Hoffmann. Can Heil's ontological conception accommodate complex properties?	75
	John Heil. Commentary	87
5	Christian Sachse. Inter-theoretic deduction of explanations	91
	John Heil. Commentary	109
6	Vincent Lam. Is a world only made up of relations possible? A structural realist point of view	111
	John Heil. Commentary	121
7	Georg Sparber. Powerful causation	123
	John Heil. Commentary	139
8	Laurent Freland. Is Heil's theory a really determinate realism? Dispositionalist realism and identity theory	143
	John Heil. Commentary	169

9 Flavia Padovani. Laws of nature, modal realism and realist lawlessness 173

   John Heil. Commentary 189

10 Michael Esfeld. From being ontologically serious to serious ontology 191

   John Heil. Commentary 207

11 Michael Sollberger. Representationalism and tactile "vision" 213

   John Heil. Commentary 231

12 Marc Aurel Hunziker. Intentionality is not only a mark of the cognitive 235

   John Heil. Commentary 249

Bibliography 251

Index 263

Notes on contributors 273

Acknowledgements

This book goes back to a symposium with John Heil in Lausanne on 9 and 10 February 2006. The symposium was part of the PhD programme of the Centre romand for logic, history and philosophy of science. In the first place, I would like to thank John Heil for having accepted our invitation and for the pain he took in responding to the students' papers. Furthermore, I'm grateful to all the participants for having submitted a written version of their paper soon after the symposium. Georg Sparber and Alain Zysset then prepared the pdf file of this book with great care. Last but not least, I would like to express my gratitude to the editors of the series "Metaphysical Research" for having accepted our book proposal, to Rafael Hüntelmann for the excellent editorial collaboration, and to the Centre romand for logic, history and philosophy of science for its financial support of this publication.

Lausanne, July 2006   Michael Esfeld

Introduction
Michael Esfeld

Fifty years after Willard Van Orman Quine published *From a logical point of view* (1953), John Heil brought out his book *From an ontological point of view* (2003). The title expresses the shift in contemporary philosophy from logical and epistemological concerns that were at the centre of the debate between logical empiricism and its critics to metaphysics. In that respect, Heil's book is a milestone in current philosophy, because it urges us to avoid loose talk, putting our ontological cards on the table. There is a lot of philosophers' shop-talk today in terms of, for instance, thinking subjects standing in relations to propositions, or facts being out there in the world, or second-order properties being realised by first-order properties, etc. If one uses such concepts – or whatever other concepts – in conceiving and expressing one's beliefs, one has to spell out what it is that makes true the beliefs that one holds true. That's what being ontologically serious means. "Truthmaking" stands in Heil's book simply for the commitment to make explicit what grounds the truth of a belief, for any belief that one holds true. Heil does not enter into a detailed theory of what truthmaking consists in, accepting truthmaking in that sense as a primitive notion.

Of course, being ontologically serious does not mean that one can or should compare one's beliefs to what there is in the world. It is a truism that one can only seek to achieve a comprehensive and coherent system of beliefs. However, that truism does not amount to putting epistemology before metaphysics. This system includes beliefs about the nature of beliefs. That truism does therefore not prevent the question of what is a belief (or a text, or a discourse to use more fashionable terms) from being a sensible one, indeed the first question to be asked and answered about beliefs, thus establishing the project of a metaphysics of mind and cognition as a central philosophical topic among others. In short, in doing philosophy, in whatever area of philosophy, one cannot but put metaphysics first.

The content of Heil's metaphysics is built around two theses: the first one is the rejection of levels of being and, consequently, the commitment to a sort of ontological reductionism. The second one is the view that each property is both categorical (or qualitative) and dispositional. The distinction between "categorical" and "dispositional" concerns predicates, not properties. Each property makes true categorical and dispositional descriptions.

The first thesis puts Heil in opposition to mainstream functionalism. In that respect, Heil's position is close to the reductive physicalism of David Lewis, or Jaegwon Kim, although Heil subscribes neither to the type identity thesis nor to epistemological reductionism (theory reduction). Moreover, Heil, in contrast to Lewis, is not a Humean. The second thesis puts him in the camp of those who seek to rehabilitate a metaphysics of dispositions or powers against the mainstream broadly Humean current as regards laws, causation, and dispositions. Both mainstream functionalism and mainstream Humeanism about laws, causation, and dispositions have come under a forceful attack in the last decade or so. The debate on these issues is again open. Heil's book is a major contribution to that debate, seeking to move contemporary metaphysics into the direction of ontological reductionism and the conception of powerful properties.

The contributions to the present symposium on *John Heil's ontological point of view* mainly focus on these fundamental issues, but also consider some of the applications, notably in the philosophy of mind. The first paper by *Simon Friederich & Giovanni Tuzet* scrutinises Heil's methodology of tying ontological seriousness to truthmaking, questioning the rationale of a primitive notion of truthmaking. The following three papers are devoted to the topic of levels of being and reductionism: *Jens Harbecke* argues against Heil that levels of being have to be acknowledged if Heil is to avoid the charge of eliminativism. *Vera Hoffmann* does not go as far as Jens Harbecke in her criticism of Heil, but maintains that it is not clear how complex properties can be vindicated within Heil's metaphysics. *Christian Sachse*, by contrast, accepts Heil's ontological reductionism and goes beyond Heil, linking ontological reductionism with epistemological reductionism (theory reduction). He sets out a proposal in that respect that is intended to avoid the objection from multiple realisability.

The following five papers discuss Heil's theory of properties. *Vincent Lam* argues that Heil's commitment to the fundamental physical properties being intrinsic properties is unjustified in the light of contemporary physics. He makes a case for structural realism, arguing against Heil that we have good reasons for believing that our world is a world made up only of relations. *Georg Sparber* seeks to rehabilitate the conditional analysis of disposition ascriptions against Martin's and Heil's arguments that are based on finkish dispositions. Against that background, he envisages adopting an eliminativist attitude towards dispositions. *Laurent Freland* claims that Heil's view of properties being both categorical and dispositional is incoherent: "categorical" and "dispositional" are descriptions that exclude each other. If both are considered as applying to the same property, we have to introduce the notion of conceptual schemes. Consequently, Heil's realism is compromised. *Flavia Padovani* considers the view of laws of nature that Heil should adopt, comparing this view to the one of Nancy Cartwright. *Michael Esfeld* seeks to combine Heil's ontological reductionism with his theory of properties, arguing that the latter opens up the perspective of a conservative reductionism in contrast to an eliminativist one.

The last two papers consider the application of Heil's ontology of properties to the philosophy of mind: *Michael Sollberger* challenges Heil's arguments in favour of intrinsic, non-representational qualia and wonders whether the admission of such qualia fits into Heil's theory of properties. *Marc Aurel Hunziker* points out that Heil's conception of intentionality wavers between the position that intentionality is the mark of mental, representational states and the view according to which there is a sort of natural intentionality characteristic of all dispositions. He argues in favour of acknowledging unconscious representational states.

Chapter 1

On being ontologically serious
John Heil

1   The veil of language

Let me say at the outset how grateful I am to Michael Esfeld, to his students and colleagues, to the *Centre romand for logic, history and philosophy of science*, and to the University of Lausanne for arranging the workshop from which the current volume sprang and for providing me with an opportunity to discover all the ways I have managed to fall short of philosophical perfection. Meanwhile, I shall avail myself of the opportunity to dig myself more deeply into holes excavated in *From an ontological point of view*.

The aim of the book was less to promote a particular ontology than to urge the abandonment of a way of doing philosophy that begins and ends with language. If you start with language, you never move beyond language. We put words to work in describing the world, but we are not screened off from the world behind a veil of language. We move around among, touch, sit on, rearrange, and ingest worldly entities. We also speak about them. When it comes to our contact with the world, language is in no sense privileged.

This all seems so obvious as not to be worth mention. Philosophical practise suggests otherwise, however. In today's philosophical climate it is common to encounter cases in which descriptions of a subject matter go proxy for the subject matter itself. Symptoms of this tendency include talk of worldly states or properties being "disjunctive" or "conditional", or as "entailing" other worldly states or properties. They include, as well, appeals to propositions, Janus-faced entities partaking of both linguistic and worldly natures, and commitments to totality or "that's-all" facts underlying universal and negative truths. Most telling of all, perhaps, we are encouraged to treat questions of the form, could A's be B's? – could statues be clouds of particles? – as implicit requests for analyses: can we analyse or translate talk of A's into B-talk?

As an antidote to these trends, I have suggested that, when defending ontological theses we philosophers focus on potential truthmakers for those theses. What I have in mind can be illustrated by reflecting on attitudes nicely exemplified by Enlightenment philosophers. Locke, Descartes, Leibniz and

Spinoza, for instance, regarded it as an open question what ontological categories items answering to ordinary singular terms and predicates belong to. This approach would nowadays be seen as bordering on the incomprehensible. But consider: for Locke, persons turn out to be, not substances, but modes, ways substances are. In this he departs from Descartes. But both Locke and Descartes agree with Spinoza that what we think of as ordinary material substances are in fact modes, particular ways material substances are organised, or perhaps local 'thickenings' of a single, all-encompassing One.

Philosophers today draw eliminativist conclusions from such doctrines. If what we call tables, for instance, are, in fact, nothing more than ways the particles are arranged, then there are no tables, only particles in motion. We know this because close attention to the table concept reveals that anything answering to that concept must have a substantial nature.

This is not at all how Locke and his Enlightenment compatriots saw it. We use the table concept to delineate salient features of our environment, features with which we enjoy extensive and ongoing extra-linguistic interactions. We are equipped to investigate these features systematically and thereby to plumb their nature. In so doing, we are not promoting eliminativist or narrowly reductionist ends, but providing a deeper account of what tables and the like really amount to. Although there is little prospect of analysing talk of tables into talk of particles in motion or fields, tables could turn out to be fleeting arrangements of particles in motion or transient goings-on in regions of space-time. I shall say more about truthmaking presently, but first I should like to illustrate the attitude I have tried to promote by reemphasising a line of argument with application to issues in the philosophy of mind and, increasingly, in the philosophy of science.

2 Multiple realisability

Few ideas in the philosophy of mind today enjoy wider support than the notion that states of mind are "multiply realisable". Arguments for multiple realisability were popularised by Hilary Putnam (1967) and Jerry Fodor (1968) as responses to attempts by Place (1956), Smart (1959), and others to identify states of mind with specific neurological goings-on. The problem is that creatures could diverge neurologically, yet answer to the same psychological descriptions. You and an octopus, we suppose, can feel pain. But you and the octopus differ dramatically in your neurological makeup. When you are in pain, what goes on inside you that might be a plausible candidate for identification with your experience of pain differs strikingly from candidate octopodean states potentially identifiable as experiences of pain. Such examples could be multiplied indefinitely and extended to merely possible creatures. There is little prospect, then, of identifying the property of being in pain with any neurological property.

One possibility is that there are no pains: pains are fictions. The possibility is one few would endorse. We are invited, instead, to conclude that the "pain property" is identifiable, not with any neurological property, but with a "higher-level" property "realised" by an open-ended collection of neurological properties.[1] Each of these realising properties plays a distinctive causal role in a complex system. Being in pain, then, is a matter of being in a state (by virtue of possessing a property) that plays the right sort of causal role. Properties playing this role are not themselves the pain property. How could they be? They differ among themselves. Properties playing the pain role are mere vehicles for the pain property. If we distinguish roles something plays from occupants of those roles, we can say that pains – and indeed mental properties generally – are "roles not occupants".[2] Once you accept this line of argument, you can see that it has applications everywhere. The special sciences appear to concern distinctive realms of multiply realised properties. Functional kinds are common in biology, for instance. Thus, having a heart is not a matter of possessing an organ with a particular kind of physical makeup; it is to possess an organ that plays a certain role. A moment's reflection reveals widespread use of functional terms in all the special sciences.

Such thoughts encourage a conception of the world as hierarchically "layered". At the fundamental level – assuming there is a fundamental level – we find entities and processes comprehended by basic physics. These are the unrealised realisers. Configurations of the elementary things realise assorted physical properties of the kind studied in chemistry and molecular biology. These properties, in turn, or their instances, realise still higher-level properties, which are themselves realisers of further properties. The upshot is a latter-day counterpart of the Great Chain of Being.

---

[1] In fact (so we are assured) properties realising pain properties – or mental properties generally – need not be neurological. An extraterrestrial creature with a silicon-based nervous system might experience pain. If an immaterial creature, an angel, for instance, could experience pain, pain would be realisable by some immaterial property. Although consistent with materialism, functionalism is not itself a species of materialism.

[2] The distinction between theories identifying states of mind with roles and theories that take mental terms as specifying occupants of those roles was originally made salient by Ned Block (1980).

3 The realisation relation

Despite the central place it occupies, philosophers exhibit very little agreement as to the ontology of realisation. Many of those who routinely invoke the concept, are blasé about making it clear what realisation amounts to. This is how it is in philosophy with doctrines concerning which there is broad agreement. What is a problem for everyone is no one's problem. Besides, it is sometimes suggested, given that the standing of the special sciences is grounded in the legitimacy of the realisation relation, we are entitled to finesse the question of what realisation amounts to. We accept quantum theory as true, after all, assuming that something about the world makes it true, even if we have no idea what that might be. Similarly, we can safely assume that perfectly respectable higher-level properties are multiply realised, without thereby incurring an obligation to spell out the details of how realisation is supposed to work.

The analogy is inappropriate, however. Quantum theory is an empirically inspired scientific theory. Talk of multiple realisation, in contrast, stems from philosophical reflections on scientific practise. To reject these reflections is not to reject the science they purport to illuminate. Doubts about multiple realisability are philosophical doubts. Proponents of multiple realisability have no business appealing to scientific practise to justify a favoured philosophical interpretation of that practise.

Invoking the realisation relation while remaining coy about its ontology is the antithesis of the attitude of ontological seriousness. In various places, I have decried what I have dubbed the Picture Theory, roughly the idea that you can "read off" ontology from language (see, for instance, Heil (2003), chapters 1 – 3). This philosophical tendency, what C. B. Martin calls "linguisticism", can be seen at work in discussions of multiple realisability (Martin and Heil (1999), § 2). We have a respectable predicate, "is in pain". This predicate can apply truly to a variety of actual and possible organisms. Further, we regard pains as causally efficacious: you seek an analgesic because your back aches. These homely observations, coupled with the idea that there is a one-one relation between predicates (or predicates figuring in causal locutions) and properties, yield the thesis that "is in pain" designates a property shared by everything to which it applies, or would apply, and in virtue of which it applies, or would apply.

So far, so good. Suppose, however, as I have supposed, it is true that both you and an octopus are in pain. Suppose, further, that your neurological state and the neurological state of the octopus are utterly different. Does this imply that your being in pain is not a matter of your being in a particular neurological state and an octopus's being in pain is not a matter of the octopus's being in a particular, but very different, neurological state? You would think that only if you thought that the pain predicate – "is in pain" – must designate a property shared by every entity to which it truly applies (and in virtue of which it truly applies).

But why suppose that? Certainly, many of the predicates we routinely deploy to express truths about the world fail to satisfy this principle. Wittgenstein (1953, §§ 65 – 70) made this point with respect to games, but it extends smoothly to most of the predicates we accept as legitimate in both everyday life and in the sciences. The predicate "is red", for instance, is satisfied by objects in virtue of those objects' possession of any of an open-ended family of similar properties. Why not suppose the same is true for psychological predicates: being in pain is not a matter of being in a single kind of state, but a matter of being in any of a family of similar states. If the functionalists are right, these states are similar by virtue of playing similar causal roles.[3] The states in question could be those identified by functionalists as realisers of the pain property.

In denying this thesis, you need not be denying the existence of pains or their causal efficacy. You are merely denying a patently implausible philosophical account of what this must mean. The pain predicate applies to distinct creatures in virtue of those creatures' possession of distinct, but similar, properties. Insofar as these properties figure in causal relations, it will be true that pains are causally efficacious. Difficulties remain of course: what of the qualitative dimension of states of mind? But the subject matter provides difficulties enough without our adding them by way of a gratuitous philosophical thesis. One way to appreciate the force of this conception is to compare the picture we get from the proponent of multiple realisability (figure 1) with the position I am recommending (figure 2).[4]

In figure 1, C_1 represents some higher-level predicate, F_1 stands for a putatively higher-level property answering to this predicate, and P_1, P_2, etc. are lower-level realisers of F_1. (C_1 might be "is in pain"; F_1, the corresponding property of being in pain and P_1, P_2, etc, distinct realisers of the pain property.)

On my view, such a conception saddles us with an unnecessary middleman, F_1. The need for F_1 arises from the assumption that realism about C_1 requires that the predicate, C_1, designates a property shared by everything to which C_1

---

[3] The resulting view resembles the kind of functionalism endorsed by two ontologically serious philosophers, David Lewis (1966, 1994b) and David Armstrong (1968).

[4] Figures 1 and 2 are borrowed from Heil (2003), p. 246. See also Kim 1993a.

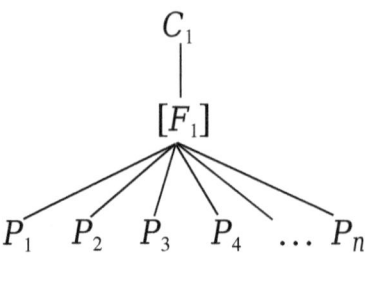

Figure 1

applies and in virtue of which it applies. Once we give up this assumption, a much simpler picture is available to us:

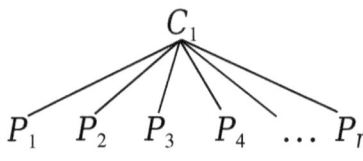

Figure 2

Here, C_1 is satisfied indifferently by any of a (possibly open-ended) family of properties, $P_1, P_2, P_3,..., P_n$.

Why prefer the latter picture to the former? The short answer is that the second better reflects the relation of mental predicates to features of the world answering to those predicates. Even philosophers unpersuaded by this line of reasoning are obliged to admit that higher-level properties are metaphysically dodgy. Ontologically candid philosophers wedded to such properties grant, for instance, that they lead to disturbing worries about "causal relevance". Cases in which higher-level properties might seem to make a causal difference appear, on closer examination, to be cases in which the realisers carry the causal burden.

Philosophers have offered accounts of "higher-level causation" that purport to evade these difficulties, but there is little agreement, even among those trafficking in higher-level properties, concerning the success of such accounts. The thought seems to be that it is just obvious that the special sciences are committed to higher-level properties and higher-level causal relations. We can relax, resting assured that someone will eventually work out the ontology of such things.

This strikes me as an especially strident form of philosophical hubris. We have the special sciences and we have a philosophical interpretation of what the world must be like in light of pronouncements of the special sciences. What is at issue is not the sciences themselves, but philosophical emendations to those sciences. Perhaps the best ontology for the special sciences is one that posits hierarchies of properties. This is scarcely obvious, however. The ontology I am proposing seems to fit scientific practise and lack manifest liabilities of the hierarchical view.[5]

4 Truthmaking

In the preceding discussion, I have helped myself to talk of truthmakers and truthmaking. The appealing idea that truths require truthmakers is one we lose sight of at our own peril. You could turn this into a doctrine or a principle and spell it out with analytical rigour. I am not convinced that this is either necessary or desirable, however. Think for a moment about definition. We define terms unselfconsciously; definitions often strike us as illuminating. The fact that no one has yet managed to produce an uncontroversial definition of "definition" does nothing to dampen our enthusiasm for definitions or their utility. The same holds for truthmaking. Attempts to provide an analytically exhaustive characterisation of truthmaking are bound to make use of terms and concepts more in need of clarification than truthmaking itself.

This is the kind of pronouncement that philosophers are trained to regard with suspicion. Surely, if truthmaking is a relation between something – a truthbearer – and something else – a truthmaker – we need some account of this relation and items it relates. David Armstrong tells us that the relation is one of necessitation: truthmakers necessitate truthbearers (Armstrong (2004a), p. 6). Is this helpful? Suppose truthmakers are, as Armstrong thinks, states of affairs. There are endless states of affairs. If every state of affairs necessitates some truthbearer, there are, as well, endless truthbearers. But what are these truthbearers? Presumably they are representations, items capable of possessing some truth value. Given their numerosity, it is implausible to imagine that

---

[5] Many kinds of hierarchy are perfectly inoffensive. Complex objects are made up of objects, which are themselves made up of objects, and so on. What are objectionable are hierarchical levels of being, property strata dependent on, but in no sense reducible to, properties at lower-levels.

necessitated truthbearers are sentences, or utterances, or beliefs harboured by finite creatures. Armstrong tells us that they are propositions.

I shall have more to say about propositions in a moment. Here I want only to note that we have moved from a simple notion of truthmaking to talk of necessitation relations between states of affairs and propositions. To my way of thinking, this is a move from the relatively clear to the much-less-clear – not a promising explanatory trajectory.

Is this just hand-waving? Consider the idea that truthmakers necessitate truths.[6] Something about this seems right. But appeal to necessitation is unhelpful unless we are clear about the nature of the necessitation in question. Suppose the *A*'s are necessitated by the *B*'s. This might be so if the *A*'s are the *B*'s, for instance, or if the *A*'s are caused by *B*'s, or if *B*'s make up the *A*'s. None of these species of necessitation appears apt in the case of truthmaking. My point is not to argue that truthmaking could not be a kind of necessitation, but only to indicate that, if you think you have made progress in characterising truthmaking in terms of necessitation, you had better be prepared to say something about the nature of the operative relation. If it were to turn out that the necessitation in question were *sui generis*, that would be bad news, a sign that we had made no analytical progress.

So we have the idea that truthmaking is a relation holding of necessity, but we are no nearer an understanding of what this relation might be. We know what it is not: it is not identity, it is not a species of causal relation, it is not a part-whole relation. Suppose, however, truthmaking were an internal relation (see Armstrong (1997), p. 199, (2004a), p. 9). To see what I have in mind, imagine two trees, *A* and *B*. *A* is six meters tall and *B* is five meters tall. This is all we need for it to be the case that *A* is taller than *B*. The taller-than relation holds between objects solely in virtue of those objects' intrinsic properties: if you have *A* and you have *B*, you thereby have *A*'s being taller than *B*. The taller-than relation is "no addition of being".

I follow Armstrong in thinking that this is how it is with truthmaking: if you have the truthmakers and the truthbearers, you have truthmaking. A conception of this sort puts the weight not on the relation between truthmaker and truthbearer – this, after all is no addition of being, nothing requiring further explanation – rather the weight falls on the side of the truthbearer. What makes it the case that a truthbearer represents the world as being a particular way?

---

[6] Another variation on this theme: "truth supervenes on being" (Bigelow (1988), chapter 19).

If we could figure that out, we would have done all we could to illuminate truthmaking.

If this is right, we can see what is problematic about the thought that truthmakers necessitate truths. Truths are not abstracta, not something in any sense brought about by worldly states of affairs. There is the world – in all its various ways – and there are representations of the world. Given the world and the representations, you have the truths.

5   Propositions

Earlier, I noted that Armstrong takes truthbearers to be propositions. More precisely, Armstrong's view is that propositions are the fundamental bearers of truth. Beliefs, utterances, sentences, and the like – concrete representations – are true only insofar as they express true propositions. You might worry about a conception of this sort on the grounds that it takes something simple – representations and ways the world is in virtue of which those representations are true – and turns it into something doubly complex. We began with the idea that truthmaking is a relation, perhaps an internal relation, between truthmakers and familiar truthbearers. We then posit propositions as intermediaries between these familiar truthbearers and whatever makes them true (see figure 3). We trade one puzzle – how are truths and truthmakers related? – for three puzzles:

(1) What are propositions?

(2) How are propositions "upwardly" related to representations "expressing" them?

(3) How are true propositions "downwardly" related to truthmakers?

I consider this an unhappy development.

Before turning to another, deeper, reason you might worry about propositions, let me pose a quiz: what do Locke, Wittgenstein, and Putnam have in common philosophically? Give up? All three defended the thesis that nothing – no *thing* – represents intrinsically. We give signs whatever significance they have by putting them to work in particular way.[7] More generally: meaning stems from use. Use includes, but need not be restricted to, conscious pursuits of intelligent, conscious agents.

---

[7] See Locke (1690), III, i–iii; Putnam (1981), chapters 1 – 2; Wittgenstein (1921), § 4.002; 1953, § 43.

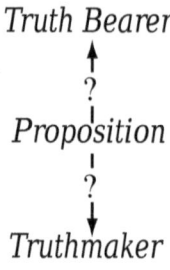

Figure 3

While disagreeing on the details, most philosophers nowadays accept the idea that use is required for meaning. But now what are propositions? Whatever they are, they are items capable of possessing a truth value. Unlike inscriptions, utterances, or beliefs, however, propositions are entities with built-in significance. Propositions mean what they mean quite independently of the activities of intelligent agents or systems. Propositions represent the philosophers' dream: entities with a definite intrinsic meaning persisting independently of the vicissitudes of finite creatures.

I submit that familiar arguments against the intrinsic meaningfulness of ordinary representations, linguistic or otherwise, extend smoothly to propositions. Propositions as philosophical posits are objectionable not, or not merely, because they are abstracta, but because they are, by our own lights, impossible entities. Or, if that seems too strong, if arguments that seem to incline us to posit propositions in the first place are right, they are impossible entities. In this regard propositions resemble unmoved movers introduced to block a regress stemming from a commitment to the principle that everything has a cause.

6 Abstracta

Propositions represent a kind of philosophical cheat, the sorts of entity that strike us as plausible only so long as we do not try to take them ontologically seriously. Many philosophers would disagree. Propositions belong to the class of abstract entities.[8] This class includes, in addition to propositions, sets, num-

---

[8] David Lewis, no friend of abstracta, regards propositions as sets of worlds. The comments here do not apply to Lewis, but they would apply to anyone who regards alternative worlds as abstracta.

bers, functions, uninstantiated universals, nonexistent individuals, and endless other "non-concrete" items. Philosophers tend to be relaxed about abstracta, in part because of the impressive standing of mathematics. Few philosophers are willing to deny the reality of numbers or sets. If such things exist, and if they are abstract entities, then we are committed already to a sizeable realm of abstracta. A purported entity's being abstract, then, cannot be held against it.

This line of reasoning is less than compelling. We accept mathematics; we suppose that many mathematical assertions are true. It is an additional matter to say what it is in virtue of which mathematical assertions are true. One possibility is that truthmakers for mathematical claims are entities subsisting in a realm "outside" space and time. This possibility is not implied by anything in mathematics, however. True, mathematicians "quantify over" numbers, sets, and the like. But quantification is a poor guide to ontology. Physicists accept quantum theory as true. Were anyone to take the trouble to translate quantum theory into first-order logic, we would find that physicists quantify over a staggering array of entities and processes. We could do this while remaining uncertain what the world must be like if the theory is true.

The same holds for mathematics. On the one hand, mathematics is an apparently self-contained enterprise. On the other hand, mathematical truths apply in the world – and perhaps in any imaginable world. It is hard to see, then, how any way the world might be could be responsible for mathematical truth. But it is no less difficult to see how a realm of abstracta could be thought to ground mathematical truth. We have access to mathematical truths, and these truths have application in the spatio-temporal world. Why should goings-on in another realm, a realm causally isolated from the spatio-temporal domain, have any bearing at all on what happens here?

All this is simply to suggest that taking mathematics seriously need not be thought to require a commitment to a universe of abstracta. If this is right, it removes an important source of comfort to philosophers fond of positing abstract entities in the course of advancing philosophical theses. The idea that abstracta are innocent until proven guilty begins to lose some of its initial plausibility.

Why worry about abstracta? Here are three reasons.

(1) We have no clear sense of what might constrain theses concerning abstracta. If you hold that a given abstract entity exists, what considerations – beyond considerations of consistency – might enter into an evaluation of this claim? If we are ontologically serious, this difficulty is important. Abstracta presumably are meant to serve as objective truthmakers for certain

philosophical claims. In this role, abstracta must be something other than creatures of thought.

(2) An old worry (Benacerraf (1973), see also Benacerraf (1965)). Mind-independent abstracta would subsist outside the spatio-temporal realm. In that case, how could we hope to gain knowledge of them, how could beliefs about abstracta come to be warranted?

(3) Abstracta are typically introduced as components of philosophical explanations. But in what sense could an entity subsisting outside the spatio-temporal realm be thought to explain goings-on within that realm?

Proponents of abstracta doubtless have responses to such worries. One sort of response, however, is bound to be unsatisfactory. The line of response I have in mind begins with a respectable domain – the numbers, for instance – proceeds through the observation that items in this domain are not identifiable with items in space and time, and draws the conclusion that the entities in question – in this case, the numbers – must be identifiable with entities outside space and time.

To my mind this kind of argument represents a failure of nerve, an unwillingness to persist in ontologically serious philosophical investigation. It is as though we began by facing a particular problem squarely: what might the truthmakers be for claims involving the numbers. This is a question a philosopher would ask in the course of pushing beyond mathematical practise into ontology. But then, having failed to locate truthmakers within the spatio-temporal world, we shrug and posit truthmakers in a non-spatio-temporal world. In so doing we resemble the bloke found looking for his lost automobile keys under a street lamp. Why there? Because, he tells us, there is more light under the lamp than where he dropped them.

7 Concluding comment

Some contributors to this volume are skeptical of various claims advanced in *From an ontological point of view* because the claims are not supported by definitive arguments proceeding from uncontroversial premises. In ontology, however, definitive arguments are few and far between. Spinoza, in the *Ethics*, develops an elaborate metaphysical edifice by deriving metaphysical theorems from fundamental axioms. But not many philosophers would locate the value of Spinoza's metaphysics in its axiomatic structure. On the contrary, the structure is erected as a scaffolding convenient for articulating metaphysical theses of abiding interest.

The test of an ontology lies not in arguments advanced in support of it, but in its applicability and power. If modes are preferable to universals, this is not because proofs for modes trump proofs for universals, still less because an ontology of modes is more parsimonious than an ontology of universals. Parsimony is, at best, a tie-breaker, and, as in baseball, there are no ties in philosophy (Cohen (1990)). If an ontology of modes is preferable to an ontology of universals, this is because modes make sense of whatever universals are supposed to make sense of, and do so less mysteriously.

I am not so naïve as to imagine that I will have convinced many readers of this volume with these observations. My aim, however, as I noted at the outset, has not been to advance a doctrine, but to encourage an attitude: the attitude of ontological seriousness. Taking up this attitude is to throw off the shackles of linguisticism, to move beyond the idea that all we need for ontology is a careful analysis of language. The veil of language is a philosophical artifact, a self-inflicted barrier to serious ontology. It is time we moved on.

Chapter 2

Inflating truthmakers. A critique of the primitive notion of truthmaking in Heil's ontological picture[1]

Simon Friederich & Giovanni Tuzet

We first summarise Heil's remarks on the notion of truthmaking and try to reconstruct the reasons that, according to him, make it necessary to work with that notion. As a first criticism we argue that, against basic intuition, many truthmakers will have to be of very large size. On the basis of this we turn to the problem of criticising certain theories which, according to Heil and others, fail to provide truthmakers for certain classes of truths; of these theories we offer alternative criticisms which are not based on the notion of truthmaking but keep the spirit of the critique in terms of truthmakers. In concentrating on the role of such truths in ordinary communication we finally suggest how to deal with them without having recourse to truthmakers.

1 Heil's conception of truthmaking

1.1 Why truthmakers?

In John Heil's ontological picture the principle underlying the talk of truthmaking is stated in the following sentence: "When a claim about the world is true, something about the world makes it true." (Heil (2003), p. 9)[2] Following Charlie B. Martin, Heil takes the expression "making a sentence true" seriously, for, according to him, it reveals a basic feature of the relations between

---

[1] We would like to thank John Heil, together with the participants in the Lausanne Symposium on his book, for the helpful discussion, and Michael Esfeld for the invitation. Helpful comments were also given by Felix Mühlhölzer (Göttingen); our English was checked by Simon Phipps (Gothenburg).

[2] Other ways of presenting it are the following: "The idea is that, when sentences, or utterances, or thoughts, or representations generally hold true of the world, they do so in virtue of ways the world is." (Heil (2003), pp. 54 – 55); "when a statement concerning the world is true, there must be something about the world that makes it true." (Heil (2003), p. 61)

world and language.[3] He postulates that for every[4] true sentence there has to exist a truthmaker, intuitively something that "makes" the sentence true. Truth of sentences can thus, according to this account, only be captured by reference to some additional entities, Heil's so-called "truthmakers".

But why take talk like "the sentence "p" is made true by X" at face-value and believe in truthmakers? Why not merely think of such talk as loosely expressing that in "p" something about X is (truly) said? What can be theoretically gained with such a notion as "truthmaker"?

As far as we can see, Heil is offering mainly two arguments in favour of the view that the truthmaker notion, taken seriously, is indeed useful if not indispensable.

(A) The notion helps to clarify why attacking such ambitious philosophical theories as for example modern (sense-data) phenomenalism and the account Gilbert Ryle has to offer on dispositions (which of course play a fundamental role in Ryle's account of mind in general).[5] The idea is that one should not want to consider a sentence as true simply because it can effectively play the role of an "inference ticket": it has to be true due to certain features of the world. We take this to correspond to the "good reason" David Lewis ((1999), p. 217) talks of in discussing Armstrong's account of truthmakers: "Now ask: when a statement S is (contingently) true, *what makes it true*? It wouldn't seem right to say: 'Well, S is just true, and that's all there is to it.'" This intuition is captured by the truthmaking principle which helps to criticise philosophical accounts and systems that do not fulfil this requirement.

(B) The notion helps to avoid hierarchically ordered properties ("levels of being") the postulation of which involves difficulties for our understanding of the alleged causal relations obtaining on each level (Heil (2003), pp. 56, 67, 73 – 74). Sentences containing predicates which (following the con-

---

[3] However, truthmaking is not to be confused with what Heil calls "Principle (Φ)", which, according to him, is a corollary of the Picture Theory of language that Heil refuses (cf. Heil (2003), pp. 26, 48).

[4] Or only some? Cf. Heil (2003), p. 60. The question whether every truth has a truthmaker is a disputed one; see, in the negative, Milne (2005).

[5] Cf. Armstrong (2004a), pp. 1 – 3, Heil (2003), pp. 61 – 62. We are not sure that Heil gives a fair presentation of Ryle's account. But in any case the account he sketches is a helpful example of a theory that does not fulfil the criterion he advances.

ception of levels of being) correspond to properties of different levels can simply have the same truthmaker(s).[6]

In the following section the (supposed) nature of truthmaking is examined; then, in the second part of the paper, the power and relevance of these two arguments are critically examined.

1.2 The nature of truthmaking

For Heil, truthmakers are "ways the world is" ((2003), p. 55), but he offers hardly any additional positive account of truthmaking, i.e. he explains merely wherein truthmaking does not consist. Truthmaking is not entailment; it cannot be explained by a simple correspondence model; it cannot be explained either in a straightforward way via supervenience (Heil (2003), pp. 36 – 37, 55, 67, 70). Rather, Heil introduces it as a primitive notion. In particular, he argues quite extensively against the thesis that the relation of truthmaking is to be understood as a relation of entailment. As far as we see, the two most important reasons he gives are the following.

(I) "Entailment is a relation holding among representations or statements of particular sorts" (Heil (2003), p. 55), but truthmakers are not representations; so, truthmaking cannot be entailment. Moreover, if truthmakers entailed representations (as for example sentences), each way the world is would – *qua* being a truthmaker – necessitate a representation. Therefore, if truthmaking were entailment, for every possible configuration of things there would exist a corresponding representation; but this is considered extremely implausible by Heil (this last argument he owes to Martin).[7]

---

[6] "If there are levels, these are levels of complexity or organisation or, alternatively, levels of description or explanation, not levels of being. Truthmakers for statements at whatever level are first-order ways the world is." (Heil (2003), p. 67)

[7] Furthermore, according to Heil, introducing propositions as intermediaries complicates the picture in the following way: "If truthbearers are concrete representations, we need some account of the relation these bear to truthmakers. If propositions are introduced as intermediaries connecting concrete representations and truthmakers, we need an account, both of the "downward" relation between propositions and truthmakers, and of the "upward" relation between propositions and concrete representations." (Heil (2003), pp. 72 – 73)

(II) Accounts of truthmaking as entailment are in need of postulating a dubious "totality fact" which appears obviously superfluous from a more natural point of view.[8]

The fundamental problem which Heil does not mention explicitly but which, as far as we see, is implicit in his whole critique of this approach (namely to characterise truthmaking as entailment), is that in order to entail representations truthmakers themselves would have to be entities equipped with truth values (entailment is a logical relation, i.e. a relation between sentences, propositions or something like that). In fact, some authors engaging in the debate do not want to conceive of truthmakers as representations, and introduce mediating propositions in order to account for truthmaking as entailment, that is for the idea that a truth is entailed by the proposition that the relevant truthmaker exists. Heil thinks that this move merely displaces the problem and introduces unnecessary complications. We share this estimation and therefore do not try to deepen the critique he offers any further. Let us move to another interesting detail in Heil's argumentation against the view that truthmaking should be understood as a form of entailment.

Take the "equivalence" or "disquotational" scheme, i.e. the principle that for every sentence "p"

"p" is true if and only if p.

Following Heil ((2003), p. 55), acceptance of this principle can also be traced back into the conception of truthmaking as entailment. In fact, even though Heil's picture does not involve a specific theory of truth, from his point of view (via applying Martin's objection against truthmaking as entailment) one could blame for example deflationary accounts of truth of being not careful enough with their ontological commitments. But, if sound, the argument could be directed against any kind of view about truth which accepts the scheme – and there are probably quite a lot of views that do.

However, the argument is disputable. The claim of someone who accepts the disquotational scheme is broadly that our understanding of the predicate "true" is partly or even mainly given by our acceptance of each instance of the principle, that is for each *given* "p" (be it a sentence, a proposition or whatever is considered to be the proper truthbearer).[9] Thus, from the acceptance of the

---

[8] Presuming that truthmaking is entailment leads to conflate representations of ways the world is and ways the world is (Heil (2003), p. 70). Such a conflating is present in Armstrong's presumption of a "totality fact" and in Chalmers' presumption of a "that's all" fact (see Heil (2003), pp. 68 – 72).

[9] Cf. in particular Horwich (1998).

equivalence scheme there does not follow any commitment to an infinity of representations whatsoever but only a commitment to endorse the scheme for each given sentence "p". It even might be the case that accepting the equivalence scheme as constitutive of the way the predicate "true" operates helps to avoid some difficulties which seem to be typical of any account postulating such entities as truthmakers. But now let us turn to our criticism of Heil's notion.

2 Is the notion of truthmaking a helpful notion?

2.1 Inflating truthmakers

The absence of a full-fledged positive account of truthmaking in Heil's ontological picture is a more serious problem than it may seem to be at first glance. Of course it is legitimate to argue that truthmaking is a primitive notion. But trying to give a thorough explication of the notion seems nonetheless of great importance.

Firstly, as long as it is unclear what to count as the truthmaker of a given sentence,[10] it is almost impossible to judge if truthmakers can do the job of making levels of being obsolete.

Secondly, it is worth noting that there are some standard arguments against a host of approaches to spell out truth as correspondence to the facts more explicitly. Truthmaking theory seems close to the spirit of correspondence theories and it seems therefore natural to inquire whether Heil's truthmakers do perhaps also fall prey to these objections and, if they do not, whether this is so only due to the vagueness of his conception. He says that they are "ways the world is" ((2003), p. 55). But what could a "way the world is" possibly be? It seems a plausible interpretation to suppose that they are either some objects or some actual "configuration of physical stuff" or at least something tied very closely to such objects or structures.

It thus seems an interesting question "how large" truthmakers ought to be. Are they restrained to a small part of the universe (except, presumably, in the case of sentences about the universe as a whole)? Or is the whole world to be considered as the truthmaker equally for each sentence? The latter option does

---

[10] Does it suffice to say they are ways the world is? Why not take them to be facts, or states of affairs, or events, or objects, or else? For example, Künne ((2003), pp. 158 – 165) claims that, according to the Austrian variant of the truthmakers theory, no truthmaker is a fact; for facts are abstract entities and truthmakers are parts of the natural order. Cf. Mulligan, Simons and Smith (1984), Armstrong (1997) and (2004a), Beebee and Dodd (2005).

not seem very attractive and it surely does not fit well with the intentions of the inventors of truthmakers. What is gained if we say that "Lausanne lies at Lake Geneva" and "Oxygen is the element occurring most frequently on the earth" have the same truthmaker? What they have in common is just that both of them happen to be true. Additionally, Heil's account of higher-level causation in terms of truthmakers ((2003), p. 45) depends on two different situations that are causally connected, namely two different truthmakers P_1 and P_2; it depends thus crucially on there being at least two different truthmakers alone for the sake of the argument. It is also worth mentioning that to let a sentence be made true by exactly those possible worlds in which it is true is not a viable option, because truthmakers are intended to be *really* existing things or structures made up of existing and not merely possible things.

So it seems that it is not a viable strategy for the supporter of truthmakers to have the whole world be the one and only one truthmaker for every sentence. Now there are well-known arguments construed by Church and Gödel and recently refined by Stephen Neale[11] to the end that for a broad class of correspondence (and maybe truthmaking) theories there exists a so-called "Slingshot argument" saying that for each of those theories necessarily all the different facts (or truthmakers) collapse into one. One would very well like to know whether Heil can avoid the problems posed by that argument.

From the Slingshot argument the following dilemma stems (Engel (2002), p. 21):

(I) if all propositions have only one truthmaker, the notion is useless;

(II) if every proposition has its personal truthmaker, the notion is idle.

David Armstrong (1997, 2004a) rejects the idea that each truth has its own personal truthmaker. The truthmaking relation is not one-one, but one-many or many-one, as the following examples show:

- (one-many) if it is true that either "p" or "q" is true, then the truthmaker for "p" is also a truthmaker for the disjunctive truth;

- (many-one) if "p or q" (inclusive *or*) is true, this truth has two truthmakers, p and q;

- (many-one) "There is at least one black swan".

---

[11] See for example Neale (1995) and (2001).

According to Pascal Engel ((2002), p. 23), this avoids the second horn of the dilemma, but not the first: in the end the world itself becomes the truthmaker of all truths.[12]

John Searle ((1995), pp. 220 – 226) denies that a proposition corresponding to a fact corresponds to every fact. For, according to him, correspondence is correspondence to facts and the substitution of logically equivalent sentences involves making reference to different facts.[13] So, Searle avoids the first horn of the dilemma.[14] Does he avoid the second? If not, is it possible to combine Armstrong's and Searle's positions in order to avoid both horns?

At any rate, since he negates that truthmaking is entailment, it can be supposed that Heil avoids the dilemma: "a state of affairs like the pillar-box's being pillar-box red does not logically entail anything." (Heil (2003), p. 63) Furthermore, since the dilemma is primarily directed to correspondence theories of truth, it can be denied that it applies also to truthmakers theories.

It is in any case natural to look for a criterion, at least a rule of thumb, specifying in which cases different sentences should be considered to have the same truthmaker. But, immediately, problems emerge. Consider negative existential claims that led such thinkers as Armstrong and Chalmers to the postulation of, respectively, a so-called "totality fact" and a "that's all" fact (related to claims of the form "There are *exactly n F*'s" which imply negative existential claims). Of special interest are those negative existential claims with an unrestricted quantifier as for example "There are no flying kangaroos (at all, that is: in the whole universe)". Which region of space-time could be considered a truthmaker for this claim which is probably true? Certainly it does not suffice to consider only Australia or its fauna as the truthmaker because the absence of flying kangaroos in any other corner of the universe should play a non-negligible role in the "truthmaking" of this sentence. As Heil rightly says, the postulation of a totality fact[15] is a very artificial move and, according to him, such a move is characteristic of a conception which thinks of truthmaking

---

[12] See in this sense Armstrong's notion of the "totality fact" ((1997), p. 198) which is, as we said, explicitly discussed by Heil ((2003), pp. 68 – 72).

[13] "Because the identity of the fact is dependent on the specific features of the fact being the same as those specified by the corresponding statement and in virtue of which the corresponding statement is true, it is false to suppose that the context "the fact that p" must preserve identity of reference under substitution of logically equivalent sentences for p." (Searle (1995), p. 220)

[14] For another way of avoiding the first horn, cf. Künne (2003), pp. 158 – 159.

[15] Such a postulation is indeed still necessary for Armstrong's recent account; see Armstrong (2004a), pp. 72 – 77.

still in terms of entailment. So, are we forced to ascribe to sentences differing in their meaning no less than "There are no flying kangaroos" and "There is no lump of uranium with a mass of more than 1000kg" the same truthmaker, namely the whole world (or, if you like, "the way the world actually is")? This seems against the intuitions of truthmaking theory.

But the question of the "extension" of truthmakers gives rise to further problems. Let us suppose that truthmakers are indeed objects or perhaps rather structures of objects in the world. The sentence "There are (at least) five coins in my pocket" is then presumably considered to be made true (if it is true) by the very coins in my pocket, that is the physical objects themselves, located quite narrowly in space, or, alternatively and perhaps more plausibly, by the "structure" or configuration of things consisting of my pocket and the coins (that is, not only the objects but also their spatial coordinates etc.). But is the presence of those bare objects or, respectively, of the bare configuration of objects really sufficient for the truth of the sentence? It does not seem so anymore if one takes into consideration that it is only the practise of paying, of assigning value to those objects which makes them "coins". But this way, a whole society of competent speakers and agents comes in and, "entering" the truthmaker, threatens to dilute and inflate it in a completely uncontrollable manner.

One may remain unconvinced by such an example and claim that the alleged role of the society should be absorbed in the meaning of the word "coin" which, so the argument, surely has to be presupposed in order to ascribe a truthmaker to the sentence. We are not sure about the prospects of a rejoinder like this concerning the above example, but in any case it will be no longer viable if we substitute for "coin" an expression like "means of payment" or simply "Euro-coin". My pocket plus its content plus one single bank which accepts my coins will not suffice for the coins being proper means of payment in the European Union. In order to become that they will need to be accepted by a much more extensive part of the society and so there is no way of narrowing down the truthmaker to an appreciable size. It seems therefore again impossible to discern the truthmaker of a given sentence from the truthmakers of different sentences.[16] But do these observations – such as the collapse of the truthmakers of all negative existential claims into one, or the "inflation" of

---

[16] Of course there are also other sentences with (potential/alleged) truthmakers of big size, such as "Prodi is the prime minister of Italy" or "Iran is an Islamic country" which involve whole societies; but here the size of the truthmaker is perhaps less damaging for the ambitions of truthmaking theory because the subject of the sentences is already an "extensive" one. Our point is that inflating truthmakers is almost always necessary even if one is dealing with small and narrowly located things such as ordinary objects or human beings.

the truthmakers of sentences on "small things" to society-like size – really pose serious problems for the theoretician defending the usefulness of truthmakers?

Of course our observations are no demonstrations of the untenability of the truthmaker notion. However, as we believe, they challenge the ability of truthmaking theory to help in criticising such theories as Ryle's on dispositions or phenomenalism. Why this? Well, what we would expect from an account of dispositions that does not let them "hang in the air"[17] – as does Ryle's – is to tie them to certain features of a person's behavior, or brain states or perhaps a sophisticated combination of those. Obviously the Rylean will not be able to identify any of these with the truthmakers of sentences on dispositions but we cannot anymore blame him for not being able to do so: that this is not possible is indeed one of the standard cases as was shown above. Further below we consider alternative ways of keeping the spirit of the "missing truthmaker objection" without making use of the notion.

Finally, to consider the second major reason to introduce truthmakers according to Heil, what about the merits of truthmakers in dealing with higher-level causation? It is difficult to say something clear about higher-level causation in a few words, but we think the problem should be assessed in each case separately by considering how and to what degree the *laws* of the higher-level theory can be accounted for by those of the lower-level theory. Causation may thus be relative to a given theoretical framework with its basic laws and may therefore be found at each level without there emerging any conflict or overdetermination.[18] The problem is not the existence and alleged causal efficacy of higher-level properties (except, perhaps, in the problem of mind, but this is in any case a very special problem) but to give, each time afresh, an account of the inter-level (if this talk is still allowed) relations. We cannot get around this often difficult task by changing the ontological framework from levels to truthmakers.

2.2 Justifying intuitions without truthmakers

Now let's come back to our intuition that if a sentence about the world is true, there has to be something in or about the world that makes it true. How should it be possible to capture the – probably sound – spirit behind this claim without

---

[17] Cf. for example Armstrong (2004a), p. 3.

[18] Consider especially the "reduction" of thermodynamics to statistical mechanics: one can very well say that a given process takes place due to the maximisation of the system's entropy; but an explanation in terms of the system's microstates is in principle possible as well. There is no contradiction but rather something like an explanation here.

engaging in talk of truthmakers? Could the "message" or the "spirit" of the truthmaking principle – the sound "realist inclination" which we do not want to miss – be captured in a more perspicuous albeit considerably different way?

The merits of the truthmaker notion are related to the possibility of giving lucid critiques of certain philosophical accounts that fail to match the truthmaking principle. As we said, famous examples include the account Ryle has on dispositions and the phenomenalist account on physical objects. Now let's look again at these examples and try to discuss the virtues of the critique in terms of truthmakers and the virtues of alternative critiques.

We will discuss the example of the *Rylean theory* first and more thoroughly. In order to do so, imagine a person, a dialogue partner, who we shall call "Hyle" to avoid confusion with the historical Ryle. Now imagine Hyle introducing a predicate F in our debate and explaining that there are no criteria when it could be truly ascribed to a thing. According to Hyle, sentences in which it occurs might however be used as reliable inference tickets. In short: Hyle sets out to explain a predicate F (of the type "being disposed to x") in a Rylean manner. Now how are we to react if he starts to talk in terms of predicates he wants to be conceived of in the sketched way?

Of course we might claim this: "Your talk of dispositions cannot be accepted because you did not manage to give it a truthmaker." However, we have already hinted to the problem this kind of critique will face because of the non-localisability of truthmakers. We will not be able to force our dialogue partner to point to something rather specific "out there in the world" as the truthmaker of his sentences which would seem desirable. If we did so, Hyle might straight forwardly declare that the truthmaker for the given sentence is already given by the *fact* that the disposition in question is instantiated here, or, if we were to disallow the suspiciously convenient reference to facts, he might alternatively reply that, as usual, the truthmaker would have to be localised "all over the society of speakers", being dependent on the totality of speakers' habitudes and expectations.[19]

Furthermore, while the proposed kind of argument in terms of truthmakers will probably not prevail in the intended manner, there is another aspect of the critique in terms of truthmakers which seems rather strange: the challenge for Hyle who defends the truth of sentences on dispositions as conceived of by himself is not to *bring about* a certain thing or a way the world might be and link the sentence to it (this would seem an at least very artificial way of

---

[19] He might also deny that his sentences need having truthmakers altogether. This case will be discussed further below.

putting the matter). The message "a truthmaker is missing" sounds as if Hyle were challenged to attach a certain object to his statement and did not manage to do so. We suspect that Hyle's problem – if he really has one – is rather a problem of commitments and entitlements in communication.[20] In order to see why this might be so, it seems promising to ask and argue in a manner such as follows: "You claim that dispositional statements are not grounded in any states of affairs. But, if this is so, what entitles me, what entitles you to use such statements as "inference tickets"? How could it be rational to build on such inference tickets if it is not possible to detect any difference from cases where it wouldn't be (i.e. to situations where the same dispositional statements were false)? Perhaps all you want to do is to recommend a certain inference ticket. But then you should not speak of it in terms of truth; probably it would be less misleading to give your talk the form of an imperative or a wish."

Another criticism might be: "If you believe in the truth of this or that dispositional statement you should be able to defend it against a person who claims the contrary. But how can you? Dispositional statements are supposed to have an empirical component, but there is nothing you could point to and, perhaps establishing some correlations by argument, provide as evidence (however weak) for your claim."

All criticism along these lines keeps the spirit of the criticism brought forward by truthmaking theory in trying to point out the way in which dispositions so "hang in the air" as is said by Armstrong. However, this critique does not depend on any notion of truthmaking, be it primitive or not.

We think that similar considerations apply to the case of *phenomenalism*. Strong support for the claim that purely phenomenal language, taken seriously, does not match the requirements of successful communication is – perhaps surprisingly – given by the logical empiricist Hans Reichenbach in his "Experience and Prediction". His label for phenomenalistically interpreted talk, that is, talk of material objects interpreted as simply an abbreviation for talk of (possible) sensations, is "strictly positivistic language": "The strictly positivistic language ... contradicts normal language so obviously that it has scarcely been seriously maintained; moreover, its insufficiency is revealed as soon as we try to use it for the rational reconstruction of the thought-processes underlying actions concerning events after our death. ... We have said that the choice of a language depends on our free decision, but that we are bound to the decisions

---

[20] This is to be understood in a rather simple and intuitive sense, as further explained in the text. It may nevertheless be backed up more systematically by inferentialist semantics and focusing on scorekeeping practise, as in Brandom (2000), cf. Esfeld (2005).

entailed by our choice: we find here that the decision for the strictly positivistic language would entail the renunciation of any reasonable justification of a great many human actions."[21] As Reichenbach makes plausible, already the requirements of everyday reasoning rule out the possibility of a reconstruction of our knowledge in phenomenalistically acceptable terms. We think that he is right on this point and phenomenalism, taken seriously, is a non-starter when it comes to the interpretation of simple human everyday talk and reasoning.

2.3 The limits of ontology

Surely doubts will be raised concerning the relevance of our criticism even by those who do not want to dismiss the problem of inflation. The benevolent reader who wants to maintain the ontological significance of the truthmaker notion might object to our reasoning: "Maybe you are right and the critique of the Rylean and the phenomenalist accounts can be formulated more accurately by reference to other notions than that of truthmaker. But all you have thereby managed to do is to give a certain methodological recommendation – how to capture a realistically inspired criticism – which will be of little if any ontological significance."

Our answer to this challenge will be that, in the first place, we are not trying to give methodological recommendations.[22] It might well be that criticising theories that fail to conform to "realist standards" is done most effectively in terms of (missing) truthmakers. A critique of that sort has the virtue of being very intuitive and easy to grasp; this might constitute a strong advantage over a critique such as the one we sketched above. What in fact we aim to show is that such a critique is "deeper" than the critique in terms of truthmakers and that this is strong evidence to think that the ontological point of view (that regards the demand for truthmakers as essential) can hardly be prior to a point of view based on consideration of ordinary communication and reasoning.

This should become more plausible if we consider the case that Hyle, the Rylean we try to force to provide a truthmaker for a certain dispositional claim, rejects the necessity of doing so. This refusal might be interpreted as a simple sign of unwillingness to accept or to meet critical remarks, but perhaps it is not an altogether irrational reaction. The argument for the inflation of truth-

---

[21] Reichenbach (1938), p. 150.

[22] Commenting on our paper in the Lausanne Symposium on his book, Heil contended not only that he wants to be neutral on what truthmakers are, but also that the truthmaking principle is to be intended as a methodological recommendation: you might be prepared to find out the ways the world is.

makers might have caused Hyle – unlike Heil, as we have learned – to reject the notion once and for all for being unhelpful, or he might lack the relevant realist intuitions without being a crazy skeptic. But now imagine that we press him further and ask the questions we proposed before instead of the question on truthmakers. If again he did not answer satisfyingly, the situation would become entirely different. Consider for example the question proposed above "How could it be rational to build on such inference tickets if it is not possible to detect any difference from cases where it wouldn't be?" and imagine that our dialogue partner were not in the least capable of pointing to such differences. Imagine further that he – uttering sentences in dispositional vocabulary – were not able to defend any such claim against a person who disapproved. It seems clear that in this case our Hyle should be embarrassed and abandon his theory; the real (historical) Ryle would surely not have claimed that for him there would be no need to provide some answers to these demands. But had he done so, it seems clear, we would be entitled to refute once and for all his theory for being incapable to explain how dispositions talk could be fruitful and perhaps it would then be wise to stop conversation on theses matters with him once and for all.

But what if Hyle managed to meet the challenge and gave satisfying answers to our questions (as the historical Ryle would probably have tried to do)? Let us consider the following case: he refuses to name anything as the truthmaker for his claim but nevertheless he comes up with a plausible story about what gives him an entitlement to his claims in dispositional terms, he tells us in which cases this or that claim should not be used as an inference ticket and how he would rationally defend it against someone who argued to the contrary.

How should we react? Different possibilities are open. We may conclude that in doing so he actually did what was necessary in order to attach truthmakers to his sentences. If we like to have the truthmaker concept as an occasionally useful concept on which no greater weight should be placed, we will probably do so. We may alternatively consider this a "constructive proof" of there being perfectly meaningful and even true sentences that failed to have truthmakers and thereby reject the truthmaking principle.

One might also remain unsatisfied with Hyle's terminology and continue demanding some truthmaker. But this would be a move which should not be considered a helpful one. According to our actual scenario everything about the application of the "Hylean" dispositional terms is now clear and they serve useful purposes in communication. We think it plausible that whoever raises further objections to those terms should be regarded as a sulking philosopher who cannot be satisfied by reasonable means. If Heil would nevertheless opt for this reaction he should come up with a much more detailed and worked-out account on truthmakers and explain exactly why the demands of that very account should be met. But, as a matter of fact, Heil does not advocate any such account but prefers to have a rather intuitive and "primitive" notion of truthmaking. It seems therefore unlikely that he would choose that road. To conclude, the considerations we have just pointed out support the view that the truthmaker notion does not help a lot in accomplishing the task it was designed to do. We argue that attention should be paid not only to the objects and structures that – intuitively – "make" truths true, but also to their emergence and way of functioning in basic communication. In the light of our above considerations this seems indispensable.

Commentary
John Heil

Friederich and Tuzet say that I embrace a truthmaking principle according to which (a) truthmaking is a primitive notion, and (b) every truth has a truthmaker. They are skeptical that truthmaking is a useful notion, and prefer to account for the kinds of consideration I advance in its favour by reference to various "conversational" constraints.

I truthmaking "primitive"? I have noted that it is unlikely that we are in a position to explicate truthmaking in simpler, clearer terms. Friederich and Tuzet regard this as an admission of failure: what role could an unexplicated primitive possibly play in a philosophical explanation?

One response to this kind of dismissal is to note that Friederich and Tuzet themselves never tell us what they mean by "definition". Following their line of argument, I ought simply to dismiss their dismissal by noting that they have not clearly explained what it is that I fall short of. Or is it that, for them, definition is a primitive notion?

Implicit in my discussion of truthmaking in *From an ontological point of view*, and explicit in chapter one in this volume, is the idea that truthmaking is an internal relation. The truthmaking relation in this respect resembles the taller-than relation: if you have the relata, you have the relation. What are the relata in the case of truthmaking? Truthmakers and truthbearers. Truthbearers are representations. I mean this to be a neutral way of referring to utterances, sentences, statements, beliefs, images, whatever you think could be capable of being true or false.

So what about the other side of the relation? What are truthmakers? Armstrong says that truthmakers are states of affairs. I say that truthmakers, or truthmakers for truths about the world, are ways the world is. There are many different views about ways the world is. Perhaps Armstrong is right, perhaps these ways are states of affairs. I say this is not something we could know just by thinking hard about truthmaking. Given a presumption that truths require truthmakers, it is up to us to determine what these might be in particular cases.

Friederich and Tuzet say that I make the Tarskian truth schema mysterious.

(T) S is true if and only if p

My worry about (T) concerns the biconditional read right-to-left. Suppose p is whatever makes S true. There are going to be lots of p's for which there are no *S*'s, no truthbearers. What do we say about such cases? Some philosophers will resort to propositions here. In chapter one, I suggest reasons to think this is a bad move. But then what is it that's supposed to be true? Friederich and Tuzet are not much interested in this question, but I suspect they ought to be. They think that our acceptance of (T) is central to our grasp of truth. But what exactly is it we are grasping?

Suppose you go with the idea that truthmaking is an internal relation between a representation of some kind and some way the world is. You will then think that (T) is a somewhat inelegant way of expressing this idea: if you have a representation, *S*, and you have the world being as *S* says it is, *p*, *S* is true. If all you have is the world, if all you have is the right side of the biconditional, you have no truths. Friederich and Tuzet say that I invoke a truthmaker argument against an ontology of levels. I wonder what argument they have in mind? An affinity for truthmaking is compatible with any ontology, including an ontology incorporating levels of being. In fact, it seems clear that proponents of the levels picture themselves appeal, implicitly at least, to truthmakers. This is clear in arguments for "multiple realisability". Failure of a one – one mapping of special science predicates and more fundamental predicates requires that we either deny that the special science predicates have truthmakers (eliminativism) or accept that those predicates designate properties distinct from properties designated by more fundamental predicates.

My suggestion is that it is a mistake to assume a one – one predicat – property mapping. One and the same property can, on a given occasion, answer to distinct predicates. This does not follow immediately upon your acceptance of a truthmaking principle. It requires rejection of the thesis that predicates concerning which we are realists correspond one-to-one with properties. Truthmaking plays a role here, but only in a way that philosophers on either side of the issue could accept.

Do I endorse a principle of the form

(P) Every truth has a truthmaker.

No. For all I know, (P) might be true – in which case there is a truthmaker for (P)! But my discussion of truthmaking is grounded in a much simpler thought. When we philosophers offer up theses that purport to express truths about the world, honesty requires that we either say what truthmakers for the theses might be or say why the truths in question don't require truthmakers.

"Possible worlds" provide a simple example. If you think that goings-on in other worlds ground modal claims while, at the same time, denying the reality of such worlds, you are trying to eat your cake and have it. If you are honest, you will need either to reformulate your account by reference to features of the "actual world", or admit that talk of possible worlds is just an oblique way of grounding modality in linguistic convention or purely conceptual matters of fact.

Is there a truthmaker argument against such a Humean view of modality? To think so would be to misunderstand the role of truthmaking in philosophical discussion. By focusing on what might make our theories true, we are forced to be ontologically candid. If you want to promote Humeanism about modality, by all means do so, but do so honestly.[1]

---

[1] David Lewis makes his version of Humeanism explicit. Others are less candid.

Chapter 3

Levels of being being there?[1]

Jens Harbecke

In this paper, I argue that Heil's ontological theory does not meet the standards it sets for itself. The author's argumentation contains a flaw in being unable to explain what "true predicate application" is. Since this concept is Heil's main tool to block the common eliminativist charges brought forward against reductionism, the consequences are severe for his entire model. In the face of these difficulties, I propose to revise a central doctrine of Heil's theory according to which there exists only "one" ontological level and I try to show why a certain conception of different ontological levels cannot be dispensed with if we want to provide a satisfying answer to the problem of multiple realisation, or "multiple reference".

1 Introduction

In his recent book (Heil (2003), all Heil references are to this book; other references are noted individually), John Heil aims to develop a general framework that defines certain adequacy standards for ontological theories. He argues that an ontology comprising different "levels of being" is a philosophically unacceptable model resulting from a fundamental misunderstanding of how our scientific theories and ordinary language work. In being "ontologically serious"[2], Heil acknowledges that many of our scientific claims and ordinary sentences are literally true and, furthermore, that there must be something about the world that makes them true. However, from an ontological point of view, the entities referred to by our special sciences and by ordinary language are hardly ever *of the same kind*. The author thereby rejects what he calls the "Picture Theory". This kind of theory postulates a "sameness of kind"-relation that maps the "same predicate application"-relation and explains truth and predicate applicability this way. The approach typically results in a multi-level ontology. Heil tries to show that the "sameness of kind"-relation is in fact not necessary

---
[1] The work on this paper has been supported by the Swiss National Science Foundation (SNF), grant nr. 100011-105218/1.
[2] Heil (2003), preface.

to ground truth and predicate applicability. In other words, the truthmaking relation is not necessarily a "bijective" relation between the structural parts of the world and those of true sentences of scientific theories or of ordinary language. In the author's view, the same explanatory power is born by an ontologically less problematic similarity relation between the referred-to entities. Since this similarity can be assumed to map the "same predicate application"-relation just the same, the original Picture Theory can be rejected without fear of explanatory loss. Although there may be unproblematic levels of complexity, ultimately, all that the world comprises is just one level that, in virtue of its particular structure, has the capacity of making true different descriptions that are in fact located on different non-reducible *linguistic* levels.

In this paper my aim will be to examine Heil's reasons for his general rejection of ontological theories that postulate levels of being. First, I shall some arguments that Heil presumes to give rise to the idea of a layered ontology and I am going to paraphrase those arguments that the author considers as defeaters of such a model. Then, I am going to investigate on Heil's positive account of how truth and reference are to be thought of in a monistic ontology. I will argue that Heil's account, to which a similarity relation among realisers is pivotal, fails to meet its own standards as the similarity relation is in fact not sufficient to ground same-predicate application. Furthermore, and with due cautiousness, I will hint that a contradiction may even await Heil at some point of his argumentation. Finally, I shall submit the thesis that levels of being – under a certain interpretation – are indispensable for an ontology that serves our explanatory purposes adequately.

2   The case for levels of being

In Heil's view, the main and initial force for accepting the model stems from a prior and tacit acceptance of a framework, which he calls the "Picture Theory". A corollary of this theory is what he identifies as the principle Φ.

(Φ) "When a predicate applies truly to an object, it does so in virtue of designating a property possessed by that object and by every object to which the predicate truly applies (or would apply)." (p. 26, varied formulations of the principle are found on pp. 27, 65, and 83).

As Heil reads it, the principle essentially expresses a correspondence theory of truth, which can be considered a very natural interpretation of the relation a true sentence bears to the world. Correspondence theories often postulate an isomorphism between statements and their referents. If a sentence is true on a particular occasion then, so it is claimed, there corresponds an entity in the world to each constituent of that sentence and it is this very relationship that explains the truth of the sentence. Additionally, it is sometimes assumed that the entities corresponding to the true sentence are of the same type on all occasions in which the sentence turns out to be true. If this assumption is correct, then, for example, for a predicate "red" a particular instance of the type property of *being red* is identifiable on each occasion in which the predicate truly applies.

Heil argues that from this natural and casual way of interpreting the truth-making relation combined with the recognition that our theories are organised on different levels a direct path leads to a layered conception of the world. On such a picture, higher-order predicates[3] refer to higher-level properties, each single predicate only referring to a single kind of property (and not to a number of arbitrarily different properties on different occasions).

According to Heil, not only folk interpretation of ordinary language displays such convictions. A widespread version of the generally respectable position of "scientific realism" results in an ontological model with very similar features. The inference underlying this more sophisticated reasoning goes as follows. There are cases in which a predicate uncontroversially applies to a number of different objects whilst, from the perspective of physical theory, there is no single physical property that all the objects referred to would have in common. In order to explain why the predicate applies to the objects, we need to invoke a homogeneous property that grounds the uniform application. Since the shared homogeneous property is evidently not a physical property, it must be a higher-level property. As a consequence, we infer that the world must comprise more than a single level. And once a single higher level is admitted, many others come easily along.[4]

Probably the best-known philosophical position promoting such a many level-view is classical functionalism. The central tenet of this theory is that any higher-order property is realised by an arrangement or configuration of lower-level properties, such that any higher-level property is possessed by an object in virtue of that object's possession of a certain arrangement of lower-level prop-

---

[3] At this stage of the argument, it is not easy to define "higher-level predicates" beyond the immediate intuitions and without circularity. As a very rough approach, we can define higher-level predicates as predicates that unify a number of cases described by other (non-equivalent) predicates. Hence, being higher-level and lower-level may be a relative matter.

[4] Heil mentions variants of this resoning, e.g. in Heil (2003), pp. 7, 23, 31, and 54.

erties. The many-levels picture and the realisation relation intertwine smoothly here, as realising and being realised is a relative matter (p. 29). It is this version of the many-levels view that Heil is going to attack.

3 Heil's arguments against the many-levels view

In this section, I review five of Heil's arguments against the plausibility of ontological models postulating different levels and I am going to evaluate each of these arguments with respect to its force. The variant of the level model that Heil chiefly attacks is the theory of functionalism.

(I) The first argument stems from Heil's analysis of the origins of the level model. Heil assumes that the motivation of accepting the level model results from a commitment to the Picture Theory. That in itself cannot constitute an argument against a philosophical tenet, of course, as virtually all philosophical theories are committed to some or other prior philosophical assumptions. However, in Heil's view the commitment to principle Φ is mostly an uncritical or "tacit" one. In other words, it is typically incorporated into level theories as an unproven supposition and as such it creates a flaw in the theorising about levels.[5]

(II) With his second argument Heil launches a direct attack on the Picture Theory, or on principle Φ. As stated above, the central tenet of this principle is the assumption that, whenever a single predicate truly applies to a number of objects (possibly in a number of different situations), the property instances in virtue of which the application holds must all be of a genuine and homogeneous kind. So, for instance, if the predicate "red" applies to a number of different objects, then, according to the aforementioned reasoning, all these objects must share a genuine and homogeneous property, i.e. the kind-property of being red. However, as Heil points out, "... it is not easy to think of a property that (a) all red things share and (b) in virtue of which they satisfy the predicate "is red"." Rather, "... objects can be red without – in any obvious sense – sharing a property in virtue of which they could be said to be red" (p. 27).

Heil's argument is interesting in a peculiar way. First of all, we can assume that what Heil intends the term "properties" to refer to are those features of objects that are detectable by physics or, perhaps, by some other relatively basic science. Among such properties are properties like "displaying

---
[5] Compare Heil (2003), pp. 7, 10, 21, 49.

charge *x*", or "displaying a mass of *x* grams", or perhaps even "displaying a texture of the kind *z*". There are good reasons for agreeing with Heil as it is highly unlikely that all red things will share any one property of such kind. However, what makes Heil's argument peculiar is the fact that the very same reasoning was used by the level theorists to establish an ontology that recognises the existence of different levels. In their view, since the searched-for homogeneous property that would explain the true application cannot be found within basic physics, it must be a higher-level property that, however, may well be "realised" by physical properties on a given occasion. If Heil now turns the same case back against the level theorists it is not clear whether this can count as an argument or whether it is simply the same reasoning only yielding a different conclusion due to different presuppositions.

(III) The third argument Heil uses to attack the level model is a variant of the famous "causal" or "exclusion argument" as it has been worked out prominently by Jaegwon Kim.[6] A pivotal tenet underpinning this argument is the idea that, whatever a property may be, it will have to endow the objects possessing it with a distinctive set of causal powers. This dictum, often called the "Eleatic Principle", suggests that properties having no causal powers are neither properties nor do they exist. Rather, each property instantiation must manifest itself through some causal impact associated with the property instantiated. It follows that, given the referent of a higher-level pedicate is a genuine higher-level property, the genuine higher-level property will have to manifest itself through some kind of causal impact. There appear to be two general cases in which such causal impact may take place. Either the higher-level property instantiation causes the instantiation of some physical property or it causes the instantiation of some other higher-level property.

In the first case, the causal impact of the higher-level property will be preempted by some physical and causally efficacious property, since, due to the principle of completeness of the physical accepted by functionalism, each instantiation of a physical property has a sufficient and complete causal history of physical property instantiations. It follows that, in order to retain its causal impact, the higher-level property instantiation will have to be identical with the preempting physical property instantiation and, in consequence, it will immediately lose its higher-level status.

---

[6] See Kim (1998, 2003).

In the second case, the caused higher-order property instantiation will always be grounded and realised by a physical property instantiation due to the realisation principle advocated by functionalism. It follows that any property instantiation causing the higher-order property instantiation will only be able to do so through causing an instantiation of the physical property that realises the higher-level property instantiation. This gets us back to the first case.

As a result, in both cases the higher-level property loses its higher-level status. All causation is grounded in the fundamental level and all higher-level property instantiations are identical to fundamental property instantiations (or at least so if overdetermination of the effect in question is excluded). Were a higher-level property instantiation to retain a higher-level status in being distinct from the lower-level property instantiation it would thereby lose its causal efficacy. However, due to the Eleatic Principle, such kind of epiphenomenalism cannot be considered a viable option. Hence, from an ontological point of view, there can only be one level, or, in that sense, no "level" at all. As Heil concludes: "The moral, it would seem, is that any purported solution to the problem of the causal relevance of higher-level properties that abandons the idea that basic-level causal transactions are autonomous is a cure worse than the disease." (p. 34)

(IV) Heil's fourth argument against the level view draws on some puzzling questions concerning interlevel relations. For the functionalist, higher-level items are distinct from lower-level items, even though they depend on them through realisation. This relation is often expressed through a principle of strong supervenience:

(S) "Necessarily, if anything, x, has α in A, then there is a property, β, in B, and, necessarily, if any x has β, x has α." (Kim (1984)).

In the given formulation (S), α represents any higher-level property and β an adequate lower-level property in the sense defined by the functionalists. As Heil points out correctly, (S) "... is a purely modal notion" and "... silent on the nature of the envisaged dependence-determination relation" (p. 37). Consequently, even if (S)'s truth is accepted there remain some questions *why* it is in fact true. The presumed distinctness of higher- and lower-level properties precludes the relation of identity. But what else is available then? Heil assumes that a proponent of the level view might appeal to a *sui generis* notion of nomological dependence. Such a "vertical" law would tie higher-level items to those located at lower levels. According to Heil, such a move would be a source of embarrassment to the level theorist, since vertical laws would not be further explicable as, for instance, common causal laws are through causal uniformity of their referents. Furthermore, such laws would seem to have an obscure character as they would tie a singular property kind on the right hand side of the law conditional to an infinity of kinds on the left hand side. It is not clear whether a so construed conditional can count as a law at all (p. 38). These flaws are problematic for level pluralism, but they are easily avoided by ontological monism.

(V) A fifth argument that Heil introduces draws on the principle of projectability. Predicates, so the reasoning goes, can figure in laws only if they are projectable. However, when a higher-level property is identifiable only with an open-ended disjunction of lower-level properties, the conditions for an application of that predicate to new cases are unclear. Consequently, it cannot designate a genuine kind of property. What Heil implicitly refers to here is a debate between Kim and Fodor on the projectability of predicates whose referred-to properties are multiply realised. According to Kim, projectability is the hallmark of lawlikeness. He says: "Lawlike generalisations ... are thought to have the following ... property: observation of positive instances, F's that are G's, can strengthen our credence in the next F's being G." This instance-to-instance accretion of confirmation is "... what explains the possibility of confirming a generalisation about an indefinitely large class of items on the basis of a finite number of favourable observations." (Kim (1992), p. 11) For illustration, Kim uses the example of jade which "... is not a mineral kind, contrary to what was once believed; rather, jade is comprised of two distinct minerals with dissimilar molecular structure, *jadeite and nephrite*." (Kim (1992), p. 11) In a thought experiment, Kim imagines an attempt of empirically confirming the generalisation "Jade is green". For such an enterprise, a certain amount of confirming observations may be taken as positive evidence for the lawlikeness of this generalisation. However, Kim imagines the following scenario: "... on re-examining the records we find, to our dismay, that all the positive instances of ["Jade is green"] ... turn out to have been samples of jadeite, and none of nephrite! If this should happen, we clearly would not, and should not, continue to think of ["Jade is green"] as well confirmed.", " ... the reasons [that "Jade is green" is not confirmed by them] is that jade is a true disjunctive kind, a disjunction of two heterogeneous nomic kinds which, however, is not itself a nomic kind." (Kim (1992), p. 12) However, Fodor has a convincing response to this argument. First of all, the reasons why we would think that "Jade is green" is not well-confirmed is not "... because "Jade is green" doesn't pass the projectability test ...; rather beause it would show that we've made a sampling error in collecting the data." So, "... what's wrong with ["Jade is green"] isn't that biased samples fail to confirm it. *Biased* samples don't confirm *anything*." (Fodor (1997), p. 152) Furthermore, Fodor points out that the jade example cannot be considered analogous to genuine multiple realisation cases. This is highlighted by the "... distinction between a multiply based property that is *disjunctive*, and a multiply based property that is disjunctively *realised*. To wit: a multiply based property is disjunctive iff it has no realiser in any metaphysically possible world that it lacks in the actual world. Jade is disjunctive because the only metaphysically possible worlds for jade are the ones which contain either [jadeite or nephrite] ... or both. By contrast, multiply based properties that are disjunctively realised have different bases in different worlds." (Fodor (1997), p. 153) Fodor deems this distinction between a functional and multiply realised property and a disjunctive property as carrying important consequences for projectability. In his view, the realised functional property, but not its physical realiser, is projectable (with respect to its effects). And this is precisely so because the conditional that contains it is metaphysically stronger, or more comprehensive, than the conditional containing the disjunction of its realisers.

So, in light of these considerations it is not clear that the projectability argument, going back to Kim and being used by Heil, has force against the functionalist level model. Peculiarly, Heil himself manifestly acknowledges projectability of higher-order predicates later in his book, when he postulates certain similarity relations between the realising properties (p. 41). As I will show later, though, this strategy is not successful.

As a conclusion of this section I would like to point out that, in my view, some, but not all, of the arguments stated by Heil as defeaters of an ontology postulating levels of being carry argumentative force. The strongest arguments are the causal exclusion argument and the argument against interlevel lawlike relations.

4 Heil's theory

In the face of all the difficulties that a layered ontology leads into, Heil aims to develop an altogether different account: one that reduces all levels to a single level (or "no level") and thus becomes a member of the family of "ontological reductionist" theories. The pivotal challenge for Heil, as for any ontological reductionist, is to give a convincing answer to those questions that the level theorist believes to be intractable for reductionism and which thereby serve as the very impetus for the development of level theories.

Heil himself calls his theory "pure realism" (p. 58), by which he means a non-eliminative monism or reductionism. A summary of this view is found in the following quotation.

> "Imagine someone who regards the world as comprising dynamic arrangements of particles. These particles possess distinctive properties. Particle complexes exhibit characteristics that stand in an unmysterious relation to properties of their constituents so arranged. Some of these complexes and some of their properties are salient to us as observers and manipulators. These we mark off with concepts expressed by predicates in our language. The concepts and predicates we deploy typically reflect perfectly genuine similarities and differences. In most cases, these similarities and differences do not depend on us, or on our concepts." (p. 57)

In this section I will present an analysis of Heil's theory that highlights what I believe to be its five central and characteristic aspects. This will serve as the basis for an evaluation of Heil's account in section 5.

(I) As was explained above, Heil rejects the Picture Theory and together with it the need to postulate levels of reality. However, in his view, this does not entail eliminativism. Tables, surfboards and stock markets do exist, and many statements involving predicates like "is a tree" or "feels pain" are literally true. But trees do not exist on a distinct ontological level; rather there is only one ontological level (p. 49) and this level serves as the truthmaker both for basic level descriptions, such as the true statements of physics, and true higher-level descriptions, such as "Trees are green". There are no levels of reality (except perhaps levels of complexity (pp. 10, 50)), but only descriptive "levels". Therefore Heil's theory is ontologically, but not analytically, reductive. As such it is not an "identity theory" in the common sense (p. 10). Presupposing such a model we can avoid the puzzles that come along with accepting the Picture Theory, as, for instance, the causal exclusion problem, the question of interlevel relations etc. "These ... are puzzles of our own making." (p. 8)

As pointed out above, Heil observes a manifold influence of the Picture Theory on philosophical analysis. In abandoning the Picture Theory outright, he paves the way to a monist ontology, whereby most puzzles associated with the Picture Theory and level models simply disappear.

(II) Only *saying* that all troubles disappear, however, is not enough, of course. Such good news are not believed until they have been proved, especially as there are a number of problems that monist theories are believed to face *in virtue* of being monist. Among such is the charge that monist theories ultimately run into various kinds of eliminativism with respect to macro-entities This general reasoning concerning the relationship of our theories can be stated in the following principle.

> "(Where G's are presumed to be uncontroversial items – those posited by the physical sciences, for instance – and F's are putatively higher-level items) if talk of F's cannot be analysed, paraphrased, wholly decomposed into talk of G's, either F's are distinct from G's or there are no F's." (p. 51)

If a theory yields a strong eliminativism with respect to all macro-items this is commonly considered a *reductio* for that theory. Is the eliminativist charge for monist theories justified, then? Heil doesn't think so. The author emphasises to be a realist about trees and surfboards, whereby he denies being an eliminativist. At the same time, he carefully avoids subscribing to a view that assigns distinctness to trees with respect to their realisers. Consequently, he is committed to rejecting the mentioned principle. But what is the alternative then? Is a realist position with respect to higher-level predicates combined with a one-level ontology intelligible? How the author conceives of such a "pure realism" is pointed out in the following passage:

> "It is close to a truism that many of the concepts we use hold of objects by virtue of properties possessed by those objects; but this does not imply either that if you are a realist with respect to a given concept you must assume that it picks out a single property shared by every object that satisfies it or that it must be possible to analyse the concept into concepts that correspond to a class of prop-

erties, any one of which suffices for the application of the concept." (p. 44, similar points are made on pp. 46, 48, 52, 53, and 73)

In other words, according to Heil, a predicate can "apply truly" (pp. 27, 48) to a number of objects, even if these objects do not instantiate a single property. To acknowledge "true application" is all that's required to be realist about predicates and so for the time being the eliminativist charge is avoided through the concept of "true application".

But of course, only shifting the whole matter onto the concept of "true application" cannot serve as an ultimate solution. "True application" is a notion that is in need of explanation itself. The point is that, even if the referents of our truly applying higher-order predicates do not satisfy a single property, it is evident that there must be *some constraints* that determine whether a predicate truly applies to an object or not, as application is not an arbitrary matter. The question why a predicate applies to a number of objects, that do not instantiate a single property is evidently not answered by the mere indication that it does. And thus it becomes clear that in order for Heil to fully avoid the eliminativist charge, he still needs to give an account of how reference, i.e. in fact multiple reference, is constrained and wherefrom it receives its non-arbitrariness.

The solution, which Heil offers is summarised under point (IV). Before it is presented, though, point (III) will show that Heil does seem to believe in a bijective mapping of our basic predicates (contained perhaps in a future theory of physics) and the basic entities of the world. Thereby it becomes obvious that the author does acknowledge the mentioned asymmetry between our basic theory and all higher-level theories.

(III) Although in general Heil's enthusiasm for the Picture Theory is markedly limited, to say the least, he does seem to approve the Picture Theory when it comes to contemporary physics (or a suitable future theory of physics). The language of physics, in his view, bijectively maps the basic entities of the world, as is evident from the following passage:

> "But consider the language of physics. Here it looks as though we have something close to what we need: a name corresponding to every kind of object ("electron", "quark", "lepton"), and a predicate corresponding to every property ("mass n", "spin up", "negative charge")." (p. 6)

A second hint is found in the following (already above-mentioned) passage. According to Heil, as a realist you do not necessarily have to assume "... that [a given concept] picks out a single property shared by every object that satisfies it or that it must be possible to analyse the concept into concepts that correspond to a class of properties, any one of which suffices for the application of the concept. This is not how our concepts work" (p. 44). At the end of this sentence Heil sets a footnote saying "Perhaps this is how concepts of a fundamental physics work" (p. 44, footnote 8). Although the word "perhaps" indicates that Heil is somewhat hesitant to fully commit himself to a Picture Theory with respect to physics on this page, taken together with the quotation from (p. 6) it becomes evident that such a model does underlie his overall theoretical scheme. From this it follows that the eliminativist charge is a true challenge for Heil that needs to be met.

(IV) In section (II) it was pointed out that Heil avoided the eliminativist charge through the concept of "true application" of a predicate, which left him with the task to demonstrate how "true application" works. Heil takes two related roads to provide an answer. The first one is to explain predicate application by similarity relations that hold between the referents of a predicate, or between the causal powers of the referents of a predicate. The second one essentially builds on the workings of our perceptual system (although it is not entirely clear that Heil seriously pursues this explanatory path).

Predicate application through similarity: On the multi-level model all objects satisfying a truly applying predicate display an instance of a single kind property. For some predicates the respective kindproperty turn out to be higher-level, and the presence of an instance of this higher-level property provides a sufficient account for the relation of true application. This option is obviously not available to Heil, as he does not accept an ontology containing higher levels. The question remains, though, whether the author can offer an equally strong explanation within his own framework. From Heil's point of view, the similarity relation between objects to which a single predicate truly applies fully provides what is needed here. Perfect similarity between objects amounts to each object instantiating exactly the same properties that are instantiated by the other object(s) in question. Sameness of properties is interpreted through a primitive perfect-similarity relation between the distinctive contributions the properties make to the powers of the objects that possess them. Similarity-but-not-precise-similarity between objects can be explained in terms of partial-but-less-than-total perfect similarity. Cases of object similarity that resist explanation within this reductive scheme may be explained through a less-than-perfect similarity relation between the constituent properties (p. 162). Less-than-perfect similarity between properties can be explained through a primitive less-than-perfect similarity relation between the distinctive contributions the properties make to the powers of the objects that possess them.

Therefore, under this scheme, all cases of perfect or less-than-perfect similarity between objects are explained through perfect or less-than-perfect similarity relations of the constituent basic properties. In other words, perfect or less-than-perfect similarity between *higher-level* objects are fully explained through perfect or less-than-perfect similarity relations of the constituent *basic* properties.

Heil thinks that once similarity is straightened out, true predicate application comes along. All that's required for true application is some kind of similarity relation between the objects referred to. In many cases this similarity will simply amount to perfect similarity or partial perfect similarity. In some other cases it will amount to less-than-perfect similarity between some of the properties displayed by the objects. So, for instance, in the case of the truly applying predicate "red":

> "As it happens, objects can be red without – in any obvious sense – sharing a property in virtue of which they could be said to be red. Tomatoes, pillar boxes, and redheads possess similar-but-not-precisely-similar properties. And this is evidently enough for the predicate "is red" to apply to them." (p. 27)

Or in the case of the pain predicate:

> "The Pain predicate applies or would apply to creatures in virtue of those creatures' possession of any of a possibly open-ended family of similar properties. These properties fall under the pain predicate because they are relevantly similar: similar, perhaps in the contribution they make to the dispositional and qualitative character of their possessors' states of mind." (p. 153)

True predicate application begins and ends where similarity begins and ends, such that there is a bijective mapping between the relation of same-predicate application and some proper similarity relation between objects. As Heil says: "Concepts, and words used to express these, are in most cases satisfied by endless similar things; and similarity grades off imperceptibly into dissimilarity" (p. 49)

Predicate application in virtue of the make-up of our perceptual system: in section 5, I will show that, ultimately, the similarity relation is insufficient to explain true predicate application and that in fact there is no such bijective mapping between similarity and true application of same predicate. But before this trickier task is carried out, I want to emphasise that a second explanatory path indicated by Heil does not provide a solution either. This path draws on the claim that true predicate application is partly due to the structure of our perceptual system. Although it is not entirely clear that Heil actually believes in this path (certain passages on pp. 40, 44 and 165 suggest the contrary), sometimes he seems to credit it some explanatory force. So, for instance, in the following quotation:

> "There is, I gather, no prospect of defining or analysing redness in terms of ... physical properties. This is due, in some measure, to the fact that the properties in question are salient – to us – partly owing to the nature of our perceptual system." (p. 44)

What is true about this statement is that the fact that the properties we perceive are perceived by us is due to the second fact that we have the appropriate capacities to perceive them. If we did not have these capacities then we would not have perceived the respective properties. What is much less clear, however, is the claim implicitly suggested by the statement that the properties owe their existence partly to the make-up of our perceptual system, or that the properties *depend* in part on our perceptual system (just as illusions depend mostly on us). When we perceive something red, then the world must offer us a sufficient basis from which we can "extract" or even "construct" our perception. It is this basis that we mean when we speak of "properties" and the basis is quite certainly not created by us. In short, creation of property perception is not to be confused with property creation. This is why reference to the make-up of our perceptual system cannot provide a promising explanation for higher-level properties or higher-level predicate application. I assume that this is the reason why Heil eventually rejects an explanation of true application in terms of perceptual make-up (p. 165).

(V) Although a hint has already been given, something needs to be said about how Heil wants to accommodate what is commonly known as the "multiple realisability" of properties. Within Heil's ontological framework this notion receives a simple reinterpretation. Literally speaking, there are no properties that are multiply realised; rather there are concepts or predicates that apply "multiply" to various different objects. The application relation is explained through certain similarity relations among the objects to which the multiply applying predicate refers. The predicates come in different "levels of abstraction" and that in itself explains in part what we really mean when we talk about multiple realisation. What we do is "... describing functional processes at an elevated level of abstraction. We can only identify egg-beaters as such because we have elected to describe egg-beaters in a relatively "abstract", non-specific way" (p. 115). In the end, the abstractness and non-specificity of our descriptions is all there is to multiple realisability, but there are no corresponding properties here, and least of all "non-specific properties".

5 Arguments against Heil

In this section I shall argue that, as it stands, Heil's model cannot serve the purposes for which it was set out. My main claim will be that there is a flaw in Heil's theory and that this flaw, due to its pivotal position in the theory, has severe consequences for the entire model. Roughly, the shortcoming consists in the fact that the set of similarity relations elaborated by Heil is altogether insufficient to provide a plausible account of true predicate application. Since the concept of true predicate application was introduced by Heil in order to deal with the eliminativist danger, it is unclear whether he can still successfully block this charge. Heil's account of multiple realisability, i.e. of multiple reference, is endangered accordingly.

(I) *Evaluating the powers of the similarity relation*: Above it was pointed out that the relation of true predicate application plays a central role in Heil's theory. As it was concluded in section 4, IV: in Heil's view, what is only required for true application "... is some kind of similarity relation between the objects referred to. In many cases this similarity will simply amount to perfect similarity or partial-perfect similarity. In some other cases it will amount to less-than-perfect similarity between some of the properties displayed by the objects" (see above, section 4, IV). In all cases, if some kind of similarity relation holds, it holds in virtue of similarity relations between basic properties, or collections of these. So, whenever a predicate truly applies to two objects these objects must stand to one another in at least one of the mentioned similarity relations, where appropriate similarity is determined by the nature of their basic properties. Furthermore they both must at least be more similar to each other than they are with respect to any object to which the predicate in question does not apply. Whether, additionally, they are required to be *dissimilar* to that third object as well is not entirely clear. But certainly, *if* the third object *is* dissimilar with respect to the first two, then the predicate cannot apply to this object. The wit is that, although these demands are undoubtedly met by some cases, they are not met by many other possible, or perhaps even actual, cases. That this is can be illustrated by the following example.

We are considering a situation in which the predicate "is red" truly applies to two objects, o_1 and o_2, that are – as far as we know – entirely red, but not to a third object, o_3, as this object is uncontroversially not red. From Heil's point of view the redness of the first two objects (which I will call two objects' "state of being red") may in some cases be realised by two states that share perfectly similar collections of properties (let's call these states e_1 and e_2). For instance, the objects will display two perfectly alike surface structures. In contrast, the surface structure of the third object (e_3) will evidently be dissimilar to the surface structures of the first two objects.

In some cases, however, the first two objects will not be perfectly similar but differ to some minimal extent even though they will still be completely and uncontroversially red. That is to say, the surface structures of the first two objects (depicted as e_1 and e_2) will be imperfectly similar to some low degree (let's call this similarity relation the "*similar^{-1} $\approx$*"-relation). But, as Heil would concede, the fact that objects o_1 and o_2 have two similar, even if not perfectly similar, surface structures doesn't keep them from being red at all. Rather, it is precisely this similarity relation that provides a sufficient explanation *why* the objects are both in the state of being red. Furthermore, the fact that the similar surface structures of o_1 and o_2 display some dissimilarity with respect to the surface structure of object o_3 (the latter relation is depicted as the "*dissimilar $\neq$*"-relation) is the explanation why o_3 is not red. But now the matter gets more complex. We can reasonably argue that, in the same way as the two slightly dissimilar surface structures e_1 and e_2 realise the state of being red for objects o_1 and o_2, each of the two surface structures can itself be realised by two slightly differing molecular states: $e_{1,1}$ and $e_{1,2}$; respectively $e_{2,1}$ and $e_{2,2}$. *Ex hypothesi*, the two molecular states realising the first surface structure, $e_{1,1}$ and $e_{1,2}$, are related by another "*similar*$^{-1}$ $\approx$"-relation as they are slightly-less-than-perfectly similar with respect to each other. But, plausibly, they both are only slightly-less-than-slightly-less-than-perfectly-similar with respect to the two molecular structures, $e_{2,1}$ and $e_{2,2}$, that realise the surface structure of the second object o_2 (this relation is depicted as the "*similar*$^{-2}$ $\approx$"-relation).

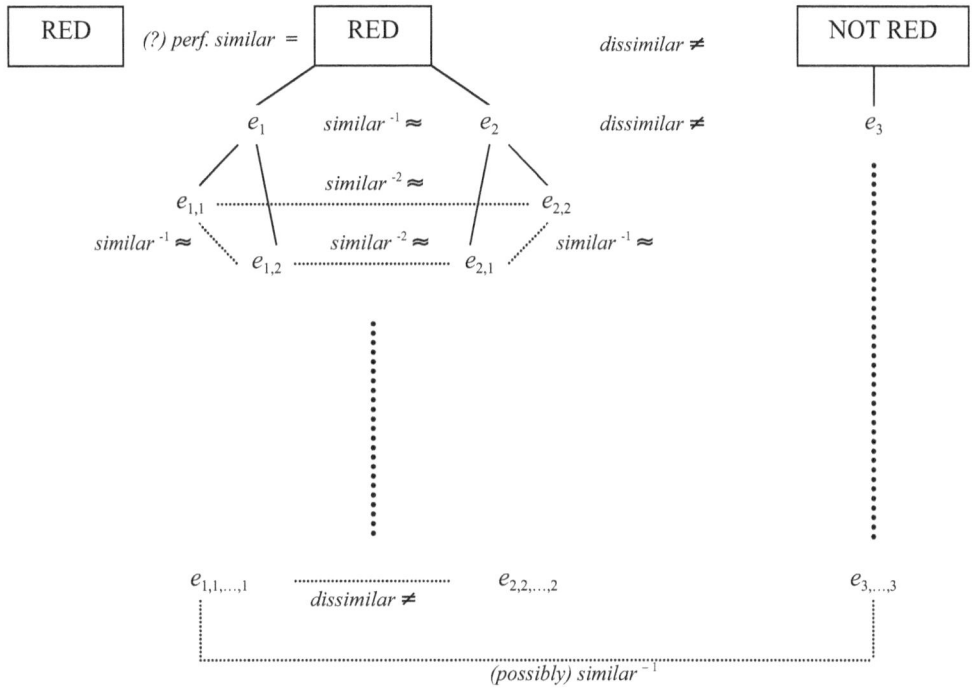

The morale of the example is that, if the same scheme is played through until we get to some basic states (collections of quarks etc.) that ultimately ground the sequence of realising states (...→ atom configurations → molecule arrangements → surface structures →...) of o_1 and o_2 and thus the state of being red, it is quite plausible to imagine that, in some cases, two states (let's call them $e_{\underbrace{1,1,...,1}_{n}}$ and $e_{\underbrace{2,2,...,2}_{n}}$) that have been identified as such basic realising states of o_1 and o_2 will lack any significant similarity with respect to each other. At the same time it is plausible to imagine a case in which one out of these two states, let's say $e_{\underbrace{1,1,\ldots,1}_{n}}$, will display some striking similarity (possibly to the extent of similarity "$similar^{-1} \approx$") to one of the basic realisers of the surface structure of the third object o_3, which by stipulation is not red.

The simple point that this example proves is that a similarity relation qualified through basic properties, or collections of basic properties (displayed by basic states), does not suffice to explain homogeneous higher-level predicate application. The reason is that even if – as is sensibly supposed – we may be able to detect some kind of obvious similarity between some (still higher-level) states that realise the presumed higher-level state (as certain similar surface structures realise the property of being red), this does not secure similarity "all the way down". Once we get to the bottom realisers of a given higher-level state, we may be unable to detect any similarity among them. Simultaneously, we may be able to detect some striking similarities between a state that realises the given higher-level state and a state that evidently does not realise the higher-level state. In other words, the similarity relation as construed by Heil does not provide a sufficient tool to explain *why* a predicate truly applies when it truly applies.[7]

This shouldn't come as a surprise, as this conclusion is at the very heart of the notion of multiple realisation. And in fact, in some parts of his book Heil himself seems to assert the possibility that the realising states of a given higher-level state, respectively the basic states satisfying a given predicate, may lack any detectable similarity. This seems to be the case in the following quotation, for instance:

> "... cases of multiple realisability are typical cases in which some predicate applies to an object in virtue of that object's possession of any of a diverse range of properties." (p. 160)

Possibly, the following quotation, taken from a discussion about the classically puzzle of "the statue and the lump of bronze", points into the same direction:

> "The truth-makers for our statue talk will be staggeringly complex, and, from the point of view of physics, hideously unruly." (p. 189)

What else could be meant by the terms "diverse range of properties" and "hideously unruly" other than a complete lack of similarity between the

---

[7] See also Pineda (2002), p. 33.

properties in question? On the other hand, Heil repeatedly commits himself to the similarity relation as the grounder of the relation of true predicate application, as it is evident from the following quotations.

> "Unlike the class of properties answering to "is the mass of an electron", the class of properties answering to "is red" is not an equivalence class, but a class of properties that resemble one another to a greater or lesser extent." (p. 143)

> "Perhaps similar properties answering to higher-level predicates are invariably either complex (but contain identical or exactly similar constituents), or simple and flatly imperfectly similar." (p. 160)

What are we to make of this? On pp. 164 – 165 Heil himself considers a variant of the argument developed above. In his version, there are three red objects possessing properties P_1, P_2, and P_3 respectively. These properties are similar but imperfectly so. Then there are three green objects possessing properties P_5, P_6, and P_7 respectively. Additionally, there are objects possessing P_4 that, too, look red to ordinary observers. As it turns out, though, P_4 is as at least as similar to P_5, as P_5 is to P_6, and as P_6 is to P_7; but it is not similar at all to P_1, P_2, and P_3. The situation is essentially the same as in the example elaborated above, only that in Heil's variant there are no mediating similarities such as those between the two surface structures (although they could be incorporated into his example as well, I presume).

Heil recognises the force of the example and he offers three ways out. On the first one, the fact that, as in the above example, objects having $e_{\underbrace{1,1,...,1}_{n}}$ and $e_{\underbrace{2,2,...,2}_{n}}$, but not $e_{\underbrace{3,3,...,3}_{n}}$ are red is explained with reference to our perceptual system. Under this approach, the objects are red in virtue of standing in a certain mutual relation together with some complex property D_1 of our colour-detection system. An object is red then, "... owing to its possessing P_1, say, and our possessing D_1" (p. 165). However, as it was already argued in section 4.IV, accounts of this kind are unpromising. The reason is simple. Even given our possession of D_1 there can be cases of the kind illustrated in the examples, and so the whole thing starts all over again.

The second option Heil considers is the simple denial that the object having $e_{\underbrace{1,1,...,1}_{n}}$ (or in his example P_4) really *is* red. We may simply be incapable of recognising that the object having $e_{\underbrace{1,1,...,1}_{n}}$ is not red. This, however, is not a good solution either. The problem is that we may find out that we – and all other actual and possible observers – are incapable of recognising that the object in question is in fact not red. This poses the question of *why* this collective misapprehension is the case. Since merely pointing at our perceptual systems doesn't help much (as shown above), we are back to asking what it is about the world that makes the collective misapprehension possible. And since it cannot be similarity, we are missing an explanation again.

Let's recall which state of the dialectics we are at now. The examples developed by Heil and myself demonstrated that, within Heil's theoretical framework, the similarity relation between basic properties is insufficient to account for true predicate application and thus to block related troubles, such as the eliminativist charge. However, alternative explanatory strategies that renounce the similarity relation have not fulfilled the hopes initially associated with them. Consequently, Heil chooses the strategy of returning to the similarity relation in trying to bolster it and make it fit for the task to be accomplished.

The author points out that, arguably, contributing the property of "being red" is a true dispositional capacity of the basic realising state $e_{\underbrace{1,1,...,1}_{n}}$ (respectively of P_4). If this disposition is included into the dispositional make-up of $e_{\underbrace{1,1,...,1}_{n}}$ (respectively of P_4) then, even if the red objects respectively having $e_{\underbrace{1,1,...,1}_{n}}$ and $e_{\underbrace{2,2,...,2}_{n}}$ (or P_1 and P_4 respectively) turn out to have no other similar properties, this disposition will serve as the creator of a sufficient similarity relation. Consequently:

> "Considered as powers or dispositions ... P_5, P_6, and P_7 are in this regard more similar to one another than they are to P_4; and P_4 is dispositionally similar to P_1, P_2, and P_3. This similarity is a perfectly objective matter; the dispositional similarity P_1, P_2, P_3 and P_4 is intrinsic to P_1, P_2, P_3 and P_4." (p. 165)

As intellectually appealing as this move may be, it remains a sleight of hand. Let's look at the facts. If you ask the physicist he will tell you that there is definitely a bigger similarity between $e_{\underbrace{1,1,\ldots,1}_{n}}$ and $e_{\underbrace{3,3,\ldots,3}_{n}}$ concerning the physical properties. If you disagree and insist that $e_{\underbrace{1,1,\ldots,1}_{n}}$ and $e_{\underbrace{2,2,\ldots,2}_{n}}$ are in fact more similar to each other than $e_{\underbrace{1,1,\ldots,1}_{n}}$ and $e_{\underbrace{3,3,\ldots,3}_{n}}$ are because of a certain further dispositional property, namely the disposition of "looking red in circumstances C", then the physicist, maintaining a certain sympathy with balky philosophers, will perhaps tell you that this may well be so. But he will also tell you that the further property of "looking red in circumstances C" detected by you cannot be physical, because he has already isolated *all* the determinate physical properties the object in question has.

In other words, if the disposition of "looking red in circumstances C" is included as a real property/disposition into the set of intrinsic properties/dispositions then the object having the property/disposition of "looking red in circumstances C" has at least one property/disposition that is not a basic-level property/disposition, namely the property/disposition of "looking red in circumstances C". Therefore, if Heil wants to maintain this corollary, he will create a tension within his theoretical framework, as it was one of the essential tenets of his theory that there are no levels of reality. If this tension can be shown to be a plain contradiction, this would obviously be a disastrous result for Heil's entire ontological programme.

If in the face of these results, Heil will probably choose to reject the claim that the disposition of "looking red in circumstances C" ought to be included into the set of genuine properties of the object's being red. Then, however, the consequences would perhaps be disastrous all the same, as this would mean that Heil lacks a working account to support one of the central tenets of his view. What "true application" really is would remain in the dark.

(II) If the conclusions of the last section are cogent, this has consequences for related matters as well. As it was argued above, if Heil cannot provide a sufficient account of true predicate application, it is not clear that he can meet the eliminativist charge. And if, as some sections of his book suggest, Heil assumes a bijective mapping between the predicates of (a future) physics and the basic entities in the world whilst true application cannot be made to work, it may in fact seem as though Heil will have difficulties in making plausible that trees exist just as much as electrons, quarks and the like do. "Pure realism" may be endangered.

(III) Similar points concern the matter of multiple realisation. Heil had reinterpreted multiple realisation of higher-level states as multiple reference/ application of higher-level predicates. However, it can be demonstrated that Heil has difficulties in explaining true predicate application (because the similarity relations endorsed by him proved insufficient), he will thereby have problems to make sense of multiple realisation or multiple reference as well.

6 Sketch of a positive account

In contrast to Heil, I believe that an ontology, which dispenses with any kind of levels of being is ultimately unsatisfying. My view is mainly based on the arguments elaborated above. Ontological reductionism, or "pure realism", has severe difficulties to provide a satisfying account of true predicate application, i.e. of multiple realisation, respectively multiple reference. This may look as a harmless flaw at first; its connection to other puzzles reveals, however, that shortcomings in this particular respect are quite consequential for the entire theory. But does that mean that I am committed to classical functionalism with its picture of distinct levels that are altogether in danger of being epiphenomenal? Not necessarily so, as I believe. In my view, the list of alternative positions sketched by Heil at the beginning of this book is not complete. On page 21, Heil claims that we have to choose between either (a) a commitment to higher-level entities together with an abandonment of causal closure, or (b) reductionism, or (c) eliminativism. What Heil has overseen is that there is actually a fourth option available (or, if we count systematic overdetermination as a further solution, there is a fifth one), and it is this option that I want to pursue. Here I can only briefly indicate what I have in mind.

In my view, it is no coincidence that Heil eventually arrives at something of an object-level model (pp. 170 – 178). In brief, Heil defines objects as "substrata" or "substances". In order to avoid arriving at an object-level theory directly (Socrates is an object/substance but his left eyebrow is a substance well. Proof: both have properties the other lacks), the author invokes a mereological relation: higher-level objects are just composed of basic ones. In order to avoid the regress of infinite composition, such a picture requires postulating basic objects. These in turn are required to lack spatial parts, as otherwise they would be further divisible. Consequently, Heil proposes the following:

> "If ... you regard simple objects as those that lack objects as parts – objects that are not made up of other objects – then there is no reason to think that there could not be simple objects with as many spatial parts as you ." (p. 174)

The question however, is whether such objects could still be called "objects" in an intelligible sense. Furthermore, aren't spatial parts objects as well as they certainly have a number of properties? So, how can an object lack objects as parts if it is thought of as having spatial parts, which, presumably, *are* objects? The answers to these questions, I presume, will not come easy to the ontological monist. And whilst it is already quite unclear whether Heil can block the eliminativist charge with respect to properties, the puzzle of avoiding the regress that the search for basic objects falls into is perhaps even more complicated for his account. The conclusion that I feel firm to draw is that some kind of a level-model for objects seems unavoidable unless we want to put our ontology into the danger of claiming that nothing exists at all.[8]

My suggestion is to treat properties and objects alike and to construe something of a level model for both. In my view, the only objects that exist are events. As a limiting approach, events can be thought of as being regions of space, which, however, are extended only synchronically, and not diachronically. All other kinds of objects can be reduced to events; a horse, for instance, ought to be thought of as an event that has the property of "being a horse", or that "horses". All that it takes such an event to be the event that it is, is to display a certain pattern of input and output events. In other words, the nature of events is defined functionally. It should be noted that such a model has already the notion of properties "built-in", that is, the relations of "bearing" or "having" between properties and objects can be dispensed with. An important feature of this model is that events can always be included into other events. This mirrors the relation of acceding complexity that Heil proposes, but only partially so. The difference is that, in my opinion, it does not make sense to ascribe something like "dependence" or "primary existence" to either the including event or the included events (this is done if an event/object is wholly defined by composition). All events genuinely exist; "higher-level" events in

---

[8] Thomas Bontly has made a similar point against the ontology of Jaegwon Kim. See Bontly (2002).

the very same way as "lower-level" events; none is asymmetrically dependent on the other. There is, of course, *something* asymmetric about their relation, but it is not dependency. Rather, the relation between the two that bears some asymmetry is the relation of inclusion. Their dependence goes both ways.[9] The central idea is that, by the inclusion relation, higher-level events cannot really be said to be discrete from lower-level events, but, arguably, higher-level events are not identical to lower-level events either. It becomes clear then that the talk of "levels" in this model is not a talk of distinct layers that are inhabited by wholly autonomous objects. However, a certain notion of levels is entertained nevertheless. Any causal relation is bound to such a level; that is, causation only goes on between events that are located on the same level of the inclusion continuity. The inclusion relation explains the fact that supervenience is true as well. Multiple realisation receives a reinterpretation by the fact that any event can be present independently (to an extent to be specified) of the nature of the events included in it. Furthermore, predicate application is explained as there exists a class of exact-same events for each truly applying homogeneous predicate.

Obviously, spelling out these claims in more detail is beyond the scope of the present paper. However, I am quite optimistic that, if such a model is presupposed, some satisfying accounts of the puzzles of multiple realisation, of similarity relations, of true predicate application and of higher-level causation can be provided.

---

[9] Many will claim that the idea of asymmetric dependency flows directly from the notion of supervenience. This is repeatedly claimed by Jaegwon Kim (e.g. Kim (2003)). However, I am convinced to be able to show that this is a consequential misinterpretation of supervenience that stems from confusing "existential dependence" with "whole determination".

Commentary
John Heil

Harbecke thinks I subscribe to (what I call) the Picture Theory when it comes to the fundamental theories. There we find something like a one – one predicate – property correspondence. In rejecting the Picture Theory, however, I am rejecting the thesis that you could in every case "read off" features of the world from features of our descriptions of the world, the thesis that there must be a one – one predicate – property mapping, the thesis that realism requires such a mapping. This leaves entirely open the possibility that, in some cases, most particularly, in the fundamental theories, predicates do line up with properties.

Here is another way to think about it. A predicate, or at any rate a predicate applicable in the spatiotemporal world, applies to objects in virtue of those objects' possession of any of a (possibly open-ended) family of similar properties. The more refined the predicate, the more similar the properties. The limiting case are those predicates satisfied by precisely similar properties. This is what we aim at in basic physics.

Harbecke holds that appeal to similarity cannot account for the application of "higher-level" predicates such as "is red". The worry is that two objects, two tomatoes, say, could be precisely similar with respect to their coloured surfaces, but, on closer examination, revealed to be less-than-precisely similar with respect to their finer-grained molecular structure. Constituent arrangements of these molecular structures, in turn, could be even less-precisely-similar. In this way, by descending to collections of fundamental entities, similarity melts away into utter dissimilarity. By eliminating higher-levels, I eliminate similarities that are supposed to ground applications of higher-level predicates.

In this context, three features of similarity deserve mention. First, similarity is an objective relation. Similarities are not merely in the eye of the beholder. The same holds for dissimilarities: A and B can be dissimilar, but appear similar to us. Imperfectly similar objects can appear perfectly similar. This is how it is with the tomatoes. Second, similarity is an internal relation: if you have the relata, you have the relation. In this regard similarity differs from, say, being a kilometer apart. Third, objects are similar by virtue of possessing similar properties; properties are similar (or not) tout court. This is especially important to keep in mind in evaluating arguments for or against reduction.

Harbecke suggests that similarity drains away as we decompose objects into arrangements of fundamental constituents. But I say that all the similarity there is between objects is to be found in those arrangements. What Harbecke's argument shows, if it shows anything, is that as we move to the basic constituents, similarities salient so long as we consider arrangements of the basic things become more difficult to discern. Imagine two similar-shaped swarms of bees. The swarms are shaped like the letter "*Q*". We can lose sight of this similarity if we attend only to individual bees. Yet all there is to the swarms are the bees in dynamical relations to one another.

If the bees seem implausible, imagine two square-shaped tangrams. The tangrams are shaped similarly. One square is made up of triangular-shaped pieces, the other from elongated rectangular pieces. We can see how each square decomposes into parts, but once we focus just on the parts, we can easily lose sight of the squares. Someone acquainted only with the parts need not be in a position to infer that, suitably organised, they would yield squares.

Notice that the squares (or swarms) will not in fact be precisely similar, but they will be similar enough to satisfy the pertinent predicates, "is *Q*-shaped" and "is square". Does this threaten to make similarity subjective? Why should it? The similarities in question, although perfectly objective, are of no interest to someone concerned solely with the constituents. What appears to us to be perfect similarity turns out not to be perfect. What might appear to us from a different vantage point to be utter dissimilarity could turn out to be imperfect similarity. Ordinary predicates and predicates figuring in the special sciences exhibit considerable latitude here. They require for their satisfaction a measure of similarity that prevents their lining up neatly with basic predicates.

Although he does not say so explicitly, Harbecke seems to think that grounding "higher-level" similarities would require an analysis of higher-level predicates in lower-level terms in a way that preserves similarity. My thought, however, is that there can be genuine similarities not describable in a fundamental vocabulary in a way that makes those similarities salient. *A* and *B* can be similar, even though this could not be deduced from an exhaustive description of the fundamental constituents of *A* and *B*. This is simply an application to similarity of the idea that realism about *F*'s does not require an analysis of *F*'s into some more basic vocabulary.

Philosophers sometimes argue as though our only contact with the world is linguistic. As Wittgenstein puts it in the Tractatus, language "reaches out" to the world (Wittgenstein 1921, § 2.1511). What it touches depends exclusively on linguistic factors. The world is hidden behind a veil of language. But this is not how it is. We walk amongst, handle, shift, grind up, assemble, ingest, buy, and recycle objects. Terms we use to refer to these objects develop in concert with these non-linguistic interactions. The predicate "is spherical" picks out shapes salient to us, but not salient to a physicist looking at particles making up the spheres. This does not mean that sphericity is merely a "construct". The predicate enables us to mark out similarities, real similarities, discernible from our vantage point, but not from the vantage point of the physicist.

Chapter 4

Can Heil's ontological conception accommodate complex properties?[1]

Vera Hoffmann

A central tenet of Heil's ontological conception is a no-levels account of reality, according to which there is just one class of basic properties and relations, while all purported higher-level entities are configurations of these base-level entities. I argue that if this picture is not to collapse into an eliminativist picture of the world – which, I contend, should be avoided –, Heil's ontological framework has to be supplemented by an independent theory of which configurations of basic entities should count as complex entities. However, such an amendment represents a substantial ontological enhancement, so that the ensuing ontological picture is not as parsimonious as Heil claims it to be.

1 Introduction

The structure of natural language sentences, like "there is a cup on the table" or "Lausanne is a city in Switzerland", usually suggests that there are objects in the world possessing certain properties or standing in certain relations to each other. From a philosophical perspective, however, these two seemingly innocent categories – the category of objects on the one hand and the category of properties and relations on the other hand – raise various puzzles. One crucial issue is whether properties should be conceived as *universals* or rather as particularised entities. More specific questions are concerned with the status of so-called *higher-level* properties, e.g., biological or mental properties, and the discussion of whether each property is to be considered as a disposition, endowing the individuals possessing it with certain causal powers, or whether there may be purely qualitative properties. With respect to objects, a fundamental issue is whether these are just bundles of properties or whether the ontology contains individual substances as *bearers* of properties.

In his book, *From an ontological point of view*, John Heil argues that these and a number of other philosophical problems arise from the (tacit) acceptance

---

[1] I gratefully acknowledge financial support by the Volkswagen Stiftung as well as by the German Academic Exchange Service while this paper was written.

of what he calls the Picture Theory, i.e., the claim that the structure of reality is revealed to us by the structure of our linguistic representation of the world (cf. Heil (2003), pp. 5 – 6). Rejecting the *Picture Theory*, Heil offers a positive account of properties and objects and argues that his alternative conception can solve philosophical puzzles which result from assuming too tight a connection between language and ontology. Concerning the ontology of properties in particular, he defends the following three theses:

(I) *Identity theory*: properties are always dispositional and qualitative at the same time (cf. Heil (2003), p. 111).

(II) *No-levels conception*: there are no higher-level properties; yet there are complex properties composed of basic physical properties (cf. Heil (2003), pp. 8, 142).

(III) *Mode theory*: properties are not universals, but particulars, i.e., tropes or modes (cf. Heil (2003), pp. 127 – 128).

Thesis (II) – the no-levels conception of reality – is a central tenet of Heil's ontological picture. According to this conception, the entities constituting the world are sparse. There is a class of basic properties and objects; what exactly these are cannot be determined by philosophical investigation alone, but only by recourse to empirical inquiry. Apart from these basic entities, there are no "higher-level" entities in the usual philosophical sense of the word, but we should still assume that there are entities which – although entirely composed of basic entities – belong to levels of higher complexity (cf. Heil (2003), p. 173).

My aim in this paper is to show that Heil's account of properties can only be upheld in its present form if it is supplemented by either an independent theory of macroscopic objects or an independent account of which entities should count as complex properties. I argue that, although Heil's theory of macroscopic objects suggests that his ontological conception should rather be supplemented by a theory of complex properties than a theory of complex objects, the theses (I) – (III) concerning the ontology of properties are better compatible with an ontology supplemented by an independent theory of complex objects. I further argue that independently of which of the two options is chosen, the ensuing conception of reality is not as parsimonious as one might hope, given the initial assumptions of Heil's no-level ontology – unless the claim that there are properties belonging to levels of higher complexity is entirely given up, which yields an eliminativism bearing philosophical problems of its own.

I give a general outline of Heil's conception of properties and objects in sections 2 and 3. In section 4, I show that Heil's three theses concerning properties should be supplemented by an account of complex entities and discuss whether this should rather be an account of complex properties or an account of complex objects. In the last section (section 5), I argue that the consequence drawn in the foregoing section could only be avoided by an eliminativist ontology, but that the latter is not an adequate option in view of the numerous successful investigations in the special sciences.

2 Heil's conception of properties

According to thesis (I), which Heil calls the *identity theory*, the received view that properties are either dispositional or categorical, not both, has to be rejected. To illustrate this conception, Heil considers the property of being spherical. Proponents of the traditional view would presumably regard this as a quality and claim that if sphericity were regarded as a dispositional property, i.e., as a power to bring about certain effects, it could not be a qualitative property at the same time. Heil argues that it is plausible to take sphericity as a disposition, for instance, as the power to roll when certain conditions are fulfilled, yet that this does not exclude that being spherical is a qualitative property as well. On the contrary, a ball's being spherical should be considered as a power and as a quality of the ball (cf. Heil (2003), p. 112).

Thesis (I) is of great systematic importance, particularly since Heil employs it to resolve problems which play a central role in the current debate in the philosophy of mind, such as the problem of mental causation and problems related to assuming the existence of qualia, i.e., purely qualitative mental properties (cf. Heil (2003), pp. 223 – 239; Heil & Robb (2003), pp. 188 – 189). The aspect which is primarily relevant to my current argument, however, is the contention that each genuine property is dispositional.

Thesis (II) consists in the rejection of the popular assumption that the world is composed of distinct hierarchically ordered levels of reality, such that, for instance, psychological properties or states belong to a higher level than neurobiological properties or states, which in turn belong to a higher level than physical properties or states. Heil contends that this view is an unfortunate consequence of the Picture Theory which implies that for each higher-level *predicate*, there must be a corresponding higher-level *property*. If the Picture Theory is abandoned, there is no reason to postulate the existence of higher-level properties which raise serious philosophical problems – notably the problem of mental causation (cf. Heil (2003), pp. 7 – 8).

Heil's positive account in this respect is that the ontology contains only basic properties which are defined as the properties of basic objects, while it is an empirical question what these basic objects are. However, it is compatible with this conception that the ontology also contains complex properties constituted by combinations of basic properties. As such they are as real as the basic properties of which they consist (cf. Heil (2003), p. 142).

This view – that there are no genuine ontological levels, but nevertheless levels of higher complexity – apparently supports a *reductionist*, but *non-eliminativist* picture of reality. What are usually considered as higher-level properties, e.g., mental or biological properties, are merely complex properties which can be directly related to the basic properties of which they consist. This holds true at least if only instantiations, i.e., tokens of these properties, are taken into account: any instantiation of a biological property, for instance, can be considered as a complex configuration of instances of microphysical properties, which is usually taken to mean that the biological is reducible to the physical. On the other hand, the so-called *higher-level properties* are still "perfectly real complex properties" (Heil (2003), p. 143) which are ineliminable in the sense that it is these complex entities, not the basic entities constituting them, which are the subject of investigation in the special sciences, such as biology or psychology.[2]

According to thesis (III), the traditional conception of properties as universals should be refuted. Instead, properties should be considered as "*particularized* ways objects are" (Heil (2003), p. 127, my emphasis). Thus, the ontology does not contain universals like whiteness or squareness, but tropes, i.e., concrete instantiations of properties, such as the whiteness of the cup standing on my desk or the squareness of the window facing me while I am writing this paper. Heil prefers the notion of mode to the notion of trope, since the latter is frequently associated with a bundle theory of objects, which he rejects (cf. section 3), while the notion of mode is purported to be more neutral concerning this point (cf. Heil (2003), pp. 127 – 128).

A crucial criterion to distinguish universals from modes is related to the conditions of their identity and individuation. The criteria of individuation

---

[2] For ease of linguistic expression in the argument to follow, I employ the notion of a higher-level property in order to describe such ineliminable, but reducible complex properties, and the notion of base-level property to signify a property belonging to the lowest level of complexity – even if this nomenclature contravenes Heil's idea of a no-levels ontology.

for universals are usually independent of the criteria of individuation for the objects instantiating them: it is possible for two numerically distinct objects to instantiate numerically identical universals. The individuation of modes, by contrast, is related to the individuation of the objects instantiating them: it is regarded as a necessary condition for the identity of modes that they are instantiated by numerically the same objects; in other words, two numerically distinct objects cannot instantiate numerically identical modes (cf. Heil (2003), p. 141). Modes can hence not be considered independently of the objects to which they belong, so that a crucial part of a complete ontological picture is an adequate account of objects. I present Heil's view on objects in the subsequent section.

3 A question of ontological priority: objects or properties?

In outlining his conception of properties, Heil seems to presuppose a basic understanding of the notion of an object, for instance, when he characterises properties as ways objects are or argues that the individuation of modes depends on the individuation of objects. However, giving an account of what objects are clearly is an ontological issue of its own.

Heil discards the view – often associated with trope theories – that objects are mere bundles of properties (hence his preference for the term "mode" instead of "trope") in favour of a substance theory of objects. In contrast to a bundle theory, according to which objects are just constituted by properties and hence derivative from properties in a certain sense, Heil's account takes objects to be the basic entities, while properties or modes are ways objects are (cf. Heil (2003), p. 172). This ontological priority of objects over modes or properties holds true at least in the case of basic objects and modes. Now according to Heil, the nature of the objects forming the basic constituents of the world can only be determined by recourse to results of the empirical sciences. These results may be incompatible with the view that the basic objects are particles and rather suggest that there are fields or even just one single object, like space-time or a quantum field. This implies that in the case of those entities which we usually regard as ordinary middle-sized objects – tables, birds, or computers – the answer to the question of ontological priority may not be as straightforward as in the case of basic objects. For it would be an injudicious consequence of the Picture Theory to assume that each singular term occurring in our natural language had to designate an object in an ontologically robust sense. Rather, middle-sized objects may just be modes, "ways the ultimate bits of the world are organized" (Heil (2003), p. 190).

Heil supports the contention that complex objects are dependent on modes, not vice versa, by the famous example of the relationship between a statue and the lump of bronze of which it is made. Evidently, these two entities differ in their modal properties, e.g., the lump of bronze would survive being smashed, while the statue would be destroyed when smashed. Now, according to the principle of the indiscernibility of identicals, x and y can only be the same object if for all properties (modes) A the following holds: A belongs to x iff A belongs to y. If this principle is taken to apply to modal properties as well, it entails that the statue and the lump of bronze are not the selfsame object (cf. Heil (2003), pp. 181 – 183). Heil argues that consequently the statue and the lump of bronze should be considered as different modes (cf. Heil (2003), p. 190).

Clearly, if the entities which we usually regard as middle-sized objects are construed in this way, the relation of ontological priority is reversed as compared to the case of base-level entities, i.e., complex properties are taken to be ontologically primary to what could still be considered as complex objects. In the following section, I investigate the consequences of this view in the context of Heil's theory of properties.

4 Complex properties and middle-sized objects

Thesis (II) entails that over and above the base-level modes whose nature can be investigated only by empirical means, there is a class of ineliminable complex modes. Now it appears plausible to assume that not any arbitrary configuration of base-level properties should count as such an ineliminable complex mode. For a strong motivation to include complex properties into the ontology is to be able to give an account of those features which are investigated by the special sciences. In biology, for instance, an organism's trying to get water may causally be explained by the dehydration of its cells. Making sense of such explanations clearly does not require that the phenomena appealed to – in this case, the organism's behaviour and the physiology of its cells – are *irreducible* to base-level entities. However, it is plausible to assume that the features occurring in such statements are not chosen in a completely arbitrary way. For instance, it would be hard to justify why a widely scattered entity, such as the conjunction of the charge of an electron in New York, the temperature of a drop of water in London, and the weight of a carbon atom in Tokyo should be regarded as a single mode which can reasonably be investigated by some special science. It should be noted that within Heil's conceptual framework, it is not possible to qualify a configuration of basic properties as a complex property iff it occurs in a meaningful explanation of the special sciences, for this would be a direct application of the Picture Theory. The general problem is hence to define an independent ontological criterion which a configuration of base-level properties has to fulfil in order to count as a complex property.

A plausible way of conceiving the relationship between complex and base-level entities is to regard a configuration of base-level properties as a complex property iff all its basic components are properties of basic objects which are part of a single macroscopic object. In fact, this is the standard view underlying numerous accounts of the relationship between macro-properties and micro-physical features, e.g., functionalist approaches or theories based on the relation of supervenience. Such a view is also appealed to by Heil when he characterises complex properties as properties belonging to complex objects (cf. Heil (2003), p. 142).

In accordance with this consideration, the problem of defining complex properties could be solved by an adequate theory of complex objects furnishing an independent criterion of which configurations of basic objects should count as a genuine complex (or macroscopic) object. For then a configuration of base-level modes could be defined as a complex mode iff all its basic components are modes belonging to base-level objects forming a configuration which, according to the criterion, counts as a single macroscopic object. If, however, in accordance with the argument presented in section 3, macroscopic objects should be taken as ontologically secondary to complex properties, such a criterion would render the account circular: modes would be considered as ontologically primary to objects, while objects would in turn be considered as ontologically primary to properties. Thus, against the background of Heil's theory of objects, trying to solve this difficulty by giving a criterion of complex objects is not an acceptable approach.

A different possibility, which is compatible with Heil's theory of objects, is to provide a criterion defining, without recourse to complex objects, which configurations of basic properties should count as ineliminable complex properties. Such a theory would clearly avoid circularity. In view of theses (I) and (III), however, the former option of defining complex properties by means of complex objects seems to be in better accordance with Heil's theory of properties.

According to thesis (III), properties are modes, not universals. As has been pointed out in section 2, this thesis implies that the criteria of identity for modes depend on the objects possessing them, such that a necessary condition of the numerical identity of a mode A with a mode B is that they belong to the selfsame object. Now thesis (II) entails that, over and above the base-level modes whose nature can be investigated only by empirical means, there is a class of ineliminable complex modes. Since, plausibly, thesis (III) applies to base-level modes as well as to these complex modes, the criteria of identity for complex modes should also depend on the objects associated with them.

Arguably, criteria of identity for base-level objects follow from an encompassing theory of what basic objects and properties are. If we hence presuppose with Heil that such an encompassing theory can – at least in principle – be given, a constraint concerning the identity of complex objects can be spelt out as follows: if a complex object x is numerically identical with a complex object y, each of the basic parts of which x is composed is numerically identical with (exactly) one basic part of y, and each of the basic parts of which y is composed is numerically identical with (exactly) one basic part of x, i.e., a necessary condition of the numerical identity of complex objects is the numerical identity of each of their parts.[3] It follows that a necessary condition of the numerical identity of the complex mode A with the complex mode B is that they belong to complex objects whose basic parts can be mapped onto each other in the way described.

This consideration, which is a natural consequence of Heil's ontological assumptions, apparently suggests an ontological priority of objects over complex modes, for it entails that the criterion of identity for modes at least partly hinges upon the criteria of identity for objects. Yet, the ontological priority of complex modes over *complex* objects is only a plausible consequence, but not a strict implication of the proposed necessary condition for the identity of complex modes. For this condition is ultimately only grounded on a criterion of identity for *basic* objects, which according to Heil's ontological picture are indeed ontologically primary to modes.

However, thesis (I), that each genuine property is dispositional and qualitative at the same time, also suggests that complex objects should be regarded

---

[3] In an earlier draft of this paper, I presented this as a criterion, i.e., as a necessary and sufficient condition, of the identity of complex modes. However, John Heil pointed out to me that the numerical identity of the parts of which they consist cannot be a sufficient condition for the numerical identity of complex objects, for numerically identical basic objects may constitute different complex objects when arranged in different ways.

as ontologically prior to complex modes, since it implies that each genuine property is dispositional. Heil considers dispositions to be *intrinsic* (cf. Heil (2003), p. 82), which (approximately) means that whether or not an object x instantiates a dispositional property only depends on the features of x itself, not on the environment in which x is located.

Throughout his book, Heil freely uses the notion of intrinsicness (cf., e.g., Heil (2003), p. 76) without giving an exact definition of the difference between intrinsic and extrinsic properties. There are various approaches to formulating a criterion for this distinction (cf., e.g., Langton and Lewis (1998), Francescotti (1999), Vallentyne (1997)), the common point of which is that the distinction between intrinsic and extrinsic properties conceptually requires a criterion defining which entities are objects. For if such a criterion were not available, the notion of regarding certain features as dependent or independent of an *object's* or *individual's* environment would be meaningless.

Since thesis (I) is particularly purported to solve problems related to the assumption of higher-level properties, especially problems related to the ontological and causal status of mental properties (cf. Heil & Robb (2003)), it must apply to complex properties or modes as well. Therefore, it entails that all complex modes are dispositional and consequently also intrinsic. However, making a distinction between intrinsic and extrinsic properties with respect to complex properties seems to presuppose a theory of which configurations of base-level objects count as macroscopic objects. For if any arbitrary configuration of base-level objects could be regarded as a complex object, the notion of intrinsicness would become completely relative: any complex configuration of base-level properties would be intrinsic to some equally complex configuration of base-level objects, such that, as a borderline case, even the distribution of all base-level properties over the whole world would be an intrinsic property of the complex configuration of base-level objects of which the world consists.[4]

There is no general objection to regarding the notion of intrinsicness as a concept which is relative to the configuration or class of objects under consideration.[5] In the particular case where macroscopic objects are to be constructed out of properties, however, such a notion yields counter-intuitive results. For

---

[4] It should noted that if base-level entities are considered, it is contentious for physical reasons whether there is a well-defined class of intrinsic properties (cf. Esfeld (2004), Lam (2006)). Since in the present context, I am primarily concerned with the nature of macroscopic or complex phenomena, however, I do not pursue this point any further.

[5] In a different context, Horgan explicitly employs such a concept of intrinsicness when he introduces the notion of being intrinsic to a particular spatio-temporal region (cf. Horgan (1982), p. 37).

according to common understanding, intrinsic properties determine the boundaries of the objects to which they belong. Thus, for instance, if the mode of having a mass of 10g, the mode of having a lengthy shape, and the mode of being 15cm long all have the same spatio-temporal location, they would usually be taken to define the boundaries of a single macroscopic object, e.g., of the pencil lying on the desk in front of me. Generally speaking, if macroscopic objects are to be defined by recourse to properties, it is the intrinsic properties which determine how the amorphous mass of particles of which the world consists should be split up into stable unities. But if intrinsicness is a completely relative notion, such that any complex property is intrinsic to some configuration of base-level objects, taking it to be a defining criterion of complex objects would result in ontological inflation: any possible partition of the world could in principle count as a complex object, which is an unwarrantable consequence.

One possibility to circumvent this problem could be to consider the difference between intrinsic and extrinsic properties as ontologically primitive and hence independent of a theory of objects. In principle, this is possible; therefore, neither thesis (I) nor thesis (III) strictly entail the ontological priority of complex objects over complex modes. However, apart from the fact that taking intrinsicness to be a primitive concept would presuppose a very uncommon understanding of the notion, either of the two options discussed – adding an independent theory of complex objects or adding an independent theory of complex (or intrinsic) properties – means adding substantial ontological claims to the purportedly parsimonious conception proposed by Heil.

5   A case against eliminativism

I have argued that if we assume that the world consists of different levels of complexity containing ineliminable complex properties (or rather modes), our ontological conception has to be supplemented by a theory either defining which configurations of basic modes should count as complex modes or which configuration of objects should count as complex objects. Yet, evidently, this consequence can be avoided by rejecting the initial assumption, so that the question is why we should not contend that all higher-level entities are in fact eliminable.

Heil's position concerning this issue seems to vary to a certain extent. On the one hand, he clearly denies that so-called higher-level properties, such as the property of being in pain, are eliminable: "I am not advocating ... a form of eliminativism about pain" (Heil (1999), p. 201, cf. also Heil (2003b), p. 14). On the other hand, the fact that he explicitly contends that "real properties are "sparse"" (Heil (2003), p. 142) and does not offer a positive criterion of complex entities seems to push his account in an eliminativist direction.

To decide this issue, consider the fact that various empirical sciences, e.g., biology or the social sciences, are primarily concerned with macroscopic phenomena. If these sciences are to be regarded as legitimate fields of research – which can hardly be denied – we must assume that the knowledge and the explanations they achieve at least partly depend on structures and regularities figuring at the macroscopic level. I have already pointed out that this does not amount to the strong assumption that the entities investigated by the special sciences are irreducible to lower-level entities. A minimal assumption which has to be made, however, is that there are certain (more or less) stable configurations of base-level entities which are regularly followed by other (more or less) stable configurations of base-level entities. I presume that what Heil considers to be complex properties are such stable configurations of base-level features.

According to Heil's account, the regularities discovered by the special sciences are not founded on strict relations between higher-level properties, but on *similarities* of objects with respect to their base-level properties. Therefore, the laws established by the special sciences usually hold *ceteris paribus* only, i.e., hold true as long as the circumstances are sufficiently standardised, but may fail to hold in some cases where the circumstances are not similar enough to the standard case (cf. Heil (1999), pp. 203 – 204). Heil proposes this account to reconcile his no-levels conception of ontology with the obviously successful practise of the special sciences. However, it should be noted that this strategy cannot be adequate without presupposing a general criterion of when configurations of base-level properties are sufficiently similar to ground *ceteris paribus* regularities. This is of particular importance in the case of multiply realisable properties: Heil's conception is explicitly purported to apply to features which occur as single properties in the regularities formulated by the special sciences, but may be constituted by very divergent configurations of base-level features. The paradigm cases here are mental properties, such as the property of being in pain. If these complex features are to occur in more or less stable regularities, there must be a criterion defining which configurations of basic properties are stable or unified enough to serve this purpose.

According to Heil, this unifying criterion is the relation of similarity, which he takes to be a basic, primitively given, notion (cf. Heil (2003), p. 151). If the

Picture Theory is to be avoided, the criterion of similarity for properties may not be epistemologically given, such that different configurations of base-level properties count as similar iff they figure in some law of the special sciences. Yet then Heil's account of complex properties involves a non-reducible ontological criterion of similarity serving as a structuring element determining which configurations of basic properties are the features to figure in the laws of the special sciences. But furnishing the ontology with such an independent ontological criterion of similarity is only one particular possibility to spell out an independent criterion defining what complex entities are.

Consequently, whenever Heil's ontological conception is constructed in a non-eliminativist way – as it should be in order to give an adequate account of the entities investigated by the special sciences –, it always has to be supplemented by an *ontological* criterion either defining which configurations of base-level objects should be regarded as complex objects or defining which configurations of base-level properties should be regarded as complex properties. I have argued that the former option squares better with Heil's general account of properties, yet not with his theory of complex objects. It should be noted, however, that whichever option is chosen, it represents a substantial ontological supplement to the overall framework, so that after all, the ontology is not quite as sparse as one might have initially supposed.

Commentary

John Heil

Hoffmann makes some valuable points that deserve more detailed consideration than I am prepared to give here. Let me first try to make Hoffmann's worry clear, then indicate a general line of response in keeping with the ontological framework provided in *From an ontological point of view*. I should say that Hoffmann is dead right to hold me accountable for being less than ontologically candid about the issues she discusses. For that I am most grateful.

Here is one way to spell out what Hoffmann is driving at. Assume that properties are modes. Modes are particular ways particular objects are. This ball's sphericity and its whiteness are distinct ways the ball is. Modes are dependent entities: a mode depends for its identity on the object of which it is a mode. The sphericity of this ball could not be transferred to another ball; if the ball perishes, so does its sphericity. All this is reasonably clear so long as we consider only the fundamental objects and their modes: the mass, charge, and spin of this electron, for instance.[1] Matters become murkier, however, when we turn to ordinary middle-sized objects: trees, planets, nerve cells, or, for that matter, this billiard ball. If the ball's sphericity is a mode, the ball must be an object. But if the ball is an object, it is a complex object. Hoffmann worries that, unless I can provide a general account of complex objects, I leave complex objects and their properties in limbo.

This worry is exacerbated by the possibility that what we ordinarily regard as objects are in fact modes: ways the particles are organised or local thickenings of the One. Suppose this is how it is with the ball: the ball is a mode. What of the ball's properties, its sphericity, for instance? The initial thought was that this was a mode. But modes are ways object are, and the ball is not an object!

Hoffmann thinks it obvious that there are complex objects, but I am less confident. I take seriously the possibility that there is just one object, or at any rate that what we ordinarily regard as objects are really modes. Suppose this were so. Would it follow that there are no trees, planets, nerve cells, billiard balls? To think so would be to invoke the Picture Theory: unless predicates

---

[1] What *are* the fundamental objects and modes? This is an empirical question. It could turn out that the world is corpuscular: there are many objects. But it could also turn out that there is but a single object: space-time, or the quantum field, or the One. In either case, we have the fundamental thing or things and ways it is or they are.

designate properties possessed by objects to which they truly apply or would apply, the predicates are empty: eliminativism!

The mistake is to imagine that, unless "is spherical" names a property, or "is a nerve cell" designates a kind of object, we are obliged to accept eliminativism. I would rather think that truthmakers for claims about nerve cells could turn out not to be objects, but ways objects are organised. Assume for a moment that the world is corpuscular. If God arranges the particles in the right way, God has created a nerve cell; different particle arrangements result in billiard balls. You might put this by saying that middle-sized objects – billiard balls and nerve cells – are objects *by courtesy*. The deep truth about billiard balls and nerve cells is that they are *not* objects. In the same vein, sphericity is a property only by courtesy. Perhaps, as seems likely, no ordinary object is in the strictest sense an object, no ordinary property is a property.

Hoffmann is concerned that a view of this kind is made ridiculous by the success of the special sciences. But I do not see the position as in any way at odds with the sciences. There are still trees, planets, nerve cells, billiard balls. What is eliminated are not the trees, planets, nerve cells, and billiard balls, but a philosophical conception of what these must be. The conception in question is in no way implied by the sciences; the sciences could be true, the story false: and in fact I think there is good reason to think the story *is* false.

This is how Locke is thinking in the *Essay* (II, ii) in his discussion of substances. For Locke, the only true substances are the corpuscles (and perhaps immaterial souls and God). Most of Locke's examples of substances – portions of gold, trees, human beings – are substances by courtesy. This does not amount to a denial of the existence of portions of gold, trees, human beings, but as Locke's attempt to get at the deep story about such things.[2]

In suggesting that I am at fault for failing to offer a general account of complex objects as a first step toward an account of complex properties, Hoffmann betrays a fundamental (though perhaps understandable) misunderstanding of the ontology sketched in *From an ontological point of view*. An illuminating account of the sort Hoffmann seeks would amount to a specification of ordinary objects in terms of the particles and their relations (or thickenings of the One). But I see no reason to be optimistic that such a task could be completed. History has not dealt kindly with analytic ventures of this sort.

You might worry that this leaves mysterious our coordination of ordinary predicates and particle-level descriptions of their truthmakers. But such coor-

---

[2] Descartes's and Spinoza's conceptions of material bodies as modes of extension resemble Locke's in this regard.

dination is not an analytical achievement. An arrangement of particles could serve as truthmaker for "this is a ball" or "this is spherical" and, in addition, for some far-too-complex particle-level description. The coordination of the descriptions is a largely extra-linguistic affair. We examine the ball and learn that it amounts to an arrangement of particles or local thickening of the One. We locate the pertinent particles non-linguistically when we locate the ball.

At best we arrive at an informal, ontologically second-class concept of objects that applies to ordinary things and serves our interests nicely. But it would be wrong to attempt to turn this second-class concept into something ontologically fundamental. The sciences do not provide grounds for such a move, nor, I think, does non-linguisticised ontology.

Chapter 5

Inter-theoretic deduction of explanations[1]

Christian Sachse

The main aim of this paper is to set out an argument for inter-theoretic deduction. My strategy will start with John Heil's claims about reality, truthmaker realism, and the completeness of physics. On this basis, I shall point out the motivation for inter-theoretic deduction. By contrast, the multiple realisation argument suggests the failure of inter-theoretic deduction. However, I shall sketch out a reductionist strategy that avoids these anti-reductionist consequences: multiply realised property types turn out to be abstract concepts. One can construct within the special sciences more detailed concepts that are coextensional with concepts that can be constructed within a fundamental physical theory. From these more detailed concepts the abstract concepts can be deduced. Hence, by means of this strategy, concepts, and thus explanations, are inter-theoretically deducible.

1   Starting point

There are no levels of being. There is just one reality. This is ontological reductionism. This is Heil's ontological point of view, and my starting premise. Any property token of the special sciences is identical with a certain configuration of physical property tokens. A property token of the special sciences may be, for instance, to possess yellow blossoms or to be conscious. A physical property token may be to possess a negative charge, or to possess a certain mass. However, a configuration of physical property tokens is a physical property token as well. Such a configuration of physical property tokens is what is intended in most cases when we say that a biological or a psychological property token is supposed to be identical with a physical property token.

There are different theories about the entities that there are in this one reality. In any case, a theory describes the world or parts of it by means of concepts. In order to describe an entity in the world, there are different concepts. Let us take "P" as a physical concept. Analogously, "B" is a biological concept, and "M" is psychological concept.

---

[1] The work on this paper has been supported by the Swiss National Science Foundation (SNF), grant nr. 100011-105218/1.

Theories are our epistemological account of the world. To describe entities in the world means to apply a certain concept to the entity in question. To describe the world in terms of physics is to apply physics' specific concepts. These concepts are different from the concepts of the special sciences. However, any concept aims to describe the entity it refers to. Thus, the concept of "charge" is what physicists tell us about charge. So is the concept of "blossoms" or the concept of "consciousness". In this context, to describe an entity e in the world by a certain theory is to apply a concept to e (e.g. "P", or "B", or "M").

Each concept has a certain extension. The extension of a concept is each and all of the entities in the world that make true an application of the concept in question. One may prefer to take property tokens of a certain property type as the truthmakers of a concept. This raises the question about the relationship between property types and concepts. To avoid the correspondence principle entailed by the Picture Theory, we should take property types as theoretical classifications (cf. Heil (2003), p. 26). Thus, any *property type* is a set of entities that can be described by one and the same *concept*. I shall take them as such in what follows.

Before we move on, let us consider Heil's truthmaker realism. In the first place, "...[when] a statement concerning the world is true, there must be something about the world that makes it true" (Heil (2003), p. 61). At least, it is suggested that there is something in the world that really exists and that makes true certain statements about the world.[2] In the second place, there are different true applications of concepts, and thus, there are *different* concepts about the world. Simplified, there are true physical, biological, and psychological concepts about entities in the world. Let us take in the following a "true concept" as an abbreviation of a "true statement", or a "true application of a concept". Taking ontological reductionism for granted, there have to be entities out there in the world that make true the application of different concepts. One and the same entity e might make true a physical ("P"), a biological ("B"), and a psychological ("M") concept.

This raises questions about the relationship between different concepts, and hence, between different theories. Since there is ontological reductionism, the truthmaker relation suggests that there are connections between true concepts. After all, concepts of different theories may be about one and the same entity.

---

[2] I should note that my argument for inter-theoretic deduction is not committed to truthmaker realism. But, given ontological reductionism, truthmaker realism provides a quite intelligible framework for my further considerations. I shall take it as such in what follows.

Thus, one is led to enquire about the difference between these descriptions. This question becomes more urgent if we accept that physics is capable to explain *any* entity in the most detailed manner. This motivates the inter-theoretic deduction of concepts. This is why I shall begin, in section 2, with a more detailed consideration about the relationship between physical concepts, and concepts of the special sciences.

Against this background, the multiple realisation argument for the widely supposed autonomy of the special sciences will be considered in section 3. In fact, Heil is opposed to inter-theoretic deduction. This position reflects the debate about the multiple realisation argument that can be traced back to Fodor (1974). The conclusion of the argument is that there are no physical concepts that are coextensional with concepts that are about so-called multiply realised property types. On this basis, inter-theoretic deduction seems not to be possible.

But still, I would like to argue for inter-theoretic deduction. My argument is based on both causal, and explanatory considerations. In conclusion, the multiple realisation argument does not exclude reductionist approaches to the special sciences. Any concept of the special sciences can be deduced, by means of sub-concepts, from constructed physical concepts. Outlining this strategy is the aim of section 4.

2 The motivation for inter-theoretic deduction

First and foremost, let us consider physics. In this part of the paper, I shall consider in which way the special sciences depend on physics. From this it follows in the end of this section that inter-theoretic deduction is well motivated.

The success of physics motivates a completeness claim for physics. By this is meant that physics is supposed to be complete in causal, nomological, and explanatory respects. At least, physicists take for granted this completeness. However, since my argument for inter-theoretic deduction is mainly based on causal, and explanatory issues, let me consider only these two completeness claims.

First, there is the *causal* completeness of physics. By this is meant that for any entity e that can be described by physics, insofar as e has a cause, it has a complete physical cause. "Complete" means physicists would never have to go beyond physical causation even if physical causation is probabilistic. "Insofar", because it might follow from quantum physics that uncaused changes are possible. Nonetheless, physicists always search for causes *within* physics.

To put it another way, there are no other, non-physical causes that could fill in any gaps that there may be in physical causation. Suppose that causal relations are probabilistic; physics still completely determines the probabilities, and physics furthermore provides the best explanation of physical causal relations. To illustrate one case in point, physicists may consider an entity e as an atom-configuration. To explain what happens when this atom-configuration changes its structure or its motion, we seek a complete cause within physics. There might be some causal influence by another atom-configuration or some waves of light for instance.

However, suppose physics turned out to be incomplete in causal respects. As a result of this, physics would be incomplete in explanatory respects as well. There would be physical property tokens with causal "aspects" that are inexplicable in physical terms. Since I shall focus on causal issues, let me take "explanation" as an abbreviation for "causal explanation". Even more precisely, the most detailed true description physics is able to give about the causal aspects of the entity in question is, in virtue of being embedded in the physical theory, a physical *explanation.*

In this context, an explanatory completeness depends on a causal completeness. If physics were causally incomplete, physics would not completely determine the probabilities of causal relations. Thus, in order to explain physically a physical property token, one would need to go beyond physics and might be obliged to have recourse to concepts of the special sciences.

Keeping this in mind, let me, secondly, outline the *explanatory* completeness of physics in more detail. By this is meant that insofar as there is an explanation of e, there is a complete explanation of e in terms of physics. "Complete" means that in order to explain, physicists never go beyond physical concepts embedded in physical theories. Physicists always search for explanations of e *within* physics. If there is no physical explanation of e, there is not an explanation in terms of the special sciences either. However, suppose physics turned out to be incomplete in explanatory respects. As a result of this, physics would be incomplete in causal respects as well. At least, this follows if we take an explanation as a *causal* explanation.

Having said this, let us recap and term this "completeness of physics". Physics is complete in causal, and explanatory respects. To put it simply, if there is a change in physical properties, there is a complete physical cause for this change as well. If there is a complete physical cause for this change, there is a complete physical explanation of the case in question as well, and vice versa (cf. Heil (2003), p. 20). This is obviously quite different in the special sciences. There, concepts about causally relevant property tokens, and hence their explanations, often include physical concepts embedded in physical theories.

Keeping this in mind, let us turn to concepts. Concepts point out what the entities they apply to have in common. Take ontological reductionism for granted. Thus, every causally relevant property token of the special sciences is identical with a certain physical property token. As a result of this, physics can describe every causally relevant property token of the special sciences. To put it another way, physics can describe these causally relevant property tokens by a physical concept. Now, let us suppose that there are some entities that are described by the *same* physical concept. In virtue of being described by one and the same concept, physics outlines what the entities in question have in common. The entities come under the same physical description. In general terms, concepts outline what the property tokens they describe have in common.

Before we turn to the motivation for inter-theoretic deduction, we should bear in mind that, by contrast to physics, the special sciences are incomplete in causal and explanatory respects. This generally means that the special sciences often include physical concepts. Nonetheless, I shall take the special sciences to describe causally relevant property tokens. Thereby, the special sciences are, even if incomplete, somehow explanatory.

On this basis, let us consider the motivation for inter-theoretic deduction. There are three steps of the argument. First, physics is supposed to give the most detailed explanation of any causally relevant property token in the world. This reflects our knowledge of physics, and takes into account ontological reductionism. In addition to this, in order to explain in the most detailed manner, physics is supposed to be complete. Second, any concept, and thus explanation, reveals what the referents of the concepts in question have *causally* in common. However, it is widely accepted that any ontological difference is based on a causal difference, and ontological identity is based on causal indiscrimination. Indeed, the argument for ontological reductionism is a causal argument (cf. Kim (2005), chapter 2). From this it follows, third, that explanations of the special sciences cannot describe something ontological out there in the world that is not identical with a physical property token. There is nothing causally relevant out there in the world beyond that what is captured by physical concepts, and thus physical explanations. If there were causal relations that were explainable in terms of the special sciences, but not in terms of physics, the "completeness of physics" would be false. Assume that this argument is cogent. Consequently, there is a systematic relationship between the physical explanations and the explanations of the special sciences. This suggests that any concept of the special sciences is coextensional with some physical concept. At least, it is not possible that, on the one hand, the concept "B" about e_1 outlines what all the entities that come under "B", say e_1 and e_2, have causally in common, but on the other hand, the physical concept "P" that refers to e_1 as well does not refer also to e_2 in virtue of outlining what e_1 and e_2 have causally in common. From this it follows that inter-theoretic deduction is well motivated. Its aim is to explain physically what concepts of the special sciences only explain in an *incomplete* manner. After all, the result of inter-theoretic deduction is to provide homogeneous physical explanations of *any* property type of causally relevant property tokens.

3 The argument against epistemological reductionism

The special sciences are considered to be about causally relevant property tokens (as is physics). Therefore, let us begin this section with some considerations on the corresponding concepts. Subsequent to this, I shall consider homogeneous explanations, and the necessity of coextensionality between concepts for inter-theoretic deduction in more detail. On this basis, the multiple realisation argument against coextensionality will be outlined.

Any concept about causally relevant property tokens can be taken to admit of a functional definition. Thus, any of its applications refers to property tokens that have at least a certain cause and/or a certain effect in common. Therefore, the concept outlines what the property tokens it applies to have *causally* in common. Let us consider a biological concept, say "B". This may apply to the entities e_1 and e_2. In addition to this, both e_1 and e_2 have causes of the same property type, and they have effects of the same property type. This means that the causes (and the effects respectively) are supposed to be property tokens that can be described by the same concept. As we have seen, any property type is a set of entities that can be described by one and the same concept. Thus, the concept "B" applies to these entities e_1 and e_2 that both have causes (and effects) of the same property type. This is why the entities come under one and the same functionally defined concept.

Bearing this in mind, let us consider homogeneous explanations. Assume that the special sciences are "somehow" explanatory. However, explanations are concepts embedded in a theory. Let me remind you that, in order not to complicate the issue, I take a "biological explanation" of e_1 to be a biological concept (embedded in a theory of biology) that e_1 makes true. This biological concept outlines salient causal relations. In an analogous manner, a "physical explanation" of e_1 is a physical concept (embedded in a theory of physics) that e_1 makes true.

Against this background, let us focus on what makes two explanations homogeneous. In general, two explanations are homogeneous if they use the same concept. For instance, the biological explanations of e_1 and e_2 are homogeneous if they explain by means of one and the same concept, say "B". To put it simply, the two entities e_1 and e_2 are biologically explained in the same way. However, to explain entities in a homogeneous manner is of epistemological interest. At least, in order to establish an epistemological account of the world, we usually seek for *homogeneous* explanations.

Let us now consider physical explanations and the aim of inter-theoretic deduction. The aim of inter-theoretic deduction is to provide homogeneous physical explanations of *types* of property tokens of the special sciences. As we have seen, the entities e_1 and e_2 are homogeneously explained in biological terms whenever they are explained by one and the same concept. Thus, biologists can point out and explain what e_1 and e_2 have causally in common. However, this explanation is incomplete. There is only, in the last resort, physics that might explain in a more detailed manner. However, in order to explain *homogeneously*, the appropriate explanations have to use the same concept. Any property token that comes under one concept of the special sciences is homogeneously explained in terms of the special sciences. Unless physics cannot, in principle, provide a homogeneous explanation of these property tokens as well, the aim of inter-theoretical deduction seems to be not feasible. Strictly speaking, whenever a homogeneous explanation is possible in terms of the special sciences, we seek for an appropriate physical and homogeneous explanation as well. At least, this is the aim of inter-theoretic deduction.

To achieve this aim, the concepts of the special sciences have to be coextensional with physical concepts. Once again, let us suppose that the entities e_1 and e_2 are homogeneously explained in biological terms. Their explanations are by means of the same concept. Let us now consider the physical explanation of e_1 and e_2. Unless the two explanations are by means of same concept, there is no homogeneous explanation in physical terms. This is why concepts of the special sciences have to be coextensional with physical concepts.

Keeping this in mind, I shall now consider the multiple realisation argument against inter-theoretic deduction. The multiple realisation argument is an argument for the possibility of non-coextensional concepts. It is possible that there are at least some concepts of the special sciences that are not coextensional with physical concepts. From this it follows that appropriate homogeneous physical explanations are not possible. Therefore, the aim of inter-theoretic deduction seems to be not feasible in general.

The multiple realisation argument proceeds as follows: on the one hand, there are entities that can be described by one and the same concept of the special sciences. Thus, a homogeneous explanation is possible in terms of the special sciences. But on the other hand, these entities differ in physical respects. For that reason, these entities are described by *different* physical concepts. This is to say that the physical explanations are not homogeneous. Strictly speaking, there are causal differences between the entities in question that are only considered in physics. Although these differences are not important from the point of view of the special sciences, the physical explanation takes them into account.[3]

Let us consider a well-known example that, among others, suggests the possibility of multiple realisation: genes are supposed to be multiply realised. This means that there may be several entities in the world that are described by biological concepts of "gene of type B". But, physicists describe these entities by different physical concepts. To put it simply, "molecular configuration of type P_1", and "molecular configuration of type P_2". From a biological point of view, "gene of type B" is a *functionally defined* concept. Thus, entities are taken to be genes of type B if they have the appropriate cause, and the appropriate effect that qualify them as a gene. However, there are physical differences possible among these entities that may not touch a biological description by means of the concept "gene of type B". In fact, there are different molecular configurations possible that are indistinguishable with respect to having the appropriate cause, and causing the appropriate effect. Indeed, the genetic code is redundant, and hence, physically different molecular configurations may obviously produce the same effects, like yellow blossoms for instance. Therefore, it seems quite clear that physical causal differences do not always imply biological functional differences. From this it follows that the concept "gene of

---

[3] I should note that the multiple realisation argument is *committed* to the "completeness of physics". Assume that "B" and "P" are not coextensional because the biological concept "B" applies to entities that differ *physically*. However, to differ physically is to differ causally. Let us suppose that physics were incomplete, and thus, there were non-physical causes for these physical differences and no physicist could explain these physical differences. Would any reference to the special sciences help? Probably not for even the special sciences *do not* distinguish between the entities in question. There would be only one type of property tokens that cause *different* effects, respectively, there would be only one concept ("B") in order to explain physical *differences*. I doubt that any physicist would be inclined to admit such causes, or explanations.

type B" is not coextensional with any physical concept. There is no homogeneous physical explanation of a gene of type B. Therefore, at least in such cases as in the case of the genes, inter-theoretic deduction seems to fail.

Before we move on to the last section, let us bear in mind the implication of any non-coextensionality between concepts: Unless there is no causal difference between entities, there is no argument to describe these entities by means of *different* physical concepts (cf. Kim (1998), p. 18 – 19). Let me take in what follows "causal" difference to refer to physical differences between entities, and "functional" differences to refer to differences that are considered by concepts of the special sciences.

4 Inter-theoretic deduction by means of functional sub-concepts

In this last section, I shall provide a reductionist strategy that avoids the anti-reductionist consequences of the multiple realisation argument. My argument contains four main steps. First of all, any physical causal difference between entities leads to functional differences between the entities in question. Thus, any physical difference is detectable in terms of the special sciences as well. To put it another way, concepts of the special sciences about multiply realised properties abstract from functional details. This is the core of my strategy, and I shall consider some possible objections before moving on to the following steps of the strategy. Given the ability to detect functional differences, second, the special sciences can introduce functionally defined sub-concepts of the mentioned concepts. These sub-concepts take into account any possible functional differences. Consequently, these sub-concepts are coextensional with physical concepts. As a result of this, third, I shall argue that any abstract concept is deducible from a more detailed concept. For that reason, fourth, any concept is deducible from one of its sub-concepts that are coextensional with physical concepts. This is inter-theoretic deduction. Against this background, the limits and possible implications of this reductionist strategy will be outlined.

Any physical difference is also detectable by the special sciences. I shall formulate the argument for this claim in two different ways.

First, let us consider a general formulation that suggests this implication. Let us take for granted that in our world, say w_1, there are many multiply realised properties. By this is meant that on the one hand, there are entities that can be described by one and the same concept of the special sciences. But, on the other hand, these entities are described by *different* physical concepts. For instance, there may be multiply realised genes, and multiply realised states of pain. Let us now consider a world that is physically distinct from our world w_1, say w_2. World w_2 is physically such that no properties of the special sciences are multiply realised. In w_2, each gene of a certain biological type is identical with a molecular configuration of one and the same physical type. The same applies to any type of pain, and so on. As a result of this, the concepts of the special sciences in w_2 are coextensional with physical concepts. Thus, the descriptions of w_1 and w_2 only differ from a physical point of view. So to speak, in w_2, there is for any biological concept "B" a coextensional physical concept "P", whereas in w_1, there are the physical concepts "P_1" and "P_2". Having said this, our present concern should be to focus on the following question: is it possible that there will never occur any difference in the description in terms of the special sciences as well? Is it possible that the description by means of concepts of the special sciences of w_1 and to w_2 will always remain the same? Since most property types are supposed to be multiply realised, I am about to question that there would never occur any difference.[4] Bearing this point in mind, let us consider the second formulation of the argument.

For any physical causal difference between entities, there is an environment conceivable in which the physical difference implies a functional difference. For instance, there is always an environment possible in which the physical differences between genes imply selective advantages, or disadvantages, and thus a functional difference (cf. Rosenberg (1994), p. 32). Let us consider this example in some more detail. Suppose that a certain type of gene, say gene for yellow blossoms, is multiply realised. Thus, tokens of this gene type are property tokens of two different physical property types, say of P_1, and of P_2. This means that the entities that are described by "gene" are either described by the concept "P_1" or by the concept "P_2". However, genes of the physical type P_1 may possess, for instance, a high resistance due to ultraviolet light. Compared to this, genes of the physical type P_2 may possess a low resistance due to ultraviolet light. Sure, this physical difference cannot be detected in environmental conditions like in our world some hundred years ago. However, there is an environment conceivable in which the physical differences in ques-

---

[4] I would like to add that Heil makes a quite similar point, even though in terms of qualities and dispositions: "Try changing a fragile object qualitatively, without altering it dispositionally. The object might remain fragile but become fragile 'in a different' way" (Heil (2003), p. 116).

tion lead to a functional difference. Consider an environment with a very intensive radiation of ultraviolet light. In such an environment, the way in which genes cause yellow blossoms depends on whether the genes are resistant due to ultraviolet light, or whether they are not resistant due to ultraviolet light. In a simplified manner, there is a difference in time and/or the need of resources in order to cause the yellow blossoms. To illustrate this point, let us say that flowers with genes that fall under the physical concept "P_1" cause yellow blossoms "as expected". Compared to this, flowers with genes that fall under the physical concept "P_2" may need more time in order to cause the yellow blossoms. These genes have to be repaired several times, and in order to repair the genes from the damages caused by the ultraviolet light, the flower needs resources that "lack" at other occasions of the flower. This is a functional difference that is detectable in biological terms and that is salient for selection. The physicist can conceive environmental conditions so that the scientist of the special sciences would detect functional differences between physically different entities. Since many functional implications of physical differences are already well-known, I doubt that there are physical differences possible that would under *no physical condition* lead to *any* functional difference.

I should note that this argument does not depend on the ability of the biologist to distinguish the environmental/physical conditions in its own terms. It is sufficient that some physicist *conceives*, and some biologist *detects* them. Detecting functional difference is a sufficient reason to introduce functional sub-concepts. To reconsider the example, it does not matter whether or not "ultraviolet light" is a biological or a physical concept. Moreover, suppose that the special sciences are not able to express the environmental conditions that lead to functional differences of, in their terms, indistinguishable entities. They only detect functional differences of property tokens of the same type. Such cases cry out for further explanations that can be only provided by physics.

Let me reconsider the two formulations of the argument in terms of concepts and explanations. Generally speaking, in order to explain different effects, different causes are suggested. Thus, whenever two property tokens of a multiply realised property type lead to different functional effects, this difference in effects is inexplicable in terms of the special sciences. After all, the special sciences recognise only one and the same type of cause for two different types of effects. Suppose that at one day, the special sciences' description of w_1 starts to differ from the special sciences' description of w_2. How could we explain this first difference since there should be just one type of cause? This problem raises questions about the *coherence* of the special sciences, and, hence, cries out for further, in the last resort physical, explanations. This problem becomes even more obvious for the second formulation of the argument. How could we *coherently* explain possible functional differences by reference to the same type of entities?

Bearing this problem in mind, I shall consider possible objections to this core of the strategy. First of all, one may maintain that the special sciences are sometimes not that precise, their epistemological classifications are sometimes vague, and maybe, that is why their laws are not strict but so-called *ceteris paribus* laws. So much the worse for any reductionist that starts from the incompleteness of the special sciences, and ends up there! This kind of objection is wrongheaded because it doesn't touch my argument: in principle, any causal physical difference leads to a functional difference that is detectable by the special sciences. And secondly, the aim of inter-theoretic deduction is not that the special sciences should explain any physical difference, or determine environmental conditions as precise as physics. To the contrary, it is physics that should explain homogeneously what is inexplicable in terms of the special sciences. And indeed, physics may explain homogeneously whenever no functional differences are possible. This is the explanatory aim of inter-theoretic deduction. Therefore, let us move on to some other possible objections.

One may employ my formulations of the argument to conceive contrary cases. For instance, one may conceive physical differences that only appear for a certain length of time. On the one hand, there certainly are environmental conditions in which many physical differences do not lead to biological functional differences. One may only think of common environments in our world in which differences in resistance due to ultraviolet light imply no functional differences. Thus, at least within a certain length of time, no functional difference may occur. In regard to this, I would like to note the following: the *possibility* of functional differences still remains. To put it in terms of Heil, there is a disposition for functional differences. Taking it for granted that there are truthmakers for dispositional talk, this is reason enough to distinguish between the entities in question.

On the other hand, there might be physical differences conceivable that disappear after a certain length of time. Genes may differ with regard to some microphysical systems, but these may decay after a hardly measurable short time. Therefore, it might not be reasonable to postulate a disposition for functional differences. How to deal, hence, with such physical differences? In regard to this, the only point I want to make here is the following one: it would be quite unlikely to take these physical differences to be relevant with respect to giving homogeneous physical explanations. That is to say, any abstraction from physical details should be admissible as long as the physical explanation remains coherent – at least, in order to provide a homogeneous explanation of types of the special sciences. To put it simply, genes may be multiply realised by different molecular configurations. But, if the physical differences are "irrelevant" in order to constitute a gene, one may leave them aside. Let me distinguish between "relevant" and "irrelevant" physical differences. "Relevant" physical differences are physical differences that make it impossible to explain homogeneously and coherently. After all, in order to explain the function of genes in physical terms, additional microphysical systems are commonly not considered. In a simplified manner, any token of a gene consists of a huge configuration of physical systems. However, any physical system, like the additional electron, can be theoretically deleted in order to provide a homogeneous explanation of genes. They are "irrelevant" in order to explain coherently. In general, physicists have to "cut" some concepts out of the conjunctions of concepts in order to reach coextensionality with (sub-)concepts of the special sciences. These are constructed "relevant" physical concepts, and I shall take physical concepts as such in order to provide inter-theoretic deduction (cf. Hooker (1981), § 3). To recap the counterarguments, either (dispositional talk of) functional differences are reasonable, or the physical differences are "irrelevant".

Let us turn to the implication of functional differences that are detectable by the special sciences. Any functional difference that is detectable by the special sciences can be considered by appropriate concepts of the special sciences. It is, hence, possible to introduce sub-concepts of concepts. These sub-concepts take into account any *possible* functional difference of "relevant" physical differences. As a result of this, the introduced functionally defined sub-concepts of concepts are coextensional with the constructed "relevant" physical concepts. Let me consider this strategy in four main steps.

First, let us recap the ability of the special sciences to detect physical differences. Any physical differences lead to functional differences. That is to say that they are detectable in terms of the special sciences. If there is a multiply realised functional property type, the appropriate property tokens differ in causal physical respects. Given the comparison of worlds with multiply realised property types to worlds without multiply realised property types, or given certain environmental conditions, any "relevant" physical differences lead to functional differences as well. Thus, they are detectable in terms of the special sciences as well.

Second, and as a result of the previous point, the special sciences are able to introduce functionally defined sub-concepts of concepts. In a simplified manner, functionally defined concepts that are about multiply realised properties do not take into account possible functional differences. Compared to these abstract concepts, their sub-concepts consider any possible functional difference of "relevant" physical differences. Let me begin with an example. To put it simply, biologists may distinguish between genes that are more resistant due to ultraviolet light and genes that are not that resistant. "Resistance due to ultraviolet light" is considered to be an abbreviation of functional differences that may occur in environments with high intensive radiation of ultraviolet light. Taking it that any "relevant" physical difference is detectable, the functionally defined sub-concepts are necessarily coextensional with these "relevant" physical concepts. Because the matter is so crucial, I am going to risk excess by restating the point once more: the special sciences can consider any "relevant" physical difference in their own terms, and hence, introduce appropriate functionally defined sub-concepts that are *coextensional* with "relevant" physical concepts. Any of these physical concepts apply to entities that do not possess "relevant" physical differences. "Relevant" physical differences are physical differences that would make impossible homogeneous and coherent explanations. Bearing in mind that the special sciences are able to introduce functionally defined sub-concepts that are coextensional with "relevant" physical concepts, let us move on and consider the relationship between concepts and sub-concepts.

To outline the relationship between abstract concepts and detailed concepts is the third step of the strategy. Clearly, any multiply realised functionally defined concept abstracts from possible functional differences that are considered by its uniformly realised functionally defined sub-concepts. In conclusion, abstract concepts are deducible from their more detailed sub-concepts. Any concept that is about multiply realised properties is deducible from each of its sub-concepts. The argument proceeds as follows: a detailed concept can be taken as a relatively long conjunction of single concepts. Taking it that the relatively long conjunction of concepts is true, any concept within this conjunction of concepts has to be true as well. Therefore, it is possible to conclude from a more detailed sub-concept to its more abstract concept. For instance, it is possible to deduce "gene for yellow blossoms" from "gene for yellow blossoms that is resistant due to ultraviolet light". To abstract from details is a theory immanent question.

Fourth, let me combine the two previous steps. Functionally defined sub-concepts are coextensional with "relevant" physical concepts. After all, since any "relevant" physical difference leads to functional differences that can be considered in terms of the special sciences, there is no argument that hinders constructing sub-concepts that are coextensional with "relevant" physical concepts. In addition to this, any abstract concept can be deduced from each of its detailed sub-concepts. Therefore, any concept of the special sciences is deducible from physics.

Suppose that a concept (or one of its sub-concepts) of the special sciences describes entities that are described by different physical concepts. Against the background of the proposed reductionist strategy, there are two possibilities: either, the biologists are not yet smart enough to become aware of the possible functional differences. This is an empirical question. Or, physicists may realise that the appropriate physical differences are "irrelevant", and hence, they can be ignored in order to formulate "relevant" physical concepts. Thus, the construction of coextensional concepts seems in principle always feasible. Therefore, taking it for granted that coextensionality can in principle always be attained, each concept of the special sciences is deducible, via the sub-concepts of the special sciences, from physical concepts.

Let me briefly recap the necessary premises and arguments for my strategy, and consider its limits and its possible implications for Heil's ontological point of view. First, any theory of the special sciences can consider, in principle, more detailed sub-concepts that take into account any possible functional differences. These are sub-concepts about property tokens without "relevant" physical differences. This argument takes for granted that there is ontological reductionism, the "completeness of physics", and that causal differences necessitate conceptual differences (and vice versa). Consequently, sub-concepts of the special sciences are coextensional with "relevant" physical concepts. Therefore, any sub-concept can be nomologically correlated with a physical concept. From this it follows that a homogeneous physical explanation is possible of the entities that are described by means of a sub-concept. Therefore, inter-theoretic deduction is in principle possible between "relevant" physical concepts and sub-concepts of the special sciences.

Second, any abstract concept can be deduced from any of its more detailed sub-concepts. From this, it follows that inter-theoretic deduction is possible from "relevant" physical concepts to concepts of the special sciences (via sub-concepts). The sub-concepts are coextensional with "relevant" physical concepts. From each of these detailed sub-concepts, the more abstract concept can be deduced. This is a theory immanent question of abstraction from details, hence, a conceptual issue. Furthermore, any sub-concept can be constructed from its more abstract concept as well. In order to construct these sub-concepts, biologists for instance, only have to take into account any possible functional differences. Consequently, "relevant" physical concepts are necessarily coextensional with these functional sub-concepts.

However, the special sciences can, by means of abstract concepts, *homogeneously* explain multiply realised property types. Contrary to this, physics cannot *homogeneously* explain these multiply realised property types. Therefore, the explanatory aim of inter-theoretic deduction might still fail. Bearing this problem in mind, let me consider a *prima facie* dilemma for Heil's ontological point of view:

Take it for granted that there is ontological reductionism, and that explanations are causal explanations. Now, it seems that there are only two possibilities: first, an abstract concept only explains *something ontological* that is captured by *each* of its sub-concepts. Since there is truthmaker realism, this would avoid eliminativism about abstract concepts. But, any sub-concept would be sufficient in order to describe and explain the world in terms of the special sciences. To favour abstract concepts is therefore only grounded in practical reasons. However, Heil is probably not inclined to claim that abstract concepts are, in principle, unnecessary. In order to avoid this consequence, let us consider the second possibility. Any abstract concept explains something ontological *over and above each* of its sub-concepts. But, how could this be possible, since each sub-concept is explanatory more detailed than the more abstract concept? Suppose two sub-concepts differ in their explanations, but nonetheless it is possible to infer from each sub-concept one and the same abstract concept. How could it be possible that this abstract concept explains something that is not captured by *each* of its sub-concepts? To put it in terms of Heil, how could concepts about dispositions explain something *over and above* concepts about qualities since dispositions are identical with qualities?

Let me reconsider this *prima facie* dilemma and the proposed strategy of this paper. Taking ontological reductionism for granted, explanations are causal explanations, and physics is supposed to be complete and to provide the most detailed explanations of any entity. However, to avoid the correspondence principle entailed by the Picture Theory, we should take any property type as a theoretical classification (cf. Heil (2003), p. 26). Consequently, we should avoid basing ontological claims on the different abilities of theories to provide true abstractions. There clearly are abstract concepts of the special sciences that provide *homogeneous* explanations of multiply realised properties. Physics is not able to explain them *homogeneously* without becoming incoherent, or false. There is no physical concept coextensional with the appropriate abstract concepts of the special sciences. However, since the strategy of this paper, and the outlined dilemma for Heil's ontological point of view is cogent, any abstract concept is, in principle, reducible to physics. The special sciences can introduce sub-concepts of each of their concepts, and these sub-concepts are coextensional with "relevant" physical concepts. In order not to eliminate abstract concepts, Heil's ontological point is necessary. To claim that any abstract concept is captured by each of its sub-concepts would be already to apply the correspondence principle entailed by the Picture Theory. To maintain that abstract concepts outline something ontological above each of their sub-concepts would be already to apply the correspondence principle entailed by the Picture Theory as well. To conclude, the lesson of the multiple realisation argument and Heil's ontological point of view is that, abstractions are, since they are true, not necessarily abstractions from ontology. This is conservative reductionism.

Commentary

John Heil

In *From an ontological point of view* I defend ontological monism and descriptive/explanatory pluralism. There is, I say, but one world that can be variously described. We err when we imagine that differences among predicates necessitate differences among properties. "Is blue" and "has molecular structure B" could both be made true by some one complex arrangement of particles. Significantly, it could turn out that "is blue" can be made true by a particle-arrangement that does not make true "has molecular structure B". You might put this by saying that objects can be blue by possessing any of a family of distinct, but similar properties.

Some philosophers take cases of this kind to establish that the property of being blue is distinct from, but "realised" by distinct physical properties: blue is multiply realisable. Sachse and I agree that this is bad ontology. We disagree, however, or apparently disagree, on what follows. I say that you can be a one-worlder without embracing the thesis that there must be an analytical relation between distinct predicates or descriptions that share the same worldly truthmaker. The idea here is neither deep nor original.

Consider mental and physical predicates. Suppose it is true of you that you are in pain. In that case, it will be true of you, as well, that you answer to some – undoubtedly very complex – physical predicate. But the pain concept and this physical concept have different rules of application. You can grasp one without grasping the other. Further, as in the case of "is blue", "is in pain" evidently applies to different creatures in virtue of those creatures possessing different properties, properties picked out by distinct physical predicates. I see no reason to think that physical and mental predicates must be coextensive, much less that mental predicates must be deducible from physical predicates.

Sachse describes this as an argument against theory reduction, but that is much too strong. I do not deny that reduction is possible, only that it is required to make sense of the idea that distinct predicates can share truthmakers. Sachse thinks that reduction is always possible, and that, were it not, the kind of ontological monism I favour would be threatened. I am not convinced.

Sachse provides a recipe for constructing predicates in a higher-level domain that will be coextensive with predicates of fundamental physics. Suppose the pain predicate applies to creatures in virtue of those creatures' possession of any of an open-ended class of distinct physical properties. Anti-reductionists take this as evidence that the pain property is distinct from, albeit dependent on, all those physical properties. But suppose we take the pain predicate to be a non-specific way of picking out all those physical properties indifferently. The physical properties differ, but not in a way wielders of the pain predicate care about. Circumstances could change, however. Minute differences could come to matter to pain ascribers. This is enough, Sachse thinks, to motivate the construction of a new predicate to mark off the difference. There are, after all, different ways of being in pain, different kinds of pain. The new predicate would belong to the higher-level vocabulary, but it would be coextensive with a fundamental physical predicate.

This gives us coextension and, Sachse contends, the possibility of deducing talk of pain from talk of the fundamental physical things. You can see how this works once you see that a creature's suffering some specific kind of pain deductively implies that the creature is in pain. This gets us from the constructed predicate to the original pain predicate. How do we get from the fundamental physical description to the constructed predicate? That will require a bridge principle that makes the coextension explicit. Well and good, but why should we care? Following Sachse's recipe, we can construct coextensive predicates to our heart's content. But it is hard to see this as anything more than an unremarkable consequence of one-worldism.

Chapter 6

Is a world only made up of relations possible? A structural realist point of view

Vincent Lam

This paper aims to evaluate the objections raised by John Heil in his recent book *From an ontological point of view* against the metaphysical conception of a world purely made up of relations. His objections are critically reviewed and rejected within the framework of a moderate version of structural realism. Ultimately, Heil's main arguments against a metaphysics of relations lack reference to the fundamental physical theories that describe the world.

In view of the recent developments of structural realism as a convincing position in the ontology of science, philosophers – like John Heil in his recent book[1] – who deny the very possibility of a world purely made up of relations must be ready to face the philosophical as well as the empirical arguments put forward by the structural realists. The minimal understanding of the world "purely made up of relations" is that there are no intrinsic properties and that the world is a network of relations at the fundamental (physical) level. I take structural realism (in a moderate version) to be precisely the metaphysical position that encompasses this view about the world.[2] However, the aim of this paper is less to defend structural realism than to carefully consider Heil's objections against the plausibility of a purely relational world. Heil only tackles this general metaphysical problem in view of the question he is really interested in, that is, the possibility of a world of pure powers. Indeed, according to Heil, the assumption of a world of pure powers comprises two aspects: first, the objects are conceived as bundles of properties. Second, the properties are conceived as purely dispositional (p. 97). On the other hand, under the assumption that dispositions are relations, discussing the possibility of a world only made up of relations amounts to discuss the possibility of a world of pure powers. According to Heil, beside some specific problems, such a relational

---

[1] Heil (2003). If nothing is specified, we refer to this work in what follows. The main discussion about relations and the possibility of a purely relational world takes place in chapter 10.

[2] I do not consider the epistemic version of structural realism, that is, as an epistemic thesis about the limits of our knowledge, see Ladyman (1998) for the distinction.

conception of the world is deeply "flawed" because of these assumptions about properties (the bundle theory and the dispositional account) and dispositions (the relational conception). However, I focus in this paper only on the problem concerning the possibility of a metaphysics of relations and I am not concerned here with the question whether dispositions or powers – if there are any – are relations or not.

In the chapter of Heil's book devoted to that problem, I read mainly six major objections against the conception of a purely relational world. I consider them in turn and try to provide an answer in the (moderate) structural realist framework. Moreover, as far as we seek for the fundamental nature of the world, I also consider these objections from the point of view of contemporary fundamental physics, which motivates part of the (moderate) structural realist answers indeed. One of the main conclusions is that, despite his "ontological seriousness", Heil does not root his ontology in the fundamental empirical sciences enough.

1 First objection

Heil first argues that relations in the (physical) world need relata, that is, things that stand in relation (p. 99). Indeed, even if, in an abstract way, it is possible to consider relations without relata (as abstract mathematical entities for instance), and as far as we are interested in the fundamental nature of (particular) entities that are instantiated in the (physical) world, relations presuppose relata to be related. Indeed, this objection is very similar to the one raised against the ontic version of structural realism: against this latter position, advocating a radical metaphysics of relations by claiming that there are no objects (and in particular no relata) but only relations (see French & Ladyman (2003)), it has been objected that it cannot distinguish between abstract (mathematical) entities and physical entities that are instantiated in the (physical) world (see Cao (2003) and Chakravartty (2003)).[3] But structural realism as a metaphysical thesis is in no way committed to such a radical move. The fundamental dependence of the relations on their relata can be captured within structural realism. However, Heil does not only point out this crucial dependence, he further concludes that the relations seem to be "dependent on their relata in a way

---

[3] Actually, the precise position of French and Ladyman may be slightly different: their main point is that the relations are ontologically primary to the relata, so that they need not be commited to a "no-relata" view. However, the precise ontological status of the relata remains ambiguous.

that excludes the possibility of relata wholly constituted by relations" (p. 99). As just explained, there are good reasons to recognise that relations require relata. However, I see no reason – and Heil does not give any – why all the properties of these relata could not consist in the relations in which they stand. This is the position advocated by the moderate version of structural realism that does recognise a (strong) mutual ontological dependence between objects (relata) and relations (see Esfeld & Lam (2006 forthcoming)): there are fundamental objects in the world, but all their properties are the relations they enter into.[4] The structures and their constituents (the relations and their relata) are on the same ontological level in the sense that both have the same (fundamental) ontological relevance (no ontological priority): on the one hand, the relations constitute all the properties of the relata (all there are to the relata) and, on the other hand, the relata are necessary to the relations in the sense that relations must (ontologically) relate relata. Such a metaphysical position is indeed motivated by empirical arguments from contemporary physics as well as by philosophical ones.[5]

2   Second objection

Indeed, Heil's rejection of objects (or relata) being wholly constituted by relational properties (or relations) finds its roots in the following argument: first, as just explained above, relations require objects that stand in the relations (the relata) and, second, these objects, whatever they are, "must have some intrinsic features which make them things in their own right" (Campbell (1976), p. 94, quoted in Heil (2003), p. 102). Objects, in order to stand in relations, must have some (qualitative) intrinsic properties over and above the relations in which they stand. Though widely spread among philosophers, this argument is not straightforward. Indeed, the structural realists object that this argument for intrinsic properties amounts to postulate unknowable and unnecessary metaphysical entities (and falls therefore victim to Occam's razor): strictly speaking, as far as they are intrinsic, these properties cannot be known and it is even questionable whether we need them in our metaphysics of nature at all. Moreover, several features of the fundamental physical theories – the the-

---

[4] In a certain sense, relations just take over the job of intrinsic propeties; in particular, this move does not commit oneself to a bundle conception of objects.

[5] See Esfeld & Lam (2006, forthcoming) and references therein. One of the main philosophical argument is the ontological parsimony, see (2) below. For a sketch of the empirical arguments from the general theory of relativity, see (6) below.

ory of general relativity (GR) and quantum mechanics (QM) – tend to show that the interpretations in terms of intrinsic properties of fundamental objects described by these theories – space-time points (see (6) below), quantum particles or fields – are rather problematic. So, one of the major arguments in favour of intrinsic properties and against a purely relational world is indeed neither ontologically parsimonious nor empirically sound.

3 Third objection

In analogy with an argument of David Armstrong against the possibility of objects only made up of Locke's primary qualities (§ 10.5),[6] Heil argues that a purely relational world provides no "coherent conception of material bodies" (p. 107). Basically, the argument is that in a purely relational world there is no (ontological) distinction between an "empty" space(-time) and a space(-time) "occupied" by material bodies (pp. 100, 109) and that this consequence is highly undesirable ("whatever our world is, it is not such a world" (p. 100)). However, I see no reason why this argument should work and even if it worked, I don't see how it would constitute an argument against a purely relational world. Indeed, the question about a metaphysics of relations, which is the position defended by structural realism for instance, should be distinguished from the question about the ontological relationship between space-time and matter. As such, structural realism (as an ontological thesis about the fundamental nature of the world) is independent of this latter question: in the structural realist framework, the space-time and material structures can be ontologically either distinct or identical (constituting the same total world structure for instance) independently of their purely structural (relational) nature. In other terms, it is possible to recognise only relations at the fundamental physical level in the sense of spatio-temporal relations and non-spatio-temporal (material) relations so that there is still a meaningful ontological distinction between space-time and matter (structures). And even if such an ontological distinction would not be possible in the framework of a purely relational world, that is, if a world made up of relations would entail a kind of ontological identity between space-time and matter (a kind of space-time substantivalism à la Spinoza), this would

---

[6] By the way, as far as Locke's primary qualities are in general naturally understood as being intrinsic properties, I don't exactly understand the sense in which "a world made up of objects possessing only the primary qualities ressembles a purely relational world" (p. 106).

in no way constitute an objection against a relational view.[7] At least, till such a space-time substantivalism à la Spinoza is shown to be incompatible with contemporary fundamental physics, which is not the case. But on the contrary, such a position still constitutes a lively option in the space-time philosophy based on contemporary fundamental physics. For instance, the difficulty to provide a clear distinction between space-time and matter within GR may speak in favour of such a position (see Rovelli (1997) and Dorato (2000) for instance). Indeed, the important points here are first that the metaphysics of relations advocated by the (moderate) structural realist can – but need not – be combined with a substantivalist conception à la Spinoza and second that such a metaphysics of relations challenges in any case the standard metaphysical view – shared by Heil – of individual objects characterised by intrinsic properties. Therefore, the world as a whole can be conceived as one unique substance (the "space-time-matter substance"), whose internal structure is purely relational in the sense of a network of relations among objects that do not possess any intrinsic properties.[8] This conception is metaphysically coherent and may well be vindicated by GR.

4 Fourth objection

As a concrete example for a purely relational world, Heil considers the proposal of Randall Dipert, who suggests to account for the purely relational nature of the world in terms of asymmetric (sub)graphs, where a (sub)graph is basically an abstract network of edges and vertices – a kind of structure indeed (see Dipert (1997)). By claiming that "the theory of graph-theoretic structure is sufficient to account for all structure in thought or world" (Dipert (1997), p. 351), Dipert advocates a (radical) metaphysics of relations: any object in the world can be understood as a subgraph of the (total) world graph, so that, all there is to the world at the fundamental level are the relations that induce the world graph.[9] However, Heil reads Dipert as suggesting that "in addition to standing in relations, objects possess dispositions to enter into new relations" (pp. 103 –

---

[7] This substantivalism à la Spinoza is actually briefly mentionned by Heil as a possibility to maintain talk about substances (about one unique substance indeed) in the framework of a purely relational world (p. 108).

[8] The internal structure can be trivially considered as being made up of intrinsic properties of the one unique substance: this is however neither metaphysically relevant nor the kind of intrinsicality that Heil wants to advocate.

[9] This is what Dipert calls "exclusive relationalism", see Dipert (1997), p. 350.

104). Heil's objection is then that it is not clear what the relationship exactly is between these dispositions – and in particular the unmanifested ones – and the (actual) relations in the world. It seems that the (actual) relations at the fundamental level cannot ground (unmanifested) dispositions. However, as such, this does not constitute an argument against a purely relational conception of the world. On the one hand, there is no need for a metaphysics of relations to be committed to dispositions: a strong commitment to dispositions (or dispositional properties) cannot constitute an argument against a metaphysics of relations. The first task of a metaphysics of nature is to account for the fundamental features of the world as described by our current best physical theories and not to vindicate a particular philosophical position – like the dispositionalist's view. On the other hand, the structural realist may well include a modal structure (or a dispositional structure) – understood as a purely relational structure – in her ontology without altering her metaphysics of (actual as well as possible) relations.

5 Fifth objection

Ultimately, Heil sees "a more fundamental difficulty" (p. 105) with any purely relational conception of the world – like Dipert's. According to him, this difficulty is actually linked with a deeper problem in philosophy, namely the (sometimes implicit) endorsement of what he calls the Picture Theory of representation. Although not exactly defined, the main idea of the Picture Theory understood in a broad sense is that (fundamental?) features of the world can be read off our (fundamental?) representations of the world (p. 6). However, Heil mainly argues against the Picture Theory understood in a more strict sense: it is a mistake to consider that the elements of our representations of the world are "lined up" with elements in the world (p. 6) and to consider in particular that every meaningful predicate of our representations of the world corresponds to a property in the world ("correspondence principle", p. 26). According to him, the Picture Theory understood in this strict sense is not metaphysically well-founded because it leads to an unnecessary (and indeed problematic) ontological pluralism (like levels of being for instance). Fair enough. Now, Heil merely extends his argument to the Picture Theory understood in a broad sense: therefore, the fact that (some of) our fundamental physical accounts of the world are purely in terms of relations does not entail that (some aspects of) the world is (are) made up of relations. But the vagueness of the definition of the Picture Theory (in a broad sense) makes this objection rather weak. The sole fact that (fundamental) physical talks are only in terms of relations does not entail that the world is only made up of relations. If that is all Heil means, then he is (obviously) right. But the (fundamental) physical accounts of the world are not "only expressed in a wholly relational vocabulary" (p. 105), they also provide strong (empirical) arguments against interpretations of (some aspects of) the world in terms of intrinsic properties and, therefore, in favour of a metaphysics of relations: namely, the famous hole argument in GR (see the sixth objection below) and the arguments against the interpretations of quantum particles as (individuals) possessing intrinsic properties (for instance, see Esfeld (2004) and references therein). In order to argue against such a metaphysics, Heil has to show that these (empirical) arguments are not sound, but surprisingly he does not even mention them.

Indeed, the very use of his objection against the Picture Theory (in a broad sense) in this context is questionable. What is at issue here is not the (problematic) ontological pluralism entailed by the Picture Theory understood in a strict sense but the fundamental nature of the world (or the nature of the world at the fundamental level in the layered view). In a scientific realist perspective (understood in a broad sense), it seems reasonable to believe that some relevant elements of the fundamental physical theories may correspond to some features of the world (oddly enough, this point is acknowledged by Heil in the footnote 8, p. 44) – the hard work being of course to identify these relevant elements. Indeed, if our fundamental physical theories about the world – our fundamental representations about the world – do not allow us to say anything about any features of the world, then it seems (obviously) impossible to know anything about the world at all. This is rather a general epistemological question that is independent of any metaphysics – be it of relations or of intrinsic properties.

6   Sixth objection

In analogy with the objection that a purely relational conception of the world could not account for physical (material) objects (see above the third objection), Heil seems to consider that such a relational conception cannot account for space-time either. Indeed, according to him, the plausibility of such a conception "depends on our depicting space (or space-time, or the (world) quantum field) as itself possessing an intrinsic qualitative nature ... but it would be hard to square a "meaty" conception of space with the thesis either that properties are purely powers or that properties are exclusively relational. Intrinsic qualities would be reintroduced through the back door" (pp. 109 – 110). I fully agree with the first part of the quotation: ultimately, we have to look at our fundamental physical representations (like GR for instance) to elaborate our metaphysics of nature (of space-time for instance). On the other hand, I claim that there are strong arguments from GR for a "meaty" conception of space-time exclusively in terms of (space-time) relations. Indeed, within GR, space-time is represented by the metric tensor field,[10] which encodes all fundamental space-time relations – the space-time structure – so that it seems reasonable to interpret space-time as a network of space-time relations.[11] Moreover, there is a wide consensus among philosophers of physics about the fact that, within GR, space-time points are not individuated independently of the metric tensor field, that is, independently of space-time relations – or independently of the space-time structure: this is generally understood as the moral of the famous hole argument (originally due to Einstein) and more broadly as a consequence of a fundamental feature of GR, namely active general covariance or invariance under active diffeomorphisms (see for instance Earman & Norton (1987), Stachel (1993) and Hoefer (1996)). Space-time points can be conceived as examples of physical relata being wholly characterised by the relations they enter into; in other terms, space-time points do not possess any intrinsic property.

Therefore, a moderate version of structural realism applied to space-time constitutes a "meaty" (possibly substantival indeed[12]) but purely relational conception of space-time (and which is coherent with our fundamental physical theory about space-time, namely GR): according to this position, space-time is a mind-independent purely relational structure, that is, a network of (space-time) relations that is not based on entities possessing intrinsic properties. In particular, space-time can be conceived as a network of space-time relations among space-time points that do not possess any intrinsic properties

---

[10] Together with the corresponding (Lorentz) connection and the 4-dimensional differentiable manifold on which it is defined (I consider the standard tensor formulation of GR).

[11] For instance, see Mauro Dorato's structural space-time realism (Dorato (2000)) and Simon Saunders' non-reductive relationalism (Saunders (2003)). The metric tensor field could also be considered as a (physical) object, very much like other physical fields. But in even in this case, it encodes all the fundamental space-time relations (and this fact makes it very unlike other physical fields indeed).

[12] Althouht purely relational, moderate structural realism about space-time is rather a kind of substantivalism towards space-time in the sense that space-time is not reduced to non-space-time (material) relations among matter (relationalism à la Leibniz) ; however, structural realism as such is compatible with any position about the relationship between space-time and matter, see Esfeld & Lam (2006 forthcoming).

over and above bearing the relations.[13] Space-time points and space-time relations are ontologically mutually dependent (they are on the same ontological level): space-time points are ontologically dependent on space-time relations – they are entirely characterised by space-time relations – and in an equivalent way space-time relations are ontologically dependent on space-time points – the relata standing in the relation (see the first objection). So, moderate structural realism about space-time is a substantival (and "meaty") conception of space-time that advocates a metaphysics of relations (at least in the case of space-time, see Esfeld & Lam (2006 forthcoming)).

7 Conclusion

To sum up, I have considered in turn what I consider to be the main objections against a metaphysics of relations advanced by Heil in his recent book about ontology. Indeed, they all receive a constructive answer in the framework of (a moderate version of) structural realism. This latter metaphysical position accounts for the ontological dependence of the relations on their relata (first objection), but rejects any commitment to intrinsic properties on philosophical as well as empirical grounds (second objection). Moreover, (moderate) structural realism is not committed to any position as regards the ontological relationship between space-time and matter: the two questions are indeed independent ones (third objection). But it constitutes an ontological thesis about the fundamental nature of the world, as the theory of dispositions does if it is considered seriously at the ontological level. Therefore, as such, dispositions alone (and in particular unmanifested ones) cannot constitute an argument against a particular metaphysics of nature – a metaphysics of relations for instance (fourth objection).[14] In the same way, Heil misses the point when he argues against a relational conception of the world on the basis that it is grounded by the Picture Theory that he explicitly rejects. On the one hand, his (main) arguments against the Picture Theory are only directed against a strict version of it. On the other hand, the purely relational view is grounded by empirical arguments from the fundamental physical theories: it is these (empirical) arguments

---

[13] A (moderate) structural realist interpretation of space-time is however not necessarily committed to the existence of space-time points.

[14] In particular, within the structural realist framework, the question of the ontological basis for modal truths can be answered in terms of a modal (or dispositional) structure (see the fourth objection); without invoking (unmanifested) dispositions at all, it could even be tackled in terms of the actual structure of the world, but this is another story.

that should actually be discussed (fifth objection). Finally, I have argued that a purely relational conception of space-time may well be vindicated by GR (sixth objection).

I hope to have shown in this paper that Heil dismisses the possibility of a metaphysics of relations too quickly. Of course, such a metaphysics, which is advocated by the moderate version of structural realism, need to be clearly worked out – for instance, a coherent identity theory for the objects must be provided. This latter task does not seem to be more problematic for the moderate structural realist than for the proponent of intrinsic properties, if we consider the fact that, in the case of a metaphysics of relations, intrinsic properties are somehow replaced by relations, which can then fulfil the role of "identity" providers. Spelling out the details is however not the purpose of this paper and would indeed require another one. So, the important point is that there are no *a priori* metaphysical reasons to reject such a relational conception. Ultimately, our ontology of the world must account for our contemporary fundamental physical descriptions of it. I claim that this is exactly the strength of moderate structural realism.

Commentary

John Heil

Lam is put off by my discussion of the idea that properties are "pure powers". In common with many other philosophers, I am doubtful that such a conception of properties is coherent. I admit that I have no knock-down argument against the view, but it is unlikely that there are very many knock-down arguments for or against substantive metaphysical theses. What I try to do is offer a number of considerations that could lead you to have doubts about properties being powers and nothing more. To treat these as botched attempts to produce a conclusive argument is both uncharitable and unhelpful.

In the course of trying to articulate worries about a world of pure powers, I suggest that these worries are, in some respects, at least, analogous to worries you might have about a world consisting exclusively of relations, a world in which relata are constituted by relations. Philosophers are moved to such views by a desire to economise ontologically. Why have objects, properties, and relations, when you can construct objects and properties from relations? So I am led from a discussion of a world of pure powers to discussion of a world of pure relations. And I remain unrepentantly doubtful that there could be such a world.

According to Lam science has already established the possibility I doubt, namely that objects could be constituted by relations. But Lam himself is none too clear about this. He admits that relations require non-relational relata – objects – but contends that physics gives us every reason to think that these objects utterly lack intrinsic properties. All there is to these objects is the relations into which they enter. This sounds like the thesis that objects are constituted by relations.

Let me say first, that I doubt that this thesis, whatever it turns out to be, is implied by physics. It is rather an interpretation of physical theories developed in an effort to understand what those theories tell us about the world: how the world must be if the theories are true. And, as in the case of quantum physics, you can accept the theory without accepting the interpretation.

One reason you might have doubts about Lam's interpretation is that it leaves us without truthmakers for counterfactual truths. If all there is to an object is relations into which it enters, what would make it true that this object would do this or that, something it is not actually doing and perhaps never will do? Lam accuses me of saddling Randall Dipert with dispositions, but my point is that there is no room in Dipert's purely relational world for dispositionality. I take this to be a *problem* for proponents of relational worlds.

Lam thinks that my conception of intrinsic properties would be inconsistent with a world of the sort envisioned by Spinoza. On the contrary. I regard the difference between Spinoza and Locke as quantitative, not qualitative. Locke thinks there are lots of objects, Spinoza thinks there is but one. If Lam is right, if the world as marked out by modern physics is Spinoza's world, it is mine as well. It would be dramatically misleading to describe such a world as a world of relations. There is a single object: the world itself, the universe, the One.[1] What we might ordinarily consider to be objects – rocks, planets, electrons – are not objects but modes, intrinsic ways the One is. Describing such a position as one according to which there are no objects, or no intrinsic properties, is at the very least highly misleading.

Lam ascribes to me an argument against a world of relations based on my rejection of the Picture Theory. Lam seems to think that rejecting the Picture Theory, abandoning the idea that you can "read off" ontology from ways we talk about the world, includes the denial that *any* statement could get the ontology right. But why should the rejection of the thesis that *every* predicate designates a property possessed by every thing to which the predicate truly applies be thought to imply that *no* predicate designates a property shared by objects to which it applies? Predicates of fundamental physics do indeed seem to designate properties. My point, made repeatedly in *From an ontological point of view*, is that this *need* not be so for most of the predicates we deploy, even respectable predicates figuring in the special sciences.

---

[1] Descartes, too, is commonly taken to hold that there is but one extended substance.

Chapter 7

Powerful causation

Georg Sparber

In this paper I shall analyse John Heil's argumentation that leads to the main thesis of his *Ontological point of view* (2003), that is, his identity thesis of dispositional and categorical properties. First, conceptual clarifications are given in order to specify the relevant meanings of the dispositional/categorical distinction. Second, the structure of Heil's argument is evaluated and a hidden premise is identified. In a next step I shall give reasons to doubt the assumption that the properties instantiated in our world are not only categorical, but also dispositional. On the one hand the negative reasons for this thesis, the apparent failure of an appropriate conditional analysis, are not convincing and on the other hand when it comes to causation there is neither epistemological nor ontological support for the claim that causal statements are made true by manifested dispositions.

1 Heil's argumentation

The set of properties can be divided in two ways. First, they can be categorical or dispositional (this distinction may not be exclusive, as Heil thinks), or they can be intrinsic or relational (this one in turn is not else conceivable than as an exclusive alternative). To my knowledge there is no reason why we should regard these two ways of classifying properties as dependent on one another. From a neutral point of view all four combinations of them are possible and might label non-empty classes of properties.

There are three central notions to consider when it comes to analysing John Heil's discussion of properties: disposition, power, causal efficacy. These three concepts are connected in the following way: powers are closely related to the notion of causal efficacy. The notion of power entails the notion of causality: there does not exist a non-causal power, such a power would be powerless. A power is always a power of something to bring about a certain effect. Causality in turn can be expressed in power-vocabulary: being a cause means having the power to act. Therefore it is at least true that power-talk is causal talk: to be a power is to be somehow linked to causation or causal relevance. The difference between categorical and dispositional properties might be expressed by their difference in power bestowing that is a difference in the way causal efficacy is executed. While dispositions have their powers built-in and bestow their powers directly on the object, categorical properties (usually referred to as qualities by Heil) bestow their powers only indirectly to their object-bearers, via the relations they enter into. Thus Heil makes an oversimplification when he identifies powers with dispositions. We should not reserve causal efficacy from the beginning for dispositions only. Heil had rather say that built-in powers are identical with dispositions.

In general, properties are related to powers. In fact, there exists a power criterion for the distinction of properties: properties are distinguished by the distinctive contributions they make to powers or dispositionalities of their possessors (Heil (2003), pp. 76 – 77). This leads to:

(PI) Necessarily, if any A and B are properties, $A = B$ just in case A and B make the same contribution to the causal powers of their (actual or possible) possessors.

(PI) is to say that two properties are identical if and only if they cannot causally behave in any way that permits to distinguish them (supposed that the indistinguishable is identical). If (PI) is combined with Heil's identity thesis (where powers are identical with dispositions) the problem arises, why and how we could conceive the existence of qualities that bestow powers on their possessors only indirectly. If there is a power (dispositional, in his talk) criterion for property identity of existing properties, should there be no qualities? They seem to be excluded by definition, and Heil admits that it "... is hard to find room for them" (Heil (2003), p. 76). But following a long philosophical tradition Heil accepts that a world lacking qualities is unconceivable. Every quality needs a relation to get causal importance. That means that pure isolated qualities have no causal relevance. It follows that there is a brute basic dichotomy between dispositions and qualities.

2 The nature of dispositions

John Heil proceeds by specifying the features of dispositions. His strategy is mainly a negative one, since he asks what dispositions are not and identifies the set of dispositions with the remaining substrate. Heil's first step is to accord dispositions an ontological status. Dispositions belong to the ontological category of properties. Then he applies commonly accepted classifications of properties to delineate the set of dispositions properly:

(I) Dispositions are not relations. This is to say that dispositions are intrinsic. For they are independent of the instantiation of other properties, especially of their manifestations (Heil (2003), pp. 79 – 81). This is an informative claim. Not only does it open the possibility of unmanifested dispositions, but it also excludes the *a priori* possibility of dispositional relations (relations, for example, that have the power to bring about other relations).

(II) Dispositions are not higher-level properties. For they would succumb to the causal exclusion principle, which would deprive them from the causal relevance they have by definition (Heil (2003), pp. 87 – 89).

(III) Dispositions are not qualities combined with contingent second-order universals (Armstrong laws). For higher-order universals need both relata to be instantiated in order to be instantiated themselves. Therefore, on a simplified Armstrong account an unperceived tomato is not red (if red is a disposition), because without perception, there is no universal relating the tomato and the perceiver. Hence, there is no disposition. Dispositions are not only non second-order but also non-contingent, that is, necessary. This means properties and their causal powers cannot vary independently (Heil (2003), pp. 90 – 92). The whole of dispositional instantiations fixes necessarily the whole causal make-up of the world.

(IV) There are qualities and there are dispositions. There is no satisfactory account of combining them while maintaining that they are different kinds of properties (Heil (2003), pp. 117 – 120). They must hence be identical.

> (IT) "If P is an intrinsic property of a concrete object, P is simultaneously dispositional and qualitative... $P_d = P_q = P$" (Heil (2003), p. 111)

3 Objections to Heil

From the set of assumptions jointly motivating the formulation of his identity theory, I shall attack the first and most basic one: the assumption that dispositions are properties. In the chronology of his argumentation listed above the power criterion for the distinction of powers is an ontological argument that already presupposes that dispositions are features of objects, that they are entities to be distinguished and classified, and that they are ways things are, i.e.

properties. There are two reasons to justify this assumption. Intuitively, our language is full of dispositional vocabulary. It is therefore plausible that those concepts refer to something in the world. Nevertheless, Heil propagates the rejection of what he calls the Picture Theory of language. This theory expresses the view that to any correctly predicated feature of an object corresponds an ontological counterpart (a property instance) in virtue of which this predication is true and that all those objects that satisfy the predicate possess the same property. Rejecting the Picture Theory of language opens up the possibility of correctly predicated dispositional concepts that are made true by something essentially non-dispositional. However, the burden of proof lies upon those who adopt an eliminativist attitude with respect to dispositions on the ontological level.

Heil's assumption that dispositions are ontological entities is backed by a reasoning Charles B. Martin presents in his 1994 paper. Martin argues as follows: there is reason to postulate dispositional properties, because the most serious and common enterprise to reduce dispositional statements to classes of counterfactual statements can be refuted. Following Martin the task for those who set out to reduce dispositional statements is double: first to show that a counterfactual account is necessary and sufficient for dispositional statements, second to show that it is not dispositional properties that make true counterfactuals. Martin refutes the first point, so he does not have to attack the second.[1] Note that Martin's argument is not logically conclusive, but only a motivation for holding that there are dispositional properties: the main enterprise to show that there are none fails. The main point of criticism Martin and Heil advance against a counterfactual analysis is the case of finkish dispositions. Finkish dispositions are supposed to be counterexamples to the prevailing counterfactual accounts of dispositions. They are supposed to be dispositions that escape counterfactual determination. The most famous example is the following one:

> The wineglass is fragile (disposition), but each time fragility is about to manifest itself God intervenes and makes the glass lose its fragility.

This refutes the first direction of implication between fragility (disposition) and its conditional analysans:

(A) Fragility $\Rightarrow$ breaks when dropped

(A) is false since the glass is fragile, but the counterfactual is false. For the second direction of implication consider the following slightly modified situation:

---

[1] For a conditional analysis of dispositional statements combined with a realist position concerning the existence of dispositional properties, see Malzkorn (2000).

Imagine a God that each time a previously non-fragile thing (a tin cup, for example) is dropped he interferes and makes it fragile.

Here we get the refutation of the implication from the conditional to the disposition:

(B) Breaks when dropped ⇒ fragility

(B) is false since the counterfactual is true, but the disposition ascription is false. Hence, counterfactuals are neither necessary nor sufficient to analyse dispositions. Since they are not further analysable in this way they must refer to something "of the kind" in the world, namely dispositional properties. There are several options to answer Martin's argument:

(I) David Lewis (1997) and others (Malzkorn (2000), Wasserman & Manley (manuscript), for example) propose conditional analyses that are finkproof: Lewis excludes the loss of the pertinent property (the dispositional basis) during the counterfactual analysis, but this approach is open to new counterexamples (Bird (1998)). Malzkorn introduces formal normality constraints that seem to exclude finkish cases. Wasserman & Manley introduce a proportionality criterion for manifestations over pertinently varying trigger-situations.

(II) Finked situations can be considered as bad or invalid counterexamples that, on a proper analysis, turn out to be mostly harmless: Gundersen (2002) and Cross (2005) favour this position, and in what follows I put forward a variant of their insights.

The examples of divine glasses and the like are often difficult to grasp for they demand a lot of flexibility and goodwill from the part of the reader. It is difficult to consider those nomologically highly inaccessible worlds, given that nomological ordering is such a central principle of counterfactual standard semantics. This somehow self-undermines the strength of the argument. Therefore, I propose to consider the following more intuitive situation (intuitive in its most honest sense as it is a scene of Stanley Kubrick's famous film *A clockwork orange* from 1971 after Anthony Burgess's 1962 novel with the same title):

The "hero", Alex, is extremely aggressive and violent. That is his disposition. Example-situations where he manifests his disposition are when someone provokes him, hits him or challenges his group internal leadership. As a most extreme manifestation of his disposition he murders a person and is arrested. The minister of interior affairs wants to make a revolutionary example in criminal treatment of him. His penalty is abated if he agrees to follow, for a short time, a brand new medical treatment (the Ludovico method) that intends to change him and make him a socially acceptable person. Alex is forced to watch ultra-violent films combined with periodical swallowing of drug cocktails. Then, after the psychosomatical treatment has come to an end, the public test in front of an illustrious audience, such as the press and the minister, takes place. Alex, on stage, is confronted with an aggressor that provokes and hits him until he gets hopping mad. He is disposed, so to say, to hit back, but every time he tries, he suddenly gets physically sick as a parrot. He lies on the floor, moans and is incapable of doing any harm. This is the result of the Ludovico method. Every time, that is the morale of finkish situations, he is about to manifest his disposition, because the appropriate triggering conditions obtain, he loses the disposition for exactly as long as those conditions obtain.[2]

The Ludovico-fink is responsible for Alex to lose his disposition right at the triggering moment. In this situation the counterfactual "Would Alex be sufficiently provoked by some aggressor, then he would hit back" is wrong because of the Ludovico-fink. More precisely, and presupposing counterfactual possible worlds semantics, there is a very (or sufficiently) similar world where Alex is provoked and does not hit back. Actually such a world would be exactly similar. Nevertheless, the dispositional statement "Alex is extremely violent and aggressive" remains true. So, at least, say Martin and Heil. When the truth values of two different statements diverge, they cannot be identical. Hence, there are dispositional situations that are not accounted for by a conditional analysis. The case of finkish dispositions cashes out the apparent tension between a disposition's actuality even if unmanifested and its pure counter-to-the-fact analysis through subjunctive conditionals.

How can then the lack of coherence in this alleged counter-example be established? In this special situation it is claimed that finkishness is a metaphysically possible scenario. First let us state the two situations that one needs to compare:

(I) The normal situation

– Alex is violent and aggressive (= has disposition V). There is a set of conditions C (the trigger conditions) that is typically sufficient for his disposition to manifest itself as A (the physical aggression and attack on someone).

---

[2] The situation is pertinent as well because it can also be regarded as a masking or antidote example in Bird's and Gundersen's sense.

- If C obtained, then V would manifest itself as A.

(II) The finked situation

- Alex is violent and aggressive (= has disposition V). There is no set of conditions C' that is typically sufficient for his disposition to manifest itself (the trigger conditions), because as soon as any set of conditions C' becomes sufficient for V to manifest itself in A, C' entails the loss of V and therefore of A.

- It is not the case that if C' obtained, then V would manifest itself as A, because C' entails that Alex loses V.

Such is the initial situation. But what does "typically sufficient" mean? In general it means to be often sufficient but not always. There are situations where it is not the case that C is sufficient for Alex's V to manifest itself as A. Think of the following un-finked (therefore type (I)) situation: Alex is V, some guy teases him, Alex wants to attack him, but a trapdoor opens and he falls in a hole. Disposition V is still there but the manifestation A has become impossible because of not satisfied but necessary physical proximity of, let's say, an arm length. What this is about could be called circumstances or context (Cross (2005)). Circumstances are also conditions for V to become manifested as A, but they are conditions of another kind than C (or equally C'). While the latter ones are properly called trigger conditions (appealing to sufficiency), the former can be qualified as background conditions commonly referred to as normality (basic necessary conditions). The most economic way of describing what we should consider as normal is a negative characterisation: the lack of interference that blocks the entailment connection between V and A given some C. If a situation is not normal, there is some blocking interference. This would qualify a fink as a sufficient feature to render a context abnormal, if added to a set of normal conditions. The context would contain an inconsistency in as much as normality is required for dispositional talk. Abnormality entails the emptiness of C'. But is it allowed to consider the fink as a part of the background conditions?

Martin and Heil intend to take the fink to be part of the trigger conditions or the overall dispositional make-up V of Alex. In our formulation of the problem the fink cannot be part of the trigger conditions C' because C' is empty. The only way to conceive C' as non-empty is when one accepts that "typically sufficient" is compatible with the existence of some counter-fink that trumps over the initial fink in making the manifestation possible again. This is no viable solution, because the pair of fink and counter-fink causally neutralises itself. It would be difficult, or even impossible, to distinguish the result from a normal type (I) situation. It is hard to imagine how finks can be parts of the trigger-conditions if "trigger" is to mean something at all in connection with the respective disposition. What if the fink should be part of Alex's overall dispositional make-up? What would the result-disposition R of disposition V be in presence of a "trumping" disposition L (the Ludovico-disposition)? I claim that whatever R might be in detail surely it satisfies the predicate non-V. This is very intuitive in the example case: Alex under the Ludovico influence is no longer violent as there is no metaphysically possible way (remember that the relation is logical entailment) he could act violently towards a person.

The hidden premise of this claim is that in order to ascribe the disposition V (violence) truly to a subject s it is necessary that some R-similar (similar in what regards the having of the finked violence) subject truly manifests V at least once. If no finked-violent subject ever could manifest violence (because there is no set of conditions jointly sufficient for this) we should not think that it is violent. Or weaker: its violence does not matter anyhow. This means that $Alex_1$ is not similar to $Alex_2$ from the point of view of his dispositional make-up. Regarding our initial example (the interacting God-fink) the same applies: God's finked glass is not fragile anymore. It is possible, however, to combine dispositional eliminativism with an account of "unmanifested disposition". This is not important in case of fancy counterexamples like ours, but matters when it comes to physically relevant properties. David Lewis's account of laws of nature, for example, integrates unmanifested laws, but does not license the inference to unmanifested actual dispositions making them true. The truth of such ascriptions might not be determined by actual, but unmanifested, dispositional properties, but rather by the lack of instantiations of the corresponding properties in our world. Unmanifested laws are non-instantiated properties.

Admittedly, it is arguable that finks are (always) components of the dispositional make-up, but if they are not, they enter at least in the background conditions that are presupposed in any case of dispositional talk. In whatever way the preferences lie, it follows from the above discussion that it is impossible that (a) a fink is truly ascribed to an object (in the general meaning that includes subjects) and that (b) the disposition it finks does not behave correctly under counterfactual analysis. Thus the amended situation (II) is either:

(II') The pseudo-finked situation 1:

- Alex is violent and aggressive (= has disposition V).
- If the situation were normal, there would be a non-empty set of conditions C' typically sufficient for V's manifestation as A. If C' were a non-empty set of conditions C' typically sufficient for V's manifestation as A, then V would manifest itself as A. This counterfactual is vacuously true, since a non-empty C' is metaphysically impossible.

or:

(II") The pseudo-finked situation 2:

- Alex is not violent and aggressive (= has disposition non-V). His having V is trumped over by the presence of the intervening Ludovico-fink, which makes it impossible for him to aggress someone.
- It is not the case that if some triggering conditions for violence C (typically the ones from case (I)) obtained, then V would manifest itself as A, because Alex does not have V.

Note that no step of the argument depends on the supposition that dispositions could not be lost or gained in time (as postulated by Martin and Heil, although for properties and not explicitly for predicates). Rather this view is adopted and constitutes a part of the premises. Even the example fits the argument in that Alex finally turns into a "normally" violent and aggressive guy again at the end of the film. In a more general context Gundersen (2002) shows that finks and more recently antidotes are no engaging counter-examples to a conditional analyses, because they either disrespect a serious principle of object composition (s having V does not imply that $s+x$ has V), or abuse to a certain point the counterfactual semantics. For valid counterexamples "... a scenario is called for in which the masker [fink or antidote] prevents the characteristic manifestation from appearing, not merely on some particular occasion, but in a systematic and non-accidental manner" (Gundersen (2002), p. 393)).

Besides this point there is a second objection to the claim that dispositional statements are typically analysed as counterfactual dependence statements advanced by Mellor (1974). His claim is inconsistent with Martin and Heil's objection because it says that strictly anything that is a true factual statement, be it dispositional or categorical, can be appropriately analysed in terms of counterfactuals. The objection to counterfactuals is then (unlike in Martin and Heil's case) that counterfactuals cover too many statements, especially not only dispositional ones. Mellor's claim provides an overall scheme to refute finkish cases:

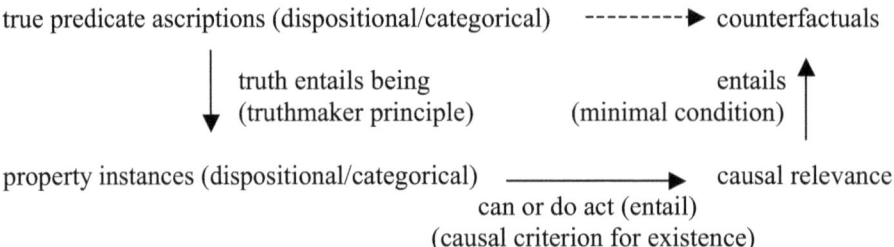

Heil is right in denouncing the analysis of the truthmaker relation as entailment, for this would be an impermissible category mix between the ontological and the linguistic domain. Entailment in the schema above therefore only stands for a general dependence relation. Note that Martin and Heil's claim for the inadequacy of counterfactual analyses of dispositional statements is turned into a challenge for them to show which true predicate ascriptions do not satisfy the inference of counterfactual truths (their finkish examples do not settle the matter). Even worse, assuming the acceptance of the truthmaker principle and the causal criterion for existence they face the problem to give intuitive examples of causal relevance that do not satisfy counterfactuals. God's intervention in making the glass unbreakable is counterfactual-proof, for example.

Counterfactuals, on a traditional Humean account, supervene on contingent laws and a distribution of qualities. It therefore depends on the conception of laws, which is independent of dispositions (like Lewis's conception as systematically privileged regularities), whether or not the truthmakers of dispositional ascriptions are dispositional properties. Given the structure of Heil's negative argumentation it is important to see that non-dispositional accounts of laws are not all equivalent to Armstrong-laws (as second-order universals). Therefore, the successful criticism of the latter does not show in any way that there are no non-dispositional laws: there might be first-order relations of structural realists or privileged regularities or simply Lewis's distribution of intrinsic properties over the whole of space-time on which the laws supervene (modulo simplicity and empirical content). So far, there is nothing that sets the friend of intrinsic properties apart from the friend of relations. They are allies against the dispositionalists.

One reason for Martin and Heil's dispositionalism, the alleged inadequacy of counterfactual analyses, is not well conceived. In any case does the construction of finkish dispositions load heavy metaphysical burden on such fancy counterexamples as enchanted glasses, namely the burden of deciding whether there are dispositions in the world or not. This fundamental question, however, had better be discussed in a broader ontological perspective (like the role of dispositions in physics and the other sciences, their philosophical prospects when it comes to reduction, and so on). Another reason in favour of dispositions is the epistemological one that pure qualities are unknowable. Their being intrinsic seems to make them impossible to grasp for the basically relational human knowledge. Even if granted, qualities are parts of regularities and relations that make it possible for a thinking subject to get in touch with them. As such unmanifested dispositions are just as unknowable as intrinsic properties deprived of their relational network. It is intrinsity that is sufficient for succumbing to the epistemological argument: qualities and dispositions are therefore on a par. The third reason in favour of dispositional properties is that once they are manifested they instantiate single-case necessary relations. On the fundamental level of properties those can be regarded as necessary law-of-nature-instances. However, the necessity that links dispositions and manifestations is first of all conceptual, not metaphysical or nomological. This point will be discussed later.

4   An outline of an alternative positive account for dispositions

The aim of this section is to sketch the framework of a positive account for dispositions through a counterfactual analysis. The idea is to indicate an *a priori* semantic reduction from dispositional to categorical vocabulary. Propositions consisting exclusively of the latter have in turn only categorical (intrinsic or relational) truthmakers. This is sufficient to make the project eliminativist. In the case of the reduction of higher-level kinds, by contrast, no semantic analysis is provided, but only extensional bridge-principles can be identified *a posteriori*. The following is an outline of an eliminativist account in the above sense:

Dispositions are names for classes of counterfactuals. Counterfactual analyses are therefore adequate and exhaustive to account for the meaning of those names. Such a reduction can be accomplished, according to a seventy years old tradition, via reduction sentences featuring a simple conditional analysis (Carnap (1936 and 1937)), Ramsey sentences composed of counterfactual relations (Mellor (2000)), or more complex variants of the simple conditional analysis (Lewis (1997), Malzkorn (2000), Gundersen (2002)). Counterfactuals are important as an expression of nomological status. Thus, laws and causal relations are typically more than simple actual truths and one needs more than material implications to fully acknowledge their status. Hence, dispositions can label laws and causal relations or even property instances that might (but did not yet) causally matter, because they fall under laws. They might label laws to the extent that the support of counterfactuals is an important feature of laws (van Fraassen (1989), chapter 2.4). They might label causal relations to the extent that to support counterfactuals is widely accepted to be a necessary condition for causation. Common examples of dispositions are:

- Fragility is the name for the law that in appropriate circumstances things of a certain molecular structure break when sufficiently struck, where sufficiency is thus specified that it does not render the statement circular.

- Alcoholism is the name for the causal relation that humans are in such a condition that they cannot resist to drink alcohol, as soon as they have the opportunity, that they feel nervous, sick, etc. when they lack the opportunity.

- Mass conceived dispositionally (intended is rest mass, not relativistic mass) is the name for the law that describes the behaviour of things as regards their resistance to acceleration. "Mass" names counterfactuals of the following kind: had the mass of thing o been a little smaller, it would have showed less resistance to acceleration (where the quantity of "less" is of course determinable).

The possibility of unmanifested basic dispositions is controversial. An eliminativist view is committed to the claim that dispositional statements about basic properties are made true by the respective, actual property instances (and the regularities they are part of). Higher-level law-like statements by contrast (like statements about genes for white blossoms, being true in winter as well) including *ceteris paribus* or normality clauses might have truthmakers that are only instantiated in the specified arrangements referred to by the clause. Heil seems to think that something merely possible in our world (the potential of producing white-blossom expressed by a gene-ascription in winter) has to have an actual truthmaker directly corresponding to the predicate. The linguistically possible is made true by the corresponding ontologically actual. Humean regularities, he thinks, do not suffice to account for the truth of such statements. This is a close tie of correspondence between the linguistic and the ontological level. Why should uninstantiated laws, for example, correspond to unmanifested dispositions? The Humean, it seems, has problems when it comes to justifying the inferences he makes from known to unknown facts. However, even if the evaluation of counter-to-the-fact statements involves vagueness and partly subjectivity, not anything is possible, given the distribution of particular matters of fact that is our world. The practical difficulties to delineate the space-time region instantiating the properties that make true such inferences are uncontroversial. Every evaluation of a causal statement on a classical Humean account involves basic regularities and big world-regions. Dispositionalists take this as a reason to plead for unmanifested dispositions each time they ask what the truthmaker for a potential behaviour ascription might be. The inference from the behaviour of one particle to the behaviour of a similar particle outside the light-cone of the former is licensed on a Humean account by means of their qualitative similarity and the degree of importance of the regularities they might therefore be part of. On a dispositionalist account this inference is licensed by means of their similarity only. In both cases similarity is primitive and not further explainable. Apart from the advantage for the dispositionalist when it comes to localise the truthmakers of disposition-ascriptions, his use of primitive similarity to license inferences is not more justified than the use the Humean makes of the same feature.

The mass case exemplifies well why many philosophers think of the basic physical properties as dispositional instead of taking them as properties governed by laws and dispositions to name those laws. To the extent that properties fall under laws the latter can be called or classified by concepts that facilitate their usage in common and scientific language. Dispositions are supposed to be necessary by those who believe in their real existence. This necessity is not nomological but conceptual. Fragility conceptually implies its counterfactual analysis, which in turn might well express relations or features of the world that are modally prioritised by being nomologically necessary. But to talk of dispositional properties would be a category mistake (Mellor (2000), p. 767).

The question of whether dispositions are identical with their basis vanishes (the higher-level question) as well as the question of whether they are intrinsic or relational: somehow dispositions are relational, because they name the nomologically possible causal network of a property instance; dispositions are neither identical nor distinct from their basis, as the disposition and the cause belong to a different category. If we take the predicate "B" that applies to the basis, they are related in the following way: $D = \{R \mid xRy$ for R a true counterfactual of a certain kind, for x satisfying "B" and y property instances$\}$. The primitive directedness (the pointing) of dispositions expresses the need for something to remain when property instances are considered independently of the relata they enter in relation to (be it of a law-like or causal kind). This is exactly Armstrong's default. Counterfactuals intimately fit the picture of property instances pointing towards a manifestation (that is a causal relation). The truthmakers of such counterfactuals have to combine the idea of stable behavioural patterns with the possibility that those patterns are sometimes or often not instantiated because the conditions to do so lack. The truthmakers need to be regularities of property instantiations in the world: regular arrangements of qualities only, an arrangement of qualities plus basic law-like relations, or only regular structure. But what makes it true that a flower has a gene to produce white blossoms, but does not execute this potentiality because it is, say, wintertime? The definition of the function of a gene incorporates the idea of its conditions of functioning (that the flower is not dead, that sunlight intensity and duration, as well as temperature are appropriate). Those conditions form a context that can be called the possibility context of normal vegetal life. Gene ascriptions for white blossoms in spring are made true by the specific DNA string, the plant having it, and the regularities (*qua* co-instantiations) of the gene with other properties of the environment or of the plant itself. To all this adds up a *ceteris paribus* clause, made true by a nomologically accessible and similar state of the world. Together, this makes true the statement held during winter, that a specific plant has a gene to produce white blossoms in spring. To the extent that the co-instantiations composing regularities are instances of categorical properties, no need for dispositional properties remains.

5 What is powerful causation?

Powerful causation for dispositionalists is the manifestation of a dispositional property instance d as m. For sure m is the effect, but what is the cause? Heil's powerful causation is an internal relation between context C, disposition D and effect M. What does D have to be in order to satisfy some minimal causation condition (e.g. simple counterfactual dependence or Lewis's influence account (Lewis (2004))? Most recently David Lewis identifies causal statements with there being a chain of influence between the cause and the effect. There is influence if and only if sometimes, small variations of the cause (C) are followed by small variations of the effect (M) and if C's and M's are counterfactually dependent. Causal responsibility comes from the object o having a certain property B often called the basis and of o standing in relations C. D then merely names $\{C\} \ \& \ \{B\} \ \Box\!\!\rightarrow \{M\}$. Gundersen rightly claims that this counterfactual relation is not implied by $\{B\} \ \Box\!\!\rightarrow \{M\}$, nor by $\{C\} \ \Box\!\!\rightarrow \{M\}$ and says more than the latter two (see Gundersen (2002), pp. 391 – 393). It is rather preferable to fully account for all the active elements in a causal relation (context, cause and effect) than to choose for example the $\{C\} \,\square\!\!\rightarrow \{M\}$ analysis for the price of leaving aside the central causally effective event. The idea to take equivalence classes for trigger-situations is given additional motivation in Wasserman & Manley (manuscript). D is sometimes saved as a cause by being identified with B, but B is not being fragile: it is rather being of molecular structure X.

This scheme might seem odd for event-ontologists. Indeed on such an account a C and a B would combine into an event E. To the extent that the truthmakers of causal counterfactuals are not properties of C, B and M only, a causal relation is an external relation: the instantiation of C, B and M is not sufficient for the instantiation of the causal relation. What might be internal, or characteristic for C, B and M is only its name. Names are given to groups of counterfactuals in virtue of so-called typifying manifestations (i.e. the typical effects). Being fragile is the name of some structure that breaks when dropped. Fragility does not mean only being of a certain molecular structure: the counterfactual is made true by laws and the events drop and break. The disposition itself does not act as a cause, and it is hardly conceivable how it could then provide explanation for M. The only explanatory function of dispositions could be that they incorporate some natural law-like necessity. This is hard to accept for anyone who believes that explanation has something to do with the causal history of things or events. It might be that law-like necessity just is systematic priority of regularities (like in Lewis (1994a), p. 478).

Therefore the feature of the glass referred to by the antecedent of the counterfactual called fragility should be the relevant cause: the molecular structure of the glass. Dispositions are only linguistic entities. As they refer to nothing dispositional in the world, there are no such entities that have their powers built-in. The trigger-manifestation-relation as the realisation of a power does not really exist. It is only a way to talk about regular causal relations. Those relations in turn are only Humean arrangements of particular matters of facts. All there is to powerful causation is a powerful name.

Commentary

John Heil

According to a traditional distinction between dispositional and categorical properties, categorical properties are those actually possessed by an object; dispositional properties are *if – then* properties, properties an object *would* possess if circumstances were such and such. The distinction confuses dispositions with their manifestations. If a grain of salt is disposed to dissolve in water, it is so disposed in virtue of something about the salt here and now, some "categorical" feature of the salt. What is non-categorically present in the salt – at least until it dissolves – is its dissolving.

Most parties to the current debate regard dispositions as categorical: whatever they are, dispositions are possessed by objects quite independently of their manifestations. In hopes of avoiding potential confusion, I recommend replacing talk of categorical properties with talk of qualities. The dispositional/qualitative distinction strikes me as more perspicuous for our purposes than the old dispositional/categorical – if – then/actual – distinction.

Sparber regards my discussion of dispositionality as philosophically naïve. He prefers Humeanism of the kind defended by David Lewis.

> "... [Every] quality needs a relation to get causal importance. That means that pure isolated qualities have no causal relevance. It follows that there is a brute basic dichotomy between dispositions and qualities." (p. 124, above)

But why should "causal importance" require relations? Sparber's Humeanism is at work here. If you are a Humean, every kind of disposition must be manifested. To say that this grain of salt would dissolve in water or this ball would roll, is to say that this grain of salt qualitatively resembles many grains that have dissolved and this ball resembles many balls that have rolled. Sparber admits that not all grains of salt will dissolve, not all balls will roll, so there are unmanifested dispositions. But if some grains could be disposed to dissolve, yet not dissolve, some balls be disposed to roll, yet not roll, why not *all* of them? It is something of an historical accident that salt exists within the light cone of water. But, if it is possible that salt never happened to encounter water, it is possible that no salt dissolves. Do we want to say that, in these circumstances, salt is not soluble?

Sparber seems happy to accept this result, but most of us would regard it as a difficulty for the Humean. Lewis recruits alternative worlds here: salt dissolves in some world, even if not in this world. But does Sparber expect us to swallow, in addition to Humeanism, an infinity of alternative worlds? Is this supposed to be simpler or more elegant than the idea that objects' properties are dispositional?

Consider this stationary ball. It is true of this ball that it would roll – and that it would reflect light in a particular way, and that it would make a concave impression were it dropped into wet sand. For many of us, and probably for all non-philosophers, these truths seem to be due to a feature of this ball: its sphericity. For the Humean, matters are different. This ball's capacity to roll depends on the rolling of other balls elsewhere and elsewhen. A Humean, like a sceptic, has a response to any opponent. But the implausibilities accumulate, leaving the rest of us looking for something better.

Sparber discusses C. B. Martin's "finkish" counterexamples to conditional analyses of dispositions.[1] These are cases in which conditions that would normally elicit a particular kind of manifestation of a disposition result either in the loss of the disposition or in its acquisition. Sparber's idea is that conditional analyses can be rehabilitated. Suppose he were right. What would follow? Not very much. We would still want to know what it is about an object in virtue of which a given conditional holds of it.

Conditional analyses seem wrong-headed, not solely because, in common with analyses generally, they inevitably fall prey to counterexamples, but because, in repairing the analyses to cope with counterexamples, we are obliged to invoke an independent understanding of dispositionality. But if we have that, what exactly is the point of the analysis? Sparber does not say.

Consider the difference between an object's losing a given disposition, D, and an object's keeping D but acquiring a new disposition, D'?, that blocks an expected manifestation of D. Any account of dispositions ought to distinguish such cases. Conditional analyses are ill-equipped to do so. You take a poison pill together with an antidote. There are two ways an antidote might work. First, it might change the chemical nature of the pill causing it to lose its disposition to do what it would otherwise do in your gut. Second, it might not affect the pill at all – the pill might not change dispositionally – but affect your gut so

---

[1] Sparber regards Martin's counterexamples as involving angelic intervention and the like, and to that extent frivolous (see p. 127, above). But Martin's actual example of an "electro-fink" is in no way exotic. You could build an electro-fink in your basement workshop: a circuit-breaker is an electro-fink.

as to block the poison's lethal manifestation. The distinction will be difficult to maintain so long as you are wedded to a conditional analysis.

On my view it is important that manifestations of dispositions are mutual affairs: a given disposition manifests itself in a particular way with a particular kind of reciprocal disposition partner. But the *very same* disposition can manifest itself differently with different kinds of reciprocal partner. Although I discuss such cases at length and highlight their importance, Sparber does not mention them. In fact he embraces uncritically the idea that the relation between a dispositions and its "trigger" is asymmetrical. I suspect that this is because he is thinking of dispositions purely counterfactually: D is a disposition to F under conditions C. But, on my view, the very same disposition, D, could be a disposition to G under conditions C'?

In response to finkish cases, Sparber takes refuge in "typically sufficient triggering conditions" (p. 129, above). So D's being a disposition to F under conditions C is not undercut by D's failing to F under C in *some* cases. But what of dispositions that are invariably blocked or that never encounter the right sort of reciprocal disposition partner? Does Sparber think that such cases are conceptually impossible? Part of the problem is that Sparber is ill-equipped to distinguish, as I do, between the disposition, a *property*, and the object that has the disposition. What an object is disposed to do depends on its overall dispositional makeup. Dispositions can cancel one another out: they can be present in the object, but certain of their manifestations are blocked or inhibited.

Sparber's talk of "triggering conditions" and "background" conditions reflects the intrusion of epistemology into ontology. A condition is relegated to the "background" not by nature, but by our interests. I strike a match and the tip ignites. Is the surrounding oxygen a "background condition"? Hardly. Dispositions inherent in oxygen are just one of the reciprocal dispositions that manifest themselves in an igniting. There is an important symmetry here that Sparber altogether misses.

Chapter 8

Is Heil's theory a really determinate realism? Dispositionalist realism and identity theory[1]

Laurent Freland

The aim of this paper is to understand Heil's position and to stress some troublesome aspects of his dispositional realism and identity theory, notably in comparison with Mumford's neutral monism stated in Mumford (1998).[2] I will use the notation (DR) and (IT) to express the following theses:

(DR) Dispositional Realism: dispositional properties exist.
(IT) Identity Theory: properties are dispositional and categorical (or "qualitative") in one

Mumford and Heil are both dispositional *realists*, and they both argue for an identity between dispositional properties and categorical properties (defined as "qualities" by Heil). In this paper, I will defend two claims. In the first part, I will show that in Heil (2003) there are only few arguments in favour of (DR) and that no thorough analysis of dispositions is actually made. I will compare Heil's and Mumford's conceptions and explain why Mumford's conception is more attractive than Heil's one. In the second part, I will illustrate how whatever non-reductionist (IT), in the framework of a full-blooded realism, leads to an inescapable metaphysical trouble and that such a trouble requires to adopt either a pure (DR) or an anti-realist standpoint. My conclusion is that realism is problematic for all non-reductionist (IT), and therefore for both Mumford's and Heil's views.[3]

1   Heil's defence of (DR).

In this part, I will defend the following claims: Heil has no well-established arguments in favour of (DR), only a strong conviction that the laws of nature

---

[1] I am very grateful to John Heil and Alexander Bird for their helpful comments on a previous version of this paper.

[2] I leave aside the issue relative to levels-of-being. Mumford adopts a continuity position with respect to levels of being. Heil defends a no-levels-of-being position.

[3] We must notice, however, that Mumford has recently changed his mind. He now seems to adopt a pure (DR) (see especially Mumford (2004b), chapter 10, sections 10.6 and 10.7).

are metaphysically necessary (section 1.1). In order to escape the relational thesis, which could lead to an anti-realist move – as Mackie points out with his double-vision criticism – Heil's simply proposes the Truthmaking Principle (TMP) and the Picture Theory (PT) criticism. Yet, this defence is only able to ensure the possibility of intrinsic non-relational properties to sustain relations (section 1.2). Heil does not actually offer any convincing account of dispositions. Therefore, to analyse these sustaining-properties, I will suggest the adoption of a token-identity functionalism, following Mumford (section 1.3).

1.1 Arguments for (DR)

The first argument relies on the (TMP).[4] According to Heil, the (TMP) is the first fundamental element for a realist defence of dispositions:

> "Nowadays few philosophers would be willing to endorse Ryle's conception of dispositionality. A large measure of the resistance issues from an implicit commitment to a truthmaker principle: if a statement concerning the world is true, there must be something about the world in virtue of which it is true." (Heil (2003), p. 62)

It is clear that the fact of posing dispositions as truthmakers grounds the truth of the conditionals in the world. This fact is not motivated by Heil. Why not positing non-dispositional entities (properties or relations) as truthmakers?[5] The (TMP) only ensures that the world is mind-independent, which is a minimal requirement for whatever realism. Truth is then an extrinsic property of sentences or beliefs. But the truthmakers are not yet determined. The (TMP) allows whatever ways (the world is) that make true conditional sentences true. Let us consider Heil's (PT) criticism. There is no bijectivity between the form of our language and the structure of the world. That our conditional statements belong to a relational idiom doesn't imply any relations or any relational entities as truthmakers:[6]

---

[4] For a criticism of this principle, see Friederich & Tuzet (this volume). I nevertheless accept this realist tool.

[5] I remain neutral, here, on the question whether such entities are able to be truthmakers for modal truths. For such a criticism, see Bird (2006 forthcoming).

[6] For Heil's criticism of relational dispositions, see below, section 1.2.

Language :   Sentences in a *relational* idiom
                        ⇩
World :   *relational* ways the world is
         or (*relational*) dispositional ways the world is

⇩: Picture-Theory's fault

But this analysis is only negative. The only available conclusion based on the TMP and the PT criticism is this one:

Language :   Sentences in a *relational* idiom
                        ↑
World :   *X* ways the world is

↑: Truthmaking relation

Furthermore, when Heil sets out to attack the relational net, he uses the (PT) criticism in the following way:

> "Let us suppose that we could represent all the truths, or all the fundamental truths using graph theory. ... Now we have a true account of the world expressed in a wholly relational vocabulary. It does not follow from this that the truthmakers for claims made in this vocabulary are relations. That would seem to follow only if you embraced the Picture Theory and imagined that we were entitled to ascribe a relational structure to reality on the grounds that our descriptions of that reality were couched in a relational idiom." (Heil (2003), p. 105)

This argument is a little odd: it gives too much to the view it is opposed to. If a *true* account of the world expressed in a *wholly* relational vocabulary is a plausible hypothesis, why supposing something more than relations? For sure, Heil would refuse such a hypothesis, but that's the point he had better focus on. If he admits the plausibility of this hypothesis, then all the dispositionalist investigation should be postponed, even if dispositions could co-exist with this representation. Indeed, a sort of principle of ontological/categorical parsimony would require to avoid the need of dispositions. Using (PT) here is problematic: the central idea of the (PT) criticism is to prevent any natural projection from predicates to properties, to make no confusion between words and things. In my opinion, whoever endorses a theory of *sparse* properties should agree with this general precaution. But here the situation is different: we suppose to have successfully translated all truths in a homogeneous, relational form. If this is possible, it would be good news. The postulation of correlated relations is in fact not a naïve projection but the best ontological decision to adopt. Besides, if a confusion between relational predicates and relations is still present, we can reduce the ontological commitment considering only the *fundamental* truths. There is absolutely no reason to proceed otherwise.[7] A (DR) proponent has to attack this hypothesis: this is the only rational target. Certainly, if we suppose that *there are* some dispositions as truthmakers, there must be an abusive projection from relational predicates to relations, and so there has to be a kind of projection as in (PT), but this is question-begging: what we want to know is whether *there are* some dispositions as truthmakers, and (PT) criticism doesn't tell us why dispositions are inescapable. So what is the real motivation for (DR)?

In Heil (2003), the most important reason to adopt (DR) is the conviction that the laws of nature are metaphysically necessary. If the laws only express a direct necessitation from properties, and if Shoemaker's thesis – the Principle of Identity (PI)[8] – is right, then the simple existence of dispositions makes sure that there is such a strong transparent metaphysical necessity in our world, without further investigation.[9] Actually, this necessity is very easy to grasp. The great advantage of this thesis relies on the fact that it prevents from quidditism: if properties have their causal powers essentially, there is no possible world in which two different properties have their powers reversed. In order to avoid quidditism, we could for instance deny that there are intrinsic properties at all. In this case, different properties with identical causal roles would represent no problem, because the properties could not be isolated from their (causal) relational net: they would become extrinsic properties. The relational realism is thus exempt from this criticism. Or we can perhaps refuse

---

[7] As Bird noticed in a private communication, this argumentation requires a strict condition. We are supposed to restrict our vocabulary only to predicates corresponding to natural relations, and that may be too restrictive (there is no property of grueness, for instance, but we can make true descriptions using "grue"). I agree, but I maintain that, without good arguments for (DR), there is no reason to suppose that these relations are "abundant" (to use Lewis's vocabulary). We only suppose that we don't look after artificial predicates in order to get this relational form, but scientific relational predicates are good proponents for natural relations.

[8] "(PI) Necessarily, if A and B are properties, $A = B$ just in case A and B make the same contribution to the causal powers of their (actual or possible) possessors." (cited in Heil (2003), p. 77) See below, section 2.1.

[9] This transparency must be understood only from a metaphysical point of view.

transworld identity for token-properties, in Lewis's way.[10] I will not discuss (PI) here, which is nevertheless the central stake between dispositionalists and categoricalists with regard to the modal status of laws and properties.[11]

1.2 The defence of the non-relational nature of dispositions

Heil's (DR), thus, is not sufficiently grounded. His strategy concerning dispositions is essentially defensive, i.e. mainly focused on proposing to dissolve some anti-realist arguments, as for instance those based on the relational nature of dispositions. In Heil's perspective, we can accept a causal (and so relational) net as a kind of derivation from the power net, the net of correlated manifestations. The most recurrent point Heil accepts to deal with is the so-called *relational* nature of dispositions. Heil's main concern, here, is to reject the relational thesis: a disposition is an intrinsic property. The operation of the mind is then not an inclusion of (causal) relations into the objects, because the nature of dispositions is not at all relational.

> "... [You] would not want "connections" among powers to reside outside those powers. It does not follow, however, that the connections reside inside the properties." (Heil (2003), pp. 123–124)

A relational nature could entail some problematic aspects. The anti-realist tradition, following Mackie, insists notably on the double-vision illusion of ascriptions of dispositions:

> "Such intrinsic powers are pretty clearly products of metaphysical double-vision: they just are the causal processes which they are supposed to explain seen over again as somehow latent in the things that enter into these processes". (Mackie (1977), in Tuomela (1978), p. 104)

According to Armstrong, the dispositionalist thesis has to confront the problem of Meinongianism, that is a relation to a non-existing thing (manifestation).[12] We could consider this argument as a specific case of double-vision. Heil would argue, against all double-vision criticism, that if we accept a (PT)-based conception, we will have to introduce the relations inside the things, so

---

[10] Robert Black, on the opposite, in Black (2000), argues that Lewis has to accept transworld identity for properties. See Mumford (2004b), p. 151.

[11] In Heil (2003) there is no real argumentation for (PI). For a critical debate, we must refer to others works. See Bird (2006 forthcoming) for a discussion of this point.

[12] Armstrong writes: "a disposition as conceived of by a dispositionalist is like a congealed hypothetical fact or state of affairs" (Armstrong (1997), p. 79).

that the double-vision emerges: some relations would need to be grounded, some relational dispositions would ground them. But if we refuse the (PT) conception, the dispositions that ground the relations are not of relational kind and therefore are not the relations "seen again and above as somehow latent in the things". Hence, the (PT) criticism (coupled with the (TMP)) is used to prevent an explanation which relies on such a projection to make dispositions redundant.[13]

Heil gives us the paradigmatic example of a key to show – paradoxically – the non-relational nature of dispositions:

> "Imagine a key with a particular shape. The key would open locks of a particular (complementary) shape. This power is intrinsic to the key. If the key "points beyond" itself to locks of particular sort, it does so in virtue of its intrinsic features. This is what it is to be a key of this shape. The key is (as Martin would put it) "ready to go". We can say this without committing ourselves to the existence of possible locks. The truthmaker for "this key would open a lock of a kind K" is not the key, a possible lock of kind K, and a relation between the key and K. The truthmaker for the assertion is just the key itself's being a particular way: its being rigid and its possessing a particular shape." (Heil (2003), p. 124)

The picture Heil rejects is exactly the double-vision view: a relation to a possible lock is only a duplication of a relation to an actual lock, located in the thing to explain the relation. I agree with Heil on this point: that a certain thing has causal roles (open the lock for a key), and therefore enters into relations, doesn't imply that this thing is relational. This is the case only if properties are founded on relations, and so are extrinsic. An extrinsic property could be a kind of monadic reduction of the relation. But if the properties are intrinsic, this fact doesn't prevent them from entering into relations without being

---

[13] Let us notice that one opportunity would be to stress on the difference between two types of relations. For Bird – as he explained in a private communication – there is no incompatibility between the intrinsicness of dispositions and their relational nature, because the intrinsicness of dispositions is only opposed to the extrinsicness of dispositions (thesis which supposes relations to particular things as being essential for dispositions) and not at all to the relational nature of dispositions (thesis which focuses on the relations between properties, and so, for Bird, *universals*). For Mumford's position, which is similar, see Mumford (2004b), pp. 170 – 174. There is actually another strategy against the double-vision illusion, and it doesn't rely on an analysis of language as Heil's strategy (referring to (PT) fault) does, but on a metaphysical distinction between particulars and universals.

relational.[14] Following Molnar, for a relation to hold, there must be a comparison between the two relata allowing the relation to supervene on the intrinsic properties of their bearers. He calls such properties "intrinsic congruence-sustaining properties" (Molnar (2003), p. 104). So, rigidity and shape could be these intrinsic congruence-sustaining properties, and the truthmakers of the relation would be the key and the lock in correlated ways (without relational structure). Yet, it is worth noticing that Heil employs the expression "to point beyond", which clearly looks like a relational term. If this expression is examined metaphysically, it leads us directly to the strong metaphysical thesis of the directional/intentional states. If Heil wants his (DR) to be a full-blooded realism, he can't adopt a "no-further-investigation" strategy. What does it mean to say "it is of the nature of F and G to yield manifestation M"?[15] For Heil, it exactly means that powers are "built-in". But if so, the double-vision appears to be inescapable in a complete analysis of powers: the ability to be directed to.[16] It is not sufficient to use the (TMP) and the (PT) criticism to avoid the relational thesis: we must also reject the intentional thesis. Another solution could be to consider the qualitative nature of the property, but then the disposition would not at all be required. The key/lock example only shows that we could be foundationalist about certain relations (key-open-lock relation), and consequently need intrinsic properties. That we need dispositions is too strong a conclusion, if the physical make-up of the thing is only what Heil refers to.[17]

---

[14] Bird adopts Barcan's formula: $\diamond \exists x\,(Fx) \rightarrow \exists x \diamond (Fx)$. See Bird (forthcoming 2006), p. 18: "I could turn the piece of paper into an origami swan. ... [For] there to be the possibility of an origami swan is for there to be a possible origami swan." So, Bird assumes the view Heil criticises. We could well think that Bird's position presents the same troubles of Meinongianism, but he could give two arguments against this association. First, dispositions are universals, and Meinongianism focuses on particulars. For a similar defence, see the reply to Armstrong by Ellis in Ellis (1999), pp. 39 – 41. Secondly, Bird uses an "all the same" dispositionalist defence: the inescapability of existent unrealised possibilities for whoever is neither a Megarian actualist or a modal realist (Lewis). See Bird (forthcoming), pp. 79 – 82, and Bird (2006 forthcoming). If Bird is right, the relational charge is impotent as an argument against (DR).

[15] Heil (2003), p. 124.

[16] Psillos thinks that there is a problematic regress of (unmanifested) powers that stops only on categorical bases (see Psillos (2005)).

[17] For Molnar and Bird, the make-up is itself dispositional. Here we have a non-vicious regress to pure ungrounded dispositions. I cannot investigate this important aspect of (DR) defence, here. In Heil's specific (DR) (in his (IT)), this argument is useless. Note that a categorical approach to these fundamental particles is possible by reflecting on symmetries. Their individuation flows from local internal symmetries. But relations (or extrinsic properties) appear to be more fundamental than qualities, here. In this sense, this is not a pretty strong argument for (IT). See Psillos (2005).

1.3 A significant silence about the causal analysis

Heil's argumentation is thus only able to ensure the possibility of intrinsic non-relational properties to support relations. This is sufficient to avoid the relational charge, but it is not sufficient to defend (DR). What would be expected is a clear dispositional defence against the double-vision argument, but a similar defence requires a precise analysis of dispositions. These considerations lead us to another point: the causal analysis. A causal account could be used to escape the relational charge and more specifically the double-vision criticism. First, the "no-further-investigation" strategy is consistent with Mumford's position. In Mumford's realism, the "to point beyond" could be interpreted as *a façon de parler* that belongs to the conditional way of characterisation. So, we can accept this stop: no further investigation is necessary because the dispositional idiom is only a (true) way of thinking about the world. There is thus no problem with respect to the nature of powers.[18] Secondly, the causal account gives another argument against the double-vision criticism with respect to the explanatory force of dispositions. The *virtus dormitiva* explanations are typical cases of double-vision. What is central for Mumford is to lay stress on the causal role of dispositions. A power's ascription could give an explanation of an actual process to complete them. It informs us that the causal process (to take aspirin, to have no more headache, for instance) is grounded on the nature of one thing (aspirin, for instance). It does not consist in saying that, say, the cause of sleeping is the sleeping power. There is a positive information, because the disposition's ascription fixes a causal origin of the process (the properties of aspirin) which otherwise would be left as a pure report of visible events. There could moreover be an explanatory gain: against the double-vision view, one could argue that the ascriptions of dispositions complete the causal claims, with some informative answer.[19]

In a purely conditional analysis of dispositional terms, we only rely on the report of some correlated events (if ... then ...) without investigating the "thing's black box". As a result, the causal report is incomplete. The things are not neutral in the processes they enter into, and so can't be redundant. For Mumford this conditional analysis is only a by-product of a good functionalist one, which posits the object that plays these causal roles in these processes. The information is only the circumscription of the cause (the aspirin), not a de-

---

[18] For Mumford's realism, see below, section 2.2.
[19] This argument is in Mumford (1998), pp. 136 – 141.

termination of it (which features of the aspirin).[20] Nowhere, in Heil (2003), do we find such a causal analysis. That is why Heil's (DR) remains indeterminate. As far as I can see, Heil would simply accept the following formulation, given by Mumford:

> "The essential point that needs to be kept in mind in the defence of a realist theory of dispositions is that conditionals are only, as Martin has said, inexact gestures towards the properties that sometimes make them true." (Mumford (1998), p. 91)

To be sure, a conditional analysis of dispositions could be used to deny their reality. In this sense, a dispositional realist could be tempted to disrupt the relation between the two.[21] But I know no other analysis of dispositions apart from these two: on the one hand, a causal analysis of dispositions, using conditional statements; on the other hand, an intentional analysis of dispositions, using a strong metaphysical theory of the nature of matter and mind. This last approach is due to Molnar, and could be summarised with Place's thesis: "the intentionality is the mark of the dispositional". This thesis is radical and it claims that the dispositions are directed to their possible manifestations. Even if we reject Mumford's interpretation of it as a new form of panpsychism[22] – because Molnar is committed to purely physical intentional states, and denies the intentional criteria of mind – it is a highly speculative theory.[23] This intentional thesis suffers from the relational charge. Actually, it seems that there is no other analysis of dispositions available to a realist than the kind of

---

[20] However, note that this argument is pretty poor concerning (DR). An anti-realist defending an event-ontology could answer that this explanation is not really an explanation, but only the indication of some actual invisible causal process (pace Ryle). A reductionist could argue that the accepted causal role related to the conditional is played by non-dispositional entities. So the power lecture could be seen again as parasitic, even if it has no strict double-vision form.

[21] See Sparber for a critical analysis of Martin and Heil's arguments (this volume).

[22] See Mumford (1999), p. 221.

[23] Ellis, who defends (DR), supports neither the first analysis nor the second one. His central notion is the notion of force. As Armstrong says, it implies directionality, but Ellis seems to refuse the intentional thesis. So Ellis' ontology is indeterminate. Notice that Armstrong is embarrassed by the notion of force: for him it is the best dispositionalist arm, which reports a kind of directed property: something dispositionalists look after. See Armstrong (1997), pp. 78 and 249.

analysis encouraged by anti-realists (eliminativists): a conditional analysis.[24] A realist would then be committed to specify the nature of the link between dispositions and conditionals, if he wanted to argue for a positive thesis, and not only for a negative one: for instance, a revised analysis which introduces a rule that excludes fink and antidotes (Bird), or a conditional analysis related to ideal conditions' specifications and which is a by-product of a functional characterisation (Mumford). Heil seems to adopt a non-committal position. He offers no criticism of the intentional thesis, but he is reluctant to avoid any quotation mark when using the directional terms. He doesn't directly criticise the causal approach, but it seems clear that he regards the proximity between a causal analysis and the relational nature of dispositions as suspicious. The reason seems to be the following: both analyses are likely to suffer from the relational charge. Heil's reluctance is explicit about the (causal) conditional analysis:

> "The inspiration for a relational conception of dispositions arises from another source: our practice of identifying dispositions conditionally, identifying them by reference to their possible manifestations." (Heil (2003), p. 81)

As this passage makes clear, Heil puts together the problem of the relations and the (causal) conditional analysis, though only one is problematic: the first one.

We will see that Mumford's position, which is a token-identity functionalism, is a better standpoint than Heil's one. Heil has some arguments to deny a functionalist thesis, but he only focuses on the functional state identity thesis (FSIT), saying that a (PT) fault allows some confusion between indeterminate predicates and higher-level properties. In a type-identity (or better sub-type-identity), there are always some dissimilarities between the particular properties, and so there is still the (PT) fault's possibility to posit a so-called set of sub-type properties where there is only one set of not-exactly similar token-properties. Furthermore, whatever may be said about this (PT) criticism of Heil, such a functionalism could not be a coherent (DR), because of the irreducible dilemma between overdetermination and causal impotence. I

---

[24] The term "analysis" is perhaps confusing, as Bird has pointed out in a private communication. I don't want to say that a kind of conceptual analysis of dispositions in terms of conditionals is required (such an analysis tends to be connected with a dispositional anti-realism, even if Malzkorn defends an opposite view – see Malzkorn (2000)), but more trivially that the way the dispositions are correlated to conditionals must be thoroughly examined.

agree with Heil on this point.[25] (FSIT) should therefore be rejected. But we could take into account another functional identity thesis. First, we could adopt a token-(IT). Heil seems to adopt a similar token-(IT), even if he doesn't say much about this point. Secondly, functionalism only focuses on the inescapable causal roles played by the things that enter into relations. Nothing prevents from having a functionalist approach if we distinguish more clearly the (causal) relational net and the things that enter into it. A token-identity-functionalism is therefore available to Heil.[26]

Nevertheless, a causal (conditional or functional) analysis, as in Mumford (1998), could be problematic for this other reason. If we have got a causal analysis of dispositions, could we have a dispositional analysis of causality? On many occasions, the opposite ontological conceptions of Armstrong and Martin are expressed in the following form: the "causal net" versus the "power net".[27] Martin thinks that the notion of disposition is more fundamental than the notion of causality. So a dispositionalist account of causality could be accepted. Any strong realist theory of dispositions has to endorse the following two claims: on the one hand, causality is a primitive notion and, on the other hand, the most fundamental features of the world are not causal processes, but powers. But is there no inescapable circularity? Armstrong writes:

> "Looking forward to the dispositionalist thesis, the thesis that the properties of particulars are nothing but powers, it may be noted that if a (singular) causal relation is necessary for the manifestation of a disposition of a particular, then, however this causal relation is analysed, a dispositionalist account cannot be given of that relation. So dispositionalists had better, on pain on falling into circularity, exclude the relation of causality from their Dispositionalist thesis." (Armstrong (1997), p. 72)

Thus, for Armstrong, no dispositional analysis of causality is possible. If the notion of causation is conceptually included in the notion of disposition (as

---

[25] I understand the footnote 8, p. 44 in Heil (2003) in this way: at the atomic level, no atom differs from another, and so perhaps a type-property could be accepted.

[26] In (FSIT), there is no real *identity* between the functional state and the categorical state, because the latter is the realiser of the former. In specification-functionalism, on the contrary, there is a real identity, because the latter is specified by the former. Such a distinction was made by Ned Block in Block (1980). But he has changed his mind, now: this sort of functionalism is not a real functionalism. One can well adopt a similar conclusion, because the functional state seems to have its own plasticity in a type-identity theory (multi-realisation). I am grateful to Heil for these clarifications.

[27] See Armstrong (1997), p. 255.

a display of dispositions), what does such a priority of dispositions mean? Molnar recognises that causality can't be defined, and that we must consider it as a natural relation (Molnar (1999), p. 190). He nevertheless maintains the possibility of a dispositionalist account of causality where the real essence of that relation is given in terms of powers of interacting objects (Molnar (1999), p. 199). The question is: is this analysis of the *essence* of causality able to make clearer what causality is? If causality is essentially grounded on a display of powers and if we know nothing about this notion of display, the essence of causality is still obscure. If we come back to causality, it is circular. We can escape circularity only by means of a metaphysical distinction between "nominal essence" (conceptual definition) and "real essence" (nature of the thing). My thesis is that any strong realist theory of dispositions has to take this consequence into account in order to avoid circularity. But then, there is no need to reject causal analysis any more. However, this doesn't seem a fruitful strategy to adopt. In fact, in the case of Mumford's realism (stated in Mumford's (1998) analysis), this circularity can be blocked without any metaphysical distinction of essences. Causality is clearly the fundamental element, used for functionalist classifications. Hence, Mumford's view is definitely more attractive. Should we urge Heil to adopt a similar view? But, as we will see in the following part, this view is a clear anti-realist move. Actually, it depends on the point of view we choose, without ontological commitment. The power net and the causal net are two non-equivalent views of the world.

2 Heil's identity theory (IT)

The first part of this paper has shown that Heil's (DR) is not sufficiently grounded: no strong arguments in favour of the existence of dispositions and no real account of their characterisation are given. More precisely, this first part has shown that Mumford's position is more attractive than Heil's one. In this part, I will show that Heil's (DR) confronts a new embarrassment with the specific (DR) he adopts, i.e. (IT). This embarrassment relies on the issue of realism, and this issue concerns also Mumford. We have seen that there is no commitment to a specific ontology with the (TMP) and the (PT) criticism, but Heil deals with a determinate ontology. Not only does he defend (DR) (dispositions exist), but he also endorses a version of (DR) (dispositions *are* qualities). So, (IT) focuses on the specific ways the world is, which are dispositional and qualitative in one. This realism is a full-blooded realism. The truthmakers are seen as being dispositions and qualities in one. Heil has a strong reason to adopt (IT): to provide an answer to Swinburne's argument. If all properties and relations reduce to powers, these manifestations of powers must themselves be analysed in terms of gaining or losing powers, and so on. There is never translation from potency to act, if we prefer the Aristotelian terms, or, to use an Armstrongian expression: "always packing, never travelling". A power brings about a power which brings about a power, in a debilitating regress (Heil (2003), p. 98). If this argument is sound,[28] a pure type of ontological dualism is the only available pure (DR) (like with Ellis and Molnar). But these theories have some metaphysical complications.[29] Hence, (IT) seems pretty attractive: a disposition is an intrinsic property that is qualitative, too. I have no objection to the possibility for (IT) to logically solve this argument. Dispositions are qualities, and qualities are always in *act*. So, no debilitating regress, here. But the problem concerns the meaning of this view. My thesis is that (IT) requires an anti-realist move, and my claims, in this second part, could be summarised in this way:

(IT) postulates an identity between dispositions and qualities, but dispositions and qualities have two conflicting "natures": if properties (as qualities) essentially have a quiddity (a non-causal intrinsic feature), they don't need their dispositional character to be also essential (direct powers "built-in") (section 2.1). So, dispositions and qualities must be linguistically relativised and a *determinate* realism could only be preserved by a metaphysical pluralism, a pluralism that holds that the way the world is, is relative to a scheme. We have thus two schemes: a dispositional one and a qualitative one. Such a metaphysical pluralism is in fact an anti-realist move (section 2.2). The only solution to preserve realism is then to refuse any contradiction between qualities and dispositions. However, this strategy is committed to the following dilemma. On one hand, a new partition inside the property could be made, but this solution would be committed to a new (PT) fault, and so couldn't be adopted. Indeed, it would be a projection of a distinction belonging to the way we talk about properties onto a distinction belonging to the world itself. On the other hand, we could accept the qualities not to receive any specific determination (no quid-

---

[28] For a criticism of this point, see Bird (2006 forthcoming).

[29] Ellis has to suppose that categorical properties and relations are dimensions of the causal set-up of power-processes (Ellis (2002), p. 172) and Molnar that powers are sensitive to categorical relations (Molnar (2003), pp. 164 – 165). Armstrong argues against similar complications (they suppose necessary and contingent causal relations, according to him). Note that Heil is logically either a foundationalist on relations (and this is a difficult position to hold, as Campbell's one), or has to accept relations (and so (IT) is redundant in order to solve Swinburne's argument).

dity, i.e. no non-causal intrinsic feature), but this lack of determination would have the following consequence: Heil should rather adopt a pure (DR), with no (IT) (section 2.3).

2.1 The meaning of "disposition" and "quality": from determination to contradiction.

Heil, like Martin, thinks that the world is a "power net". But what is a power? It is a real intrinsic property, which is qualitative, too. This thesis is called "identity theory" (IT) as we have seen, and it is formulated in this way by Heil:

> "(IT) If P is an intrinsic property of a concrete object, P is simultaneously dispositional and qualitative; P's dispositionality and qualitativity are not aspects or properties of P; P's dispositionality, P_d, is P's qualitativity, P_q, and each of these is P: $P_d = P_q = P$." (Heil (2003), p. 111)

The (IT) represents a particular form of (DR), but a surprising one.[30] To argue for an identity thesis and to claim that "a quality is a disposition" is tantamount to saying that "Caesar is a prime number", something which could be seen as a category mistake. (IT) would be a realist thesis, but a meaningless one. Why could it be meaningless? The principle of identity stated by Shoemaker (PI) gives the following definition of properties:

> "(PI) Necessarily, if A and B are properties, $A = B$ just in case A and B make the same contribution to the causal powers of their (actual or possible) possessors." (cited in Heil (2003), p. 77)

Heil's position is a complicated one. As such, he refuses (PI), because qualitative properties exist, and the qualitativity is not by itself identified by causal powers. So, a similar principle should be applied to dispositional properties only and we can consequently consider a variation of (PI):

> (PI*) Necessarily, if A and B are *dispositional* properties, $A = B$ just in case A and B make the same contribution to the causal powers of their (actual or possible) possessors.

Therefore, I propose to define a disposition as follows:

---

[30] We could say, with Martin: "This is perhaps a surprising identity, but frequently it happens that different representations turn out to one's surprise to be of the identical entity." (Martin (1997), p. 216 cited in Molnar (2003), p. 154)

(D) A disposition is a property that has powers "built-in".

What is a quality, then? A quality is an intrinsic property, but this requires some additional characterisation, because also a disposition is an intrinsic property. Heil explains that non-dispositionality could have causal powers, but only indirectly. So let us accept the following possible determination of qualities:

> "The idea is to distinguish properties that themselves amount to causal powers [dispositions] from those [qualities] that bestow powers on their possessors, if at all, only indirectly: via contingent laws of nature, for instance." (Heil, (2003), p. 79)

Unfortunately, this determination is only a negative one: a quality must have a determinate feature of what it is, independently of powers (and laws). About non-causal differences, Heil writes:

> "Surely causally idle properties would 'make a difference' to theirs possessors, just not a causal difference: such properties would have no effect on what their possessors do or would do." (Heil (2003), p. 78)

Accordingly, I give these two definitions of a quality:

(Q_1) A quality is a property without powers "built-in" but only in-directly connected, via laws, to some powers (negative determination).

(Q_2) A quality has an intrinsic non-causal feature (positive determination).

Now, a pure disposition is a property that is only a disposition and nothing else. A pure quality is a property that is only a quality and nothing else. But for Heil, there are no pure powers and no pure qualities.[31] Indeed, Heil proposes (IT) and thus claims:

> "P's dispositionality, P_d, is P's qualitativity, P_q, and each of these is P: $P_d = P_q = P$." (Heil (2003), p. 111)

Hence, we have the implication: (IT) + (PI*) → (PI).

That is why Heil actually adopts (PI). Thus, to be a real property means to be a disposition. The Eleatic Principle could be used in this specific way: to be a real property means to directly bestow causal powers to its possessors. Here, we have to face a perplexity, though: it seems that the ways the terms

---

[31] For pure powers, see Swinburne's argument in Heil (2003), p. 98 and the introduction to this part. For pure qualities, see Heil (2003), p. 118, and here below, section 2.3.

are defined make them look like opposite. What we are looking for is a kind of compatibility between dispositions and qualities if they are identical entities: a property is dispositional and qualitative. Let us have a look at the terminology: we can accept the definition of dispositions as fundamental: they are powers "built-in" (D). But that is not the case for qualities. For the fact of being identical to dispositions, qualities have powers too, but "being identical to" doesn't imply an "indirect connection". So, qualities have powers "built-in", too. If we come back to our citation from p. 79 (see above, this section), I must admit that I didn't speak of qualities: (Q_1) must be refused. There is still the positive determination (Q_2): as such, a property could (directly) bestow some causal powers and some non-causal intrinsic features to its possessor, but is it possible without making a partition of the property or admitting second-order properties?[32]

To be a quality means to be able to claim: I am what I am (Q_2). To be a disposition means to be in the condition to claim: I am what I (could) do (D).[33] But could we say: I am what I am *and* I am what I (could) do? Note that if I am what I am, it is sure that I could not do everything.[34] According to my qualitative nature, there are some things I can do, and other ones I cannot do. So, we could say: what I am (and I am what I am) determines what I (can) do. This is only to emphasise the causal relevance of properties. Causal relevance

---

[32] Let us accept this point. Accepting second-order properties is not an open option to Heil, because of his (PT) criticism and his no-levels-of-being thesis. With respect to the partition of the property, it could be argued that the truthmaker of a dispositional ascription is not wholly the property but one of its sides, and similarly for the qualitative ascription. But then, what is the modal status (necessity/contingency) of the relation between the two? If only contingent, why not a pure dispositionalism? If necessary, why presupposing dispositions (the qualities make the job)? This is an Armstrongian argument. Molnar talks of redundancy (Molnar (1999), p. 150), Armstrong only of a strange totally brute necessity (Armstrong (1997), p. 251). I think Armstrong is right, because there are some other differences: unmanifested powers only for dispostionalism.

[33] Armstrong gives a clear formulation: "Properties and relations are thought of by philosophers as having a nature that is self-contained, distinct from the powers that they bestow. We shall call this position Categoricalism. Others think of them as having a nature that essentially looks beyond the particulars they qualify, outward to potential interactions with further particulars, and where this nature is exhausted by these potential interactions. This view may be called Dispositionalism." (Armstrong (1997), p. 69)

[34] This claim is relative to one world, to solve the problem of quidditism. See above, section 1.1.

could be allowed as in Armstrong's way.[35] However, (PI) presupposes the contrary, too: what I (can) do determines what I am. And so, eventually: what I am is *identical* to what I can do. But this is in contradiction with the fact that, nevertheless, I am what I am! This is the problem of the conflicting "natures" of these properties.

2.2 The anti-realist move.

To avoid this conclusion, Heil proposes a strict identity criterion, with a *double-view* conception:

> "The human mind, as Locke noted, has a capacity for "partial consideration". We can consider an object's properties as dispositions or powers or we can consider them as qualities. In so doing we consider, not two kinds of property, but the selfsame properties in two different ways." (Heil (2003), p. 124)

If the two "natures" are incompatible, we have to reject the material mode, and use a formal one. The concept "disposition" has universal application to intrinsic properties. The concept "quality" has universal application to intrinsic properties. This is quite delicate for Heil's view, because he clearly looks for a full-blooded realism. Heil says: "I prefer to associate realism with mind-independence".[36] And I could agree with him, but the question is to know if we are not left with a kind of noumenal world. In this case, the intrinsic properties are mind-independent, but they remain indeterminate if not considered according to the two different ways just mentioned. Let us consider Mumford's position on this issue. He writes:

> "There are two senses of ontology that are relevant when we are considering the constitution of the world: the first concerns how the world really is and the second consists in how we think the world is. Concepts may determine our ontology in this second sense but obviously leave ontology of the first kind intact. I am thus accepting a division between the world and our conceptualisation about the world. Whatever the world is actually like is unaffected by the way we con-

---

[35] However, this categoricalist position is not out of trouble: either the non-causal feature is a substantial one (but then qualities would have a problematic quidditas); or the non-causal feature only points out the self-identity of the qualities. In this case, this feature would be required for whatever entities. For this second problem, see Bird (2006 forthcoming).

[36] Heil (2003), p. 11.

ceptualise, describe, and think about the world." (Mumford (1998), p. 194)

Mumford is a realist, but the couple dispositional/categorical is related to "how we think the world is" and not to "the world in itself". This sort of dichotomy allows for a full-blooded realism on the world-side, but the question, in the end, is whether our inquiry succeeds in finding the world's *true ontology*, as Heil aims at. For Mumford, the analysis of dispositions clearly stays on the language-side:

"I have been trying to guard against taking the dispositional-categorical distinction to be anything more than a distinction in the way we talk about instantiated properties or states of the world. The danger is projection of this distinction onto the world such that it is taken to be a division in reality rather than a division in ways of talking about reality." (Mumford (1998), p. 192)

Heil is not committed to an analogous projection since there is not a dualist ontology, with two type-properties (as in Molnar (2003) and Ellis (2002)). Such a projection would be a (PT) fault for him. But even if we avoid a projected dualism, can we say that dispositions and qualities are the salient features *of the world*? It is pretty difficult, if there are only some ways to consider the same particular properties inside the world's net.

To be more precise, the "seeing as", or "considering as", is a kind of relativistic scheme. Whatever realism Heil wants to endorse, it turns out not to be a full-blooded realism, i.e. a perfectly objective one, independent of any considerations from our side. If we accept a weak realism, or a *relativistic realism*, so to speak, this doesn't imply that these ontologies are not correct.[37] There is more than one language in which to describe the world though the world exists independently of such languages (see Mumford (1998), p. 194). But once again, the intrinsic property, as an independent item, is neutral, indeterminate, and dispositions and qualities are only predicates. The true determination is only a true application of predicates. What about the so-called real intrinsic *disposition* (the intrinsic property as disposition)? This way the property is, is relative to a scheme (dispositional view). What about the so-called real intrin-

---

[37] Fetzer gives the following formulation: "The world exists as an entity apart from our beliefs about it, but the properties of the world are linguistically relativised in the sense that there is more than one language in which it may be described; hence, there is no unique descriptive language." (Fetzer (1977) in Tuomela (1978), p. 164)

sic *quality* (the intrinsic property as quality)? This other way the property is, is relative to another scheme (qualitative view).

Relativistic realism (Fetzer, Mumford) :

Contradiction
Dispositional Scheme (DS)   ↔   Qualitative Scheme (QS)
(true determination) ↘   ↙ (true determination)
Intrinsic Property

Actually, if determinate ways properties are, are relative to some schemes, then the world of properties as determinate requires a metaphysical pluralism, and we rely on a kind of relativistic Kantianism as developed by Lynch, a position which can be defined through the following claims (stated in Lynch (1998)):

(I) Truth concerns the way the word is.

(II) Pluralism holds that the way the world is, is relative to a scheme.

(III) So pluralism implies that truth is relative to a scheme.[38]

Furthermore, if the predicates are contradictory predicates, the (TMP) becomes a problematic principle in a weak realism, because one and the same property cannot make true two opposite predicates, without making truth itself relative to a certain scheme. This problem is solved by adopting a metaphysical pluralism. The (TMP) is preserved, but only if the truthmaking relation is relative to one specific world (the dispositional world or the qualitative world).

Pluralist Kantianism (Lynch):

Dispositional predicates   Qualitative predicates
↑   ↑
The dispositional way   The qualitative way
the property is   the property is
(DS) ↖ (Kantian problem) ↗ (QS)
Intrinsic Properties   ↑ :Truthmaking relation

---

[38] See Lynch (1998), p. 137. Mumford says: "Properties themselves are just properties simpliciter, which should be thought of neither "really" categorical nor "really" dispositional, but which can be denoted in those ways." (Mumford (1998), p. 191)

Lynch avoids anti-realism by saying that the concept of truth is nevertheless not a relative concept. But the anti-realist move is very close to it. For Heil, all these differences could not support a realist standpoint, as he criticises the internal realism of Putnam (see Heil (2003), p. 56). Even if we reject an epistemic characterisation of truth, the pluralist Kantianism of Lynch, and the relativistic realism of Fetzer and Mumford are too weak to pretend to be full-blooded realisms. I argue that a double-view, step by step, runs into an anti-realist position. Heil writes:

> "I can't, however, bring myself to believe that there is no correct ontology, only divers ways of carving up ontological space." (Heil (2003), p. 3)

But here, we have two opposite ontologies of properties, a qualitative one and a dispositional one. What is the right scheme to choose? It depends on our purposes of determination.[39] In my opinion, Heil does not escape some sort of extrinsic *relational* properties.[40] To "carve-up" the world (as qualities or as dispositions) is something we do anyway. With no mind to *consider* the property, the property is what it is, but it remains indeterminate: not really a quality, not really a disposition. In this sense, being a power is the kind of thing which is a secondary property, in a traditional Lockean interpretation. We understand why Heil urges Locke to be a proponent of the identity thesis.[41] Mumford's neutral monism accepts a minimal sense of realism, i.e. a relativistic realism. But in a strong realist perspective, all weak realism is assimilated to anti-realism. Heil claims to be a strong realist: such relativisation is thus a perfect anti-realist move!

Anti-realism:

Mind

↙   ↘

Dispositional scheme   Qualitative scheme

↘   ↙

intrinsic property

---

[39] I explain the *power* to open the door with the *qualitative* make-up of the key. I can continue and explain also the *qualitative* make-up of the key with some underlying *powers*. Hence, I use both the two schemes (alternatively) in my explanation.

[40] See Molnar (2003), p. 155.

[41] Heil (2003), p. 79 footnote 3, pp. 82, 113.

2.3 The dilemma

We have seen that Heil, in the end, turns out to be paradoxically committed to an anti-realist standpoint. The first way to ensure a strict *ontological* identity, and so a full-blooded realism, is to deny any contradiction in the two ontological applications, and therefore to fuse these different "nominal essences" into only one "real essence": a property *is* qualitative *and is* dispositional. But this is impossible without simplifying the identity up to dissolve the qualitative realism. In (PI), the nature of what I am is wholly determined by these powers. The solution is to deny this: what I am is only partially determined by these powers. If this was the case, what I am could be differently investigated: a qualitative consideration, for instance, that reports a qualitative feature in the rest of the essence. If a property is a disposition, the powers "built-in" are nevertheless really existent: an unmanifested power is something pertaining to the essence of the property: a kind of occurrent potentiality. If so, we come back to a partition of the property, reflected in the essence: a qualitative side (intrinsic differences) and a power side (occurrent potentialities). Partial essence takes the place of partial consideration, but the ontological division comes back, as in the double-side thesis or in the double-aspect thesis. The three following solutions are very similar, according to the (PT) strategy of Heil:

	Dispositional true ascription ⇩	Qualitative true ascription ⇩
1	dispositional-side of property	qualitative-side of property
2	dispositional property of property	qualitative property of property
3	dispositional-part of essence of property	qualitative part of essence of property

I see no reason to adopt one and refuse the others, with PT strategy.[42]

A second solution would be to give up all the specific determinations of qualities, to dissolve the contradiction. That is what Heil should do. For instance, as display of powers, the causal relation is necessary (the modal way the causal relation is, is relative to the dispositional scheme); as nomic interaction between qualities, the causal relation is contingent (the modal way the

---

[42] For the double-aspect view, there is a double-PT fault: one PT fault for a projection of a distinction in language onto a partition in the world, since two different properties are supposed to coexist as second-order properties; another PT fault for the adoption of higher-levels, since second-order properties belong to a *higher level-of-being*, and that levels-of-being derive from PT fault.

causal relation is, is relative to the qualitative scheme). But the realist question is, actually: is the causal relation necessary or contingent? This contradiction between contingency and necessity is troublesome for Mumford (1998) but not for Heil (2003), because according to him, the causal relation must be necessary.[43] We have seen that he could do this only by giving up one of the two determinations of qualities, (Q_1). Now, here is a second aspect, about the modal status of properties, aside from causal (necessary or contingent) interactions. As quality, a property is in act (the occurrent way the property is, is relative to the qualitative scheme); as disposition, a property is in potency (the occurrent way the property is, is relative to the dispositional scheme). But the realist question is: is the property (apart from its relations) in act or in potency? The actuality of a property is related to the non-causal feature. Heil could choose the dispositional answer, but he would consequently have to give up the second determination of qualities, (Q_2), and the identity relation would therefore be coupled with an absolute, indeterminate term. Some claims of Heil seem to show that this is the implicit solution: in order to be a strong realist, Heil has to dissolve qualities, and then be able to give some dispositional features. Let us try to show this step. When Heil rejects the purely qualitative properties, he says:

> "A pure quality, a property altogether lacking in dispositionality, would be undetectable and would, in one obvious sense, make no difference to its possessor." (Heil (2003), p. 118)

Here, the quality is not pure, and therefore makes a causal difference. The question, then, is: does it make a non-causal difference, too? It seems not! If a pure quality makes no difference at all, a non-pure quality (and so a dispositional quality) makes only some causal ones. So, the positive determination of qualities fails. Conclusion: there is no determination at all.

It is clear that Heil has to accept real, non-causal differences in order to posit qualities as ontologically determinate items. A (non-pure) quality makes non-causal differences to the possessor (and makes causal differences to himself – his behaviours – and his environment – including the observer – as a result of his dispositionalities). Actually, it is problematic to accept non-causal differences. Heil could argue that "to make a non-causal difference" is ontologically vacuous. If a quality makes a difference, how could that difference possibly not be a causal one (one way or another), if "to make a difference" is definitely a causal connotation of causation? But if a quality makes causal differences only,

---

[43] See section 1.1.

it has causal relevance *by itself*. "By itself" is ambiguous. Yet, there are only two ways to understand it. As an ontological claim, it could derive from (IT). For Heil, a quality must receive causal relevance from its own dispositionality. In this sense, this job could be done by pure dispositions only: they qualify the particular, anyway! Analogously, if "by itself" means a real independent causal relevance of qualities, what we need are relations (if a purely qualitative property could never be isolated from causal efficacy). We can then say: "to be a real quality is to have causal relevance". Nevertheless, this real property would not be a disposition. A quality would then tend to be an extrinsic property, and, as a result, we would have a relational realism. One way or another, there is no possible determination of intrinsic qualities without postulating some specific non-causal features.

We have seen that a tension would appear between the two different "natures" of properties, and it is therefore difficult to ensure any reality of qualities. To conceive properties looks like conceiving them either in dispositional/causal way (first option) or in relational/causal way (second option). Heil should be urged to choose the first one. The only way to speak of qualitativity, and so to develop a qualitative scheme about it, is a new "partial consideration": there are no non-causal differences in the world, but I can consider some differences *as* non-causal. When I conceive some qualities to determine some causal powers, I consider these qualities without the power/causal net they are bound to. Qualitative considerations are only idealisations or abstractions. The ascription of dispositions seems to overlap the ascription of qualities. From a realist point of view, there is no reason to presuppose qualities, if the only job of (indeterminate) qualities is their ability to give an answer to Swinburne's argument. If so, it is quite *ad hoc* to postulate an entity in order to provide a solution to that argument. Is this not a wrong projection from "quality" to quality, thus the same kind of (PT)'s fault that Heil criticises?[44]

One could say that my claims, here, refer to all identity theses, but this is not true. On the opposite, I maintain that the metaphysical problem of the conflicting natures is solved by whatever reduction: there are *no real* qualities in a dispositionalist reductionism, never mind the so-called identity thesis. Armstrong is neutral about two theses: either an identity thesis with categorical reductionism that states that, with respects to laws, there is an identity between dispositions and categorical properties (with asymmetrical relation: the categorical is more fundamental), or a kind of supervenience thesis, which includes

---

[44] The following formulation is significant: "I shall use "qualitative" to designate intrinsic qualitative properties of objects ..." (Heil (2003), p. 79)

laws. We could say that Armstrong is deflationalist without being a strict eliminativist on dispositions. Yet, this nuance should be neglected here: what is central is that there are eventually no real powers. I agree with Armstrong when he says that

> "Martin gives unmanifested powers a reality I deny them. I do not deny that there are innumerable truths about the might-have-been corresponding to Martin's unmanifested powers. I believe that I have provided reasonably satisfactory truthmakers for these truths." (Armstrong (1997), p. 256)

We should then be aware of all the implications of a strong identity thesis (not a reductionist version of it): a quality is a disposition *with all the expected features of dispositions*. What is central for (DR) is the foregoing pretension: that occurrent unmanifested powers exist. To reject this means to be a qualitative reductionist, and that provides a solution to the metaphysical problem. Parallely, what is central for a qualitative realism is the forgoing pretension: that occurrent independent qualities exist. To adopt a dispositional reductionism is to refuse any independent qualities, and that again solves the metaphysical problem. The only effective distinction between eliminativism and reductionism just relies on a problem of true or false denotations. The metaphysical problem finds a solution in both cases. Indeed, true qualitative denotations don't imply qualities, true dispositional denotations don't imply dispositions, but for a realism that aims at being a strong one, either one or the other must be the good implication, neither both (contradictory ontological identity) nor none (anti-realist move). So there is no way to escape this anti-realist shift if we reject pure dispositions: we have to accept the double-view, with complete contradictory schemes. I argue that Heil's realist worries would better have to focus on this double-view consideration.

3 Conclusion

I have shown that the realism of Heil meets some difficulties and that it is important to analyse all his ontological commitments, and the metaphysical problems they hide. The main one is constitutive of (IT). As I have pointed out, two conflicting natures of properties are compelled to be strongly related by the strongest possible relation: identity. To avoid such a trouble, we must stress the double-view conception endorsed by Heil, and therefore accept a less strong metaphysical thesis: a kind of neutral monism which presupposes a *relativistic realism*. In doing so, some difficulties are avoided too, and a kind of token-identity functionalism can be maintained. This move is furthermore in agreement with the (PT) suspicion (no projection into the world!). But this type of realism implies in fact an anti-realist standpoint, and a pure (DR) represents therefore a better solution. Mumford took a similar realist step in Mumford (2004b). Heil should rather adopt an analogous viewpoint too, if he would like to remain a full-blooded realist. Yet, this analysis gives us no strong arguments in favour of (DR). The core of the opposition lies on the status of modalities, as Heil puts it in defending a metaphysical necessity. Unfortunately, there is no strictly conclusive argument in Heil (2003). Besides, if a strong realism is needed, a kind of well accepted bijectivity between the language and the world is then mandatory, and the (PT) criticism must be rejected. But how could it be otherwise, if realism means not only mind-independence, but also a full determinate realism?

Commentary
John Heil

Freland is disturbed by the lack of a decisive argument for what he calls dispositional realism (DR).[1] Sorry: there *are* no such arguments. Indeed, it is unlikely that anything approximating a decisive argument is available for any substantive metaphysical thesis. The best we can reasonably hope for is the articulation of a position that makes the best sense of the world in light of our scientific and everyday beliefs about it. If you want to evaluate dispositional realism, then, look at its costs and benefits.[2]

Much of Freland's paper comprises arguments that various grounds I offer for my conception of dispositionality are consistent with positions at odds with mine. But these other positions are in the same boat; none is privileged. The question is not, which is supported by a decisive argument, but which best fits our considered worldview. In this context, ties leave us dissatisfied.

I defend the idea that properties of concrete objects are at once dispositional and qualitative: properties are powerful qualities. The idea is neither new nor original. It appears to have been held by two Enlightenment luminaries, Locke and Spinoza. More recently, it has been embraced by C. B. Martin.

Why should anyone be attracted to the thesis that properties of concrete objects are at once dispositional and qualitative? You might begin by thinking of a paradigmatic quality: shape. To focus matters, think of the shape of this tomato, the tomato's sphericity. Most philosophers and all non-philosophers would regard the tomato's sphericity as a paradigmatic quality of the tomato. But now think about what the tomato would do in virtue of its sphericity: it would roll, it would reflect light so as to look spherical, it would make a concave imprint in soft clay. This makes the tomato's sphericity out to be a power or disposition.

I say both impressions are correct: the tomato's sphericity *is* a power and to say this is not to deny that it *is* a quality. In so saying, I am assuming what many philosophers do not: that dispositionality and qualitativity are not mutually exclusive. Being the one is compatible with being the other. I go further: being the one *is* being the other. Is this outrageous?

---

[1] I must show that "dispositions are inescapable" (p. 146, above).

[2] Think here of Lewis's alternative worlds. You might or might not like them, but few philosophers would reject them solely because they are not implied by uncontroversial premises.

It will seem to be outrageous if you define dispositionality or qualitativity so these are mutually exclusive as Freland does on pp. 152 – 153. I am careful not to do so. Think of David Armstrong's "headless woman". Not seeing that the woman has a head is not to see that she does not have a head. The general point here is that characterising something as an *F* is not thereby to characterise it as *not* being a *G*. The fact, if it is a fact, that you could define dispositionality without mentioning qualitativity, does not entail that what is dispositional is not qualitative as well.

Freland offers quotations in which I seem to violate these strictures, speaking of qualities as inert (p. 156, above). But the quotations in question are ones in which I am discussing competing views. I agree: if you define dispositionality so as to exclude qualitativity, and you define qualitativity so as to exclude dispositionality, the identity thesis is hopeless. But I do not do this. In fact I offer no rigorous definition of either.

Freland regards this omission as a serious flaw. I give only a "negative" characterisation. The idea that we do not know what we are talking about until we precisely define it is one I reject. The idea finds a home in the philosophers' thought that our access to the world is exclusively linguistic. But it is possible to point to examples of dispositions and qualities, and it is possible to see that these examples are apparently consistent with the identity thesis. There might be some interest in moving on to provide exacting definitions of the terms, but informative non-circular definitions are hard to come by. An interesting exercise would be to define "definition" (see chapter one, above).

I believe that understanding a philosophical view involves going with that view as far as possible, to the point where you feel its pull. Going with a view, figuring out where it leads, what it can do for us, is not the same as endorsing that view. Without this kind of sympathetic understanding you will never be in a position to appreciate what is important in philosophy.

Let me mention another route to the identity thesis, the thesis that properties are powerful qualities. One popular view of dispositions turns them into "higher-level" properties "realised by" distinct, "lower-level" qualities (Prior, Pargetter and Jackson (1982), see Heil (2003), § 9.2). Here we have a quality, the "realiser", plus a "realised" disposition (see the figure on the next page). The relation is contingent on external laws of nature (see my reply to Padovani, below).

Now suppose you were skeptical about multiple realisation, or suppose you liked functionalism – not the "functional identity" version which distinguishes realised properties from their realisers, but the "functional specifier" version.

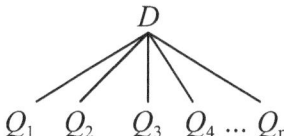

D would then collapse into $Q_1, Q_2, Q_3, Q_4, ..., Q_n$. You would have powerful qualities!

A final point. Even if you thought that, in virtue of possessing certain qualities, objects possessed certain powers, why go along with my contention that the relation is one of identity? In the first place, I am skeptical that the relation could be contingent. I doubt that it is contingent that spherical objects would roll, would reflect light so as to look spherical, would make concave impressions in soft clay. Yes, I know: many philosophers would deny this. But then I would be interested in getting clear on why they would deny it. Suppose, however, you go with me on the necessity. What kind of necessity do we have? Is it simply an opaque necessary covariation? Such necessities ought to make us uneasy. Identity is otherwise. If the quality *is* the power, it is no wonder they co-occur. If you are willing to take seriously the idea that qualities and powers are necessarily related, you should be open to the idea that the relation could be identity.

In *From an ontological point of view* I distance myself from talk of "aspects", rejecting the characterisation of my view as a "double aspect" view. My thought was that aspects must be properties – what else? And the idea very definitely was not that qualities and powers are paired properties. If we take aspects as Spinoza did, however, the result is an identity thesis. Spinoza thinks of qualities and powers as aspects – two among an infinitude of aspects – of the One. The relation among aspects is strict identity!

So, if we have identity, why aspects? In discussing these matters, I invoke Locke's notion of abstraction or "partial consideration". Freland thinks that this introduces an epistemic element into the account, threatening anti-realism. But this is to misunderstand abstraction. You can consider a triangle as a three-sided figure without considering its having three angles. This is so despite the triangle's being, of necessity, both. This in no way suggests that trilaterality or triangularity is in any way mind-dependent. The human mind has a capacity for abstraction, to consider in isolation what could not exist in isolation.

My idea is that we have two ways of considering properties: as powers and as qualities. We can consider sphericity qualitatively or in terms of what contribution sphericity makes to the powers of spherical objects. This in no way makes sphericity, the quality or the power, mind dependent.

Chapter 9

Laws of nature, modal realism and realist lawlessness

Flavia Padovani

One of the most interesting aspects of Heil (2003) consists in the rejection of the traditional opposition between dispositional and categorical properties, parallel to a no-level view of reality. I argue that, from an epistemological perspective, this demands a definite stance on the real meaning and role that laws of nature play in this account. Unfortunately, this issue is not treated by the author in due detail. I will show that an adherence to a "mixed" categorical-dispositional interpretation of properties is incapable of adequately reflecting the business of science, unless some additional explanation is provided of how scientific law statements tell us something about the real world.

1 Introduction

There is no agreement on how to define univocally the term "law of nature". On the one hand, it seems difficult to find a commonly shared idea of what a "law" is; on the other hand, it is unclear what exactly we should understand by "nature". Whether a law is, with Hume, a mere statement expressing a regularity that we find in nature, or whether it is the product of an artificial construction;[1] whether it represents a necessary[2] or a contingent feature of the world, a second-order universal;[3] whether it should be understood within the adopted

---

[1] Below, I will briefly discuss this position, typically supported by Cartwright (1999) and endorsed by Heil.

[2] As, for instance, in the accounts given by Bigelow, Ellis & Lierse (1992) and Shoemaker (1998).

[3] See the conceptions of laws – formulated independently – by Dretske (1977), Tooley (1977) and Armstrong (1978).

deductive system[4] or whether we can do completely without this notion:[5] these are all questions that crucially involve some additional understanding of the scientific practise in which such laws are stated.

In general, within the realm of realist views (to which Heil's belongs), the idea of a law tends to connote some form of necessity. Whether it is an objective or subjective necessity, or whether it is based on a probabilistic or universalistic interpretation of the conjunction between events, is a further question.

In this paper, I will follow Mumford ((2004b), p. 15) in distinguishing three types of metaphysics of laws:

(I) The first one could be defined "Humean lawlessness". According to this conception, the world appears to be "composed entirely of modally inert distinct existences". Laws are mere statements with no objective necessity.

(II) The second one, called "nomological realism", considers laws as modal, whereas the (categorical) properties are non-modal. So "laws are added to animate the non-modal existences".

(III) The third one is Mumford's own position, which he labels "realist lawlessness". In this case, there is nothing at a non-modal level: all existences are modal, so "laws are never required for their animation".

As we will see, Heil's position fits in the third type, which is rather innovative. Heil's view on laws of nature is not committed to any of the perspectives traditionally implied by those theories, which consider properties as either categorical or dispositional. One of the most interesting aspects of Heil's book consists in the rejection of the traditional opposition between dispositional and categorical properties, parallel to a no-level view of reality. But as far as laws of nature are concerned, Heil seems to be oscillating between a loosely necessitarian and a regularist account. According to the author, there are ways

---

[4] This is the position defended by Earman, namely the so-called Mill-Ramsey-Lewis account: "Roughly, the idea is that the laws of this world are the axioms or theorems of the best deductive system, where a deductive system is an axiomatizable, deductive closed set of true statements and where the best such system is the one that achieves the best compromise between simplicity and strength. Scientific theorizing can be seen as a *groping* towards the optimal system. I emphasize the world "groping". Even with respect to a limited domain of inquiry – say, gravitational physics – scientists don't consider all possible theories (= deductive systems) of the domain. For given our limited computational powers and limited imaginations we are lucky if we can explicitly produce more than a handful of theories that would be judged as minimally adequate." (Earman (1993), p. 416)

[5] The notion of law of nature can be absorbed by other notions, like symmetry and probability, according to van Fraassen (1989).

to accommodate the apparent contingency of laws of nature into his account without giving up the idea of properties having dispositionalities built-in. One such way is given by interpreting dispositions as capacities, as it is done in Cartwright's well-known account.

Nevertheless, the attempt to propose a reconciliation between the two conceptions does not turn out to be very illuminating in Heil's book. In fact, as we will see, it amounts to taking no real position on the essence of laws of nature. There are aspects that still remain in need of clarification. What is the relation between dispositions, at an ontological level, and laws at an epistemological one? Are natural laws mere statements serving to express the manifestations of capacities of objects? Or are they some sort of particular entities *capable* of detecting and/or finally determining capacities? In the first case, Heil would be a dispositional realist who defends a "realist lawlessness". In this case, he should give an additional explanation of the actual scientific practise involved in stating laws, if these laws are supposed to express the dispositionalities of the objects. In the second case, the author would take on a full-blooded modal realism with respect to all existences, which would collide with the role somehow active played by the laws of nature.

2 The framework

2.1 Heil's ontological picture

Heil's ontological point of view can be briefly summarised as follows.[6] In contrasting the defectiveness of the traditional – although at times implicit – adherence to the Picture Theory (PT)[7] of representation, Heil commits himself to an allegiance to (C.B. Martin's) truthmaker principle; an attitude also defined as "ontological seriousness". According to this view, when a statement is true, there must be something about the world that makes it true. Reality is not structured in a hierarchy of levels, and it is mind-independent. To be a realist does not mean to be committed to a (multi-)level conception of being. Objects are property-bearers, whereas properties are understood as *ways* objects are and they contribute "in distinctive ways" to their powers or dispositions, i.e. to the intrinsic features of the objects. Powers and qualities are not to be understood as aspects of the property; rather, they *are* the "selfsame property differently

---

[6] See Heil (2003), pp. 11 – 12, chapters 9 – 11.
[7] "The core idea is that the character of reality can be "read off" our linguistic representation of reality." (Heil (2003), p. 7)

regarded". Properties are modes (ways of an object), not universals. There is no "metaphysical superglue" to attach properties to the object to which they refer. Hence, objects are not bundles of properties.

2.2 Motivation for this point of view

Heil's motivation for his ontological point of view can be neatly captured by the following passage:

> "An adequate conceptualisation of the world and our place in it is founded not on the analysis of concepts, but on an adequate ontology. Ontology is not an analytical enterprise. ... [In] engaging in ontological investigation we are endeavouring to make sense of issues we should otherwise find perplexing. The issues in question arise in the sciences, in the humanities, and in everyday life. To this extent they include an ineliminable *empirical* element. My belief is that, if we get the ontology right, these issues will take care of themselves in this sense: the remaining questions will be largely *empirical* hence susceptible to techniques we standardly deploy in answering empirical questions." (p. 3, my emphasis)

Basically, this means that the status of ontology appears to be prior to that of science and, respectively, to that of philosophy of science. Indeed, Heil suggests that such a point of view could solve some of the troubles encountered in certain PT (but not only)-based theories. If, in other words, a primacy is to be accorded to ontology, we should think that, in general, science and philosophy of science have to align with ontology, in a way such that solving certain empirical issues will become a simple question of finding the right techniques to do it.

3 Laws of nature

3.1 Which account? Shoemaker vs. Armstrong?

Heil proposes a (neo-Lockean) reading of properties as primary qualities: they are *both* qualitative *and* dispositional. A criticism one could pose against traditional interpretations of dispositions is that they support a conception of the powers as constructed "top-down" from laws of nature, i.e. that they support the idea that

> "... objects' possession of causal powers depends on laws of nature that could vary independently of objects' intrinsic properties. ... Such properties could bestow a power on their possessors, but only given certain laws of nature" (p. 79).

If categorical properties bestow powers on their possessor, it cannot be "only indirectly, by virtue of their standing in an appropriate relation to a contingent law of nature" (p. 87). The refusal to adopt the traditional dispositional/categorical distinction entails that the top-down option be rejected in favour of a "bottom-up" line of interpretation. This, of course, implies an ontological independence of the nature of objects from the theories that incorporate them and on which our knowledge of them relies.

Thus, in sections 9.4 – 5, Heil presents the problem to solve by his account of properties as dispositional and categorical as follows:

> "What is upsetting about the thought that the possession of certain properties could endow objects with powers or dispositions non-contingently? Might it be possible to reconcile the sense that things might have behaved very differently from the way they do in fact behave with the thesis that property bestow powers non-contingently?" (p. 92)

The dispute concerns the nature of properties. We may understand dispositions as built into the properties or, on the opposite, we may consider them as a contingent addition to the object's properties. So we first have to clarify whether properties are modally connected to powers, or whether dispositions are to be thought of as varying independently of properties. Thus, we can have a basis on which we can rectify an account of laws of nature. If, on the one hand, we concede to Armstrong that laws of nature are contingent, but, on the other hand, we also want dispositionalities to be built into properties, we run the risk of having contingency go "by the board" (p. 93). Here, Heil's view on laws of nature seems to be oscillating between contingency à la Armstrong and necessity à la Shoemaker. According to Armstrong, laws of nature are to be interpreted as higher-order necessitation relations (but owing to contingent laws of nature) among universals (properties). Shoemaker (1998) (but also, for instance, Bigelow, Ellis & Lierse (1992)), on the contrary, holds that laws of nature are necessary truths. Heil seems to express a similar view in the following quotation:

> "God does not create the objects and properties and then adds the laws. Instead, laws of nature "logically supervene" on the properties: when God fixes the properties, He thereby fixes the laws" (p. 93).

According to this passage, the truth of laws of nature is rooted in the objects and there is no contingency involved between properties and laws of nature. Yet, Heil wants to preserve some form of contingency for laws of nature and properties. Thus, the central challenge for Heil seems to consist in reconciling Armstrong with Shoemaker, or in combining some form of contingency with a bottom-up account of laws.

3.2 Where and why do we need to have contingency?

Heil's conception of laws is meant to combine Armstrong's and Shoemaker's positions. But the question for modal realism remains: if powers do all the work, and necessity is *in* nature, where should we place contingency? Why do we need to introduce a contingent aspect in this conception of laws? As Heil sees it, a certain form of contingency is wholly compatible with a necessitarian view of laws à la Shoemaker. The author points out that

> "[the] apparent contingency of natural processes might be due, not to those processes (or laws governing them) being contingent, but to two other factors. First, our ignorance concerning the processes or laws means that beliefs as to what the laws are are invariably fallible. Second, even on a view that grounds laws of nature in the properties, there is room for a contingency of sorts: it will be contingent what the laws are if it is contingent that salt dissolves in water, but it would be contingent that salt or water exist at all. Perhaps this is all the contingency we need" (p. 94).

Under the conception expressed here, dispositions are not necessary in themselves.[8] They are necessary to their bearer, but they are not necessarily actualised. So, the "requirement" of contingency is primarily put in the *manifestations* of powers.

> "Dispositions can be conditionally characterized in a way that invokes their actual or possible manifestations. But this does not turn dispositions into manifestations. The existence of a disposition does not in any way depend on the disposition's standing in a relation to its actual

---

[8] I will not discuss this aspect here.

or possible manifestations or to whatever would elicit those manifestations." (p. 83)

Heil's solution to the problem presented at sections 9.4 – 5 is set out to preserve contingency of laws by the contingency of the manifestations of powers, which is evidently compatible with a bottom-up view of laws. To put things this way, however, doesn't seem to give Heil any particular advantage over Shoemaker's position. But is this really all he wants to say about contingency?

Actually, there is a further sense in which contingency plays a role for laws of nature, which has less to do with a metaphysical point of view and more with a purely epistemological one. On a metaphysical conception, we have contingency in the occurrence of the dispositionalities of objects. But in an epistemological conception, we also have some form of contingency with respect to the law *statements* of empirical science. What is meant here is the fact that, very generally, our scientific practise dictates that all we will ever be able to discover are *ceteris paribus* laws. In other words, we will never be able to have knowledge of laws that mirror the necessity in nature perfectly. And this has nothing to do with the fact that we may be unaware of certain dispositionalities because they never happen to occur in our world or our environment. All the law statements we come up with are open to revision, which is partly due to the fact that reality is much too complex for us to be able to wholly explain it. To gain knowledge of laws is therefore bound to make approximations.

"So long as you consider only the properties of the very simple things in controlled settings, such law statements could be expected to imply generalizations that would hold with something like perfect uniformity. Once you move beyond the very simple things, however, uniformity gives way to approximation or worse. This is the realm of *ceteris paribus* laws and defeasible generalizations." (p. 95)

This is a crucial point as it constitutes a shift to an epistemological level. It is in this way that Heil oscillates between two conceptions of laws of nature. Looked at from an ontological point of view, the author believes in a necessary connection between laws and properties. But from the viewpoint of epistemology, he allows for a certain kind of contingency, namely the one between law statements and their referents.

3.3 A possible reconciliation: dispositions as capacities

In the end, Heil proposes a view that aims to reconcile Armstrong's and Shoemaker's interpretations, thereby preserving his own conception of properties as both qualitative and dispositional. If we consider objects as having powers built-in, the world in which they are could well be represented as a "power net", following Martin's expression. The behaviour of objects embedded in a power net would result from the interactions or reciprocal influences of objects' properties. Such a net should express the whole set of interactions among powers.

A possible way to understand this is, according to Heil, to substitute "capacities" for "dispositions" . To illustrate what he means, the author quotes a passage from Alan Chalmers:

> "Once we interpret laws as describing capacities we should not expect them to describe happenings in the world. Happenings in the world are usually the outcome of several capacities acting in conjunction in complex ways, so a law that accurately describes one of those capacities cannot be expected also to describe the outcome of its interaction with other capacities. The fact that the tendency of a leaf to fall is sometimes swamped by the effect of the wind is no reason to doubt that the gravitational tendency continued to act in that circumstance and, moreover, continued to act in the exact, quantitative way specified by the law of gravitation." (A.F. Chalmers, quoted by Heil (2003), pp. 96 – 97)

What is Heil's position on this? Both the idea of dispositionalities as built-in powers, and the rejection of the idea of lawlike relations holding over and above objects, can be maintained by adopting Cartwright's interpretation of dispositionalities as capacities. Contingency is preserved at an epistemic level, whereas laws are construed "bottom-up" from dispositions that are necessary but contingently manifested.

In the ontological picture given by Heil, the reality of the objects is irreducibly tied to a specific concept of their properties (as qualitative *and* dispositional). Dispositions become manifest in the interactions among objects. Nevertheless, their existence is in no way depending on their actualisation. Moreover, they are ontologically independent from the epistemic dimension, in the sense that their existence is not depending on our knowledge of them, be they occuring or not. What kind of relation do laws of nature bear to objects within the framework of this ontology? Laws of nature appear to be expressions of some intrinsic necessity of the objects, but they are not to be thought of as ontological entities.

If all the necessity is *in* nature, in the end, laws of nature play an extremely marginal role in Heil's ontology. We will discuss these aspects in the next section.[9]

4 Modal realism and realist lawlessness

What is the essence of laws of nature from this perspective? In Armstrong's view (1985), pp. 88 – 95, laws are second-order relations holding between universals; they are abstractions from particulars which instantiate the laws; they are universals *in re*. Hence, they are entities of a certain sort, not merely statements (from which they have to be distinguished and of which they are the truthmakers). In Shoemaker's theory, properties are first-order, they incorporate powers or dispositions, and they ground the truth of law statements. The necessitation relation represented by the laws is true in virtue of the objects' first-order properties.

In Heil's ontology, the properties have necessary connections with other properties, but they are not necessarily actual or manifested. Laws are in nature, in the objects of the world. Modal properties (powers, dispositions, capacities) are self-governing. The possibilities they make are made from within. In this sense, Heil is a modal realist.

What kind of items are the laws of nature in Heil's book? Are they statements or entities? Heil does not explicitly address this issue, but his actual position can be inferred from his interpretation of properties and from his adherence to a no-level view of reality. All existences have to be modal. If dispositions or capacities do all the work, laws of nature are metaphysically redundant and are not required to "animate" the existences. Laws, *per se*, have no metaphysical existence then. They result from dispositions but only in the sense that they express them, so to speak. Given the manifest ontological redundancy of laws, they can be nothing else but mere statements, whose truthmaker is found in the interactions of the objects' dispositionalities (or capacities) in the power net.

---

[9] However, laws of nature play an important part in Heil's rejection of the level conception when discussing the problem of the "causal relevance" of higher-level properties. See his (2003), section 4.2, pp. 32 – 34. I will not deal with this question, but will mention it again below, in section 5.

One can well maintain a realist lawlessness. But can we be satisfied with this? Is the task of depicting dispositions by the law the only one that is consistent with this interpretation of laws?

5 The double nature of laws of nature

From an ontological point of view, we have seen that laws are redundant. So why do we need the law talk? What can laws be? What is their role, if any?

We have seen, in section 2.2, that Heil seems to accord ontology a primacy in establishing the truth about the world. In this respect, if we manage to produce a *true* ontology, the *empirical* issues arising in other domains, from science to everyday life, should "take care of themselves"; that is to say that they should be solvable by means of purely empirical techniques.

What about the role of physics, for example? Physical laws *do* play a fundamental role, here:

> "The physical world is evidently 'causally closed': we take physics to uncover exceptionless laws governing our world's fundamental constituents. This suggests that, whenever a physical event occurs, it has a wholly physical explanation. ... [The] physical world is causally closed. The behaviour of the basic constituents is wholly determined by fundamental physical laws." (p. 20)

In this sense, laws of physics are essential in determining the behaviour of basic constituents. This seems to imply the possibility for physical laws to have a precise and active role. But then the difficulty arises of how the laws can determine dispositions or capacities if they are still to be thought of as being determined by these very dispositions or capacities?

Furthermore, we need to ask how in Heil's framework capacity claims can serve to reconcile the idea that properties are intrinsically qualitative and irreducibly dispositional at once with the assumption that laws of nature are constituted bottom-up. To tackle this question, we first have to understand what is meant by capacities. In fact, what are *capacities*?[10] Cartwright, in her (1999), still defends the claim that capacities are prior to laws: they are causal powers, irreducible, ontologically primary and causally active constituents of the world.

---

[10] In what follows, and given the little attention paid by Heil to this matter, I will take Cartwright's position as naturally supported by Heil. To be sure, in the very first footnote of his book he explicitly admits that "much of what [he has] to say here is consistent with ... Cartwright's dappled world" Heil (2003), p. 17.

Capacities, in Cartwright's view, are different from what is usually understood by disposition terms, i.e. as something "tied one-to-one to law-like regularities". As she points out, capacities "are not restricted to any single kind of manifestation. Objects can behave very differently in different circumstances" (Cartwright (1999), p. 59). But in Heil (2003), where properties are both dispositional and categorical, capacities can well be substituted to dispositions, provided that we keep in mind that modality is in the objects. In a similar spirit, Mumford ((2004b), p. 150) maintains that causal powers are *exhaustive* of properties. The nature and identity of a property is connected with its nomic or causal role. Hence, nomic and causal roles are intimately linked. The nomic roles essential to properties provide the identity criteria of properties.

We want to know how the world is constituted. Law statements should indicate what capacities are and how they work. But Cartwright's (and also Heil's) point is that scientific laws hold only *ceteris paribus*.

> "To ascribe a behaviour to the nature of a feature is to claim that the behaviour is exportable beyond the strict confines of the *ceteris paribus* conditions, although usually as a 'tendency' or a 'trying'. ... [The] laws of contemporary science are, to the extent that they are true at all, at best true *ceteris paribus*. In the nicest cases we may treat them as claims about natures. But we have no grounds in our experience for taking our laws – even most fundamental laws of physics – as universal. Indeed, I should say *'especially* our most fundamental laws of physics', if these are meant to be the laws of fundamental particles. For we have virtually no inductive reason for counting these laws as true of fundamental particles outside the laboratory setting – if they exist there at all. ... Reality may well be just a patchwork of laws." (Cartwright (1999), pp. 33 – 34)[11]

In Cartwright's dappled world, we must not look at the scientific laws to determine what capacities are. It is rather the other way around. If we are looking for laws, we should rather ground them on the capacities we identify in nature.

---

[11] Incidentally, Heil's position does not seem to align with Cartwright's one in this respect. Apparently, in discussing the issue of causal relevance of higher-level properties, Heil appears to endorse the view that laws of physics do determine the basic constituents of our world. In facts he refers to the laws of physics or chemistry as "strict or exceptionless", be they deterministic or probabilistic. And adds: "... we evidently regard the actions of the basic items as wholly determined by basic laws. ... When you move to the basic entities – the electrons and quarks – matters are different. Laws governing such entities leave no room for outside disruption. At the basic level, there is no 'outside'." (pp. 32 – 34) But see also the passage of p. 20 quoted above.

Capacities are thus responsible for our account of the behaviour of things in the world. But laws of nature hold only insofar as things with *stable* capacities are put to interact in appropriate circumstances and instantiate certain regularities thereby. Therefore, according to her, what we consider to be a regular behaviour in nature should be traced back to a so-called *nomological machine* (Cartwright (1999), p. 50). As she explains it,

> "[it] is capacities that are basic, and laws of nature obtain – to the extent that they do obtain – on account of the capacities; or more explicitly, on account of the repeated operation of a system of components with stable capacities in particularly fortunate circumstances. Sometimes the arrangement of the components and the settings are appropriate for a law to occur naturally, as in the planetary system; more often they are engineered by us, as in a laboratory experiment. But in any case, it takes what I call a *nomological machine* to get a law of nature" (Cartwright (1999), p. 49).

The regularities that we are used to rely on arise from very specific arrangements of things. Regularity and lawfulness are introduced only by those "machines". Laws (and theories) are true only *ceteris paribus*.

But this seems like a vicious circle! Where is the ground for regularity? How can we detect "stable capacities"? If we think that aspirin has the capacity to relieve headaches, this comes after a regular association between event-types has allowed us to infer a connection between taking aspirin and the vanishing of the headache. If capacities are supposed to be stable, we should have good reasons to expect that, given that capacities are primary and irreducible constituents (or *ways*, to put it with Heil) of the objects, they should not hold *ceteris paribus*.

The contingency was located by Heil both in the manifestations of capacities and in our mode of detecting them. The evident problem, here, is that strictly universal claims about capacities cannot be made.[12] So we cannot say what makes a claim about capacities true because such claim cannot hold outside "the realm of *ceteris paribus* laws and defeasible generalizations" (Heil (2003), p. 96). What is the nature of capacities if they are ontologically prior to laws and if we cannot properly define them given the contingency of our laws?

Here we face a central issue, which is widely left unexplained in Heil (2003). Heil appears to accord to the laws of nature some sort of "double" attitude. We have uniformity (and possibly universality) in cases in which the settings are

---
[12] See Psillos (2006).

perfectly controlled. But the settings don't mirror reality in its complexity. Moreover, capacities have a "multi-track" character in the sense that they can manifest themselves differently, according to, or depending on, the settings. Cartwright herself, in her (1999), oscillates[13] between a thesis of laws as causal powers of things and a thesis of laws as of *some* kind, i.e. as artefacts, outputs of nomological machines. Individuating capacities is not at all a "neutral" activity, indeed. If the laws are not restricted to detection but are also *actively* involved in "realising" or in making properties being realised, they cannot possibly be mere statements. How can a law bring capacities to existence? Or, stated more forcefully, how can a law have the *capacity* to bring a capacity to existence? I agree with Psillos in underlining that

> "... properties are what they are because of the laws they participate in. ... If it is the case that *no laws, no properties*, or if properties and laws are so intertwined that one cannot specify the former without the latter and conversely, then some laws had better be true. For if they are not, then we cannot talk of properties either" (Psillos (2006)).

So the question, in the end, is: what kind of existence do the laws of nature have? In Heil's book, we are left with two options about laws: (I) laws *qua* statements (epistemological option); or (II) laws *in* powers (ontological option).

(I) As we have seen, the only meaning maintained by Heil is the first one: laws are ontologically redundant, but they can be interpreted as statements, formal expressions (whatever this could mean) of relations holding among objects. In this case, we can interpret laws *qua* statements as:

- (i) having a *descriptive* or explanatory meaning: laws should bring to existence what capacities are and the way they work. But is the idea of laws *qua* statements a good candidate to account for the metaphysics of their instances? It does not seem so, from an epistemological perspective, as we can only rely on a somehow defective and imperfect knowledge. So if laws are *supposed* to explain what is out there in the real world, they will never manage to accomplish this task if not either in an approximate or in an artificial fashion.

- (ii) *determining* or detecting capacities: this is actually more worrisome, because if laws are intended according to Cartwright's model, we run the risk of falling back into the situation she describes, where laws, and

---
[13] Mumford (2000), and (2004a), p. 131.

the whole machinery producing them, are not neutral towards the individuation of capacities. A nomological machine makes laws end up being of some (not natural) kind. What kind is this? If we accept that laws are mere descriptions in this second sense, Heil should explain *what kind of object* they are, and why we should conform to them.

(II) Otherwise, from the ontological perspective, we can accept (with Mumford and as it seems to be suggested naturally by Heil) that laws do not exist *per se* and that they *are* dispositions. This is all good as it stands; but how do we get to know the laws? Hence, we are back to point (I).

The very problem of this double nature of laws is actually to understand what the relation between (I) and (II) is. We can coherently maintain a realist lawlessness, in a world where capacities do all the work. But it remains unclear how we can then know the laws in such a world, speak about them and above all use them confidently. The epistemological option is to be taken seriously; otherwise, the motivation for this ontological point of view turns out to be quite unsound.

6 Conclusion

The interesting perspective offered by Heil (2003) in rejecting the traditional opposition between dispositional and categorical properties, parallel to a no-level view of reality, requires modal realism and a realist lawlessness. From such a point of view, laws of nature are ontologically redundant, but it is still not clear what role laws of nature should play in the epistemology that matches this ontology. This is indeed a central issue that, unfortunately, is not addressed by the author. Heil's reference to dispositionalities as capacities, and to Cartwright's position, does not shed much light on it.

Laws, although metaphysically redundant, are central in epistemology. If we assume that we need a nomological machine to get a lawful regularity, the nomological machine somehow produces the laws. And on these laws the way that we define and interpret the power net depends in turn. But we are left with an apparent discrepancy between ontology and epistemology. The double nature that is accorded to the laws of nature calls for some clarification. What is the relation between the two pictures of laws we have obtained? We need to know what guarantees the identity between the regularities we detect and the regularities in nature. How can laws *in* things be mirrored by the laws we elaborate *with the help of* the nomological machines? We cannot use laws to explain the dispositionalities of objects if these are what grounds the laws. We could avoid thinking that there is an identity between the laws *in* nature and the laws *of* science and take the mutual relation to be a weak correlation. In this case, there would be some reciprocal influence of both kinds of laws. What we could then know about dispositions would be something that we have cooperated in creating. But this would sound even more complicated. And, even worse, we would be left with an unexpected result. If scientific laws cite kinds of objects that are kinds only for us at an epistemic level, what happens with the the full-blood realism from which we had started?

One final remark. Didn't ontology, on Heil's account, have some priority in making sense of the world? Wouldn't the remaining questions simply have to "take care of themselves" once the right ontology was given? The issues arising in scientific methodology are maybe "largely empirical and hence susceptible to techniques we standardly deploy in answering empirical questions" (Heil (2003), p. 3). Nevertheless, they raise some problems that should be held in due consideration also by an ontological point of view. Otherwise we have a perfect ontology but quite distant from the scientific practise. Unfortunately, these issues don't seem to find a clear answer within Heil's ontology.

Commentary
John Heil

What are laws of nature? Here is one possibility: laws are rules objects are set by God to obey. Philosophers nowadays would be unlikely to accept this characterisation. Suppose we subtract God from the picture: laws are rules objects obey. This makes the laws external to the objects and contingent. You could keep the objects, but change the rules.

Although few philosophers would own up to such a view, I suspect that this is how many of us have thought of laws in our less reflective moments. We have a vague picture of objects obeying rules (the laws). This is understandable so long as we have God in the picture. God does not simply make the rules; God *enforces* them. God *sees to it* that the objects behave as they are supposed to behave. The subtraction of God from the picture, however, removes the steering mechanism. We are left with objects moving about, changing *in accord with* rules, but not moved about by some external factor. The objects just do what they do. Luckily for us, what they do is often orderly and predictable. Laws are reduced to regularities expressed in universal generalisations.

Something has gone wrong. Surely something *makes* the objects behave as they do, something ensures that they behave in accordance with laws formulated by the sciences. But what could this be? What could be responsible for the orderliness we observe in nature?

According to D. M. Armstrong, objects behave as they do owing to their properties. Armstrong takes properties to be universals, identical across their instances. Laws are second-order relations holding among the universals. The F's *necessitate* the G's, hence every instance of F brings about a G. Laws are contingent in the sense that you could have had the F's and the G's without the F's necessitating the G's. This would be so were the second-order relation absent.

I am uncomfortable with this picture for a couple of reasons. First, I do not know what to make of universals. I do not understand what it is for something to be wholly present in – identical across – each of its distinct instances. In common with most philosophers who discuss these issues, I can talk the talk, but I really have no idea what I am talking about. I am not going to accept a position I do not understand.

Second, I am strongly impelled to think that the objects behave as they do owing exclusively to particular ways *they* are. Objects' dispositionalities (or powers, or capacities) determine what they do and, significantly, what they *would* do. What are the alternatives? Manipulation by God? Aimless, but miraculously orderly behavior?

Suppose I am right about dispositionality. Where would this leave the laws? Padovani is correct: if you take the dispositional picture seriously, laws are not coercive entities that play a role in objects' behavior. Objects behave as they do because they are as they are. Objects are self-governing. This does not mean that each object is a law unto itself, a Leibnizian monad. An object's behavior results from its dispositionalities and dispositionalities of other objects. Behavior (broadly construed so as to include change generally) is the mutual manifestation of reciprocal dispositionalities. If the world is corpuscular, the dispositionalities of complex objects are grounded in dispositionalities of their parts. If the world is not corpuscular, if ordinary objects and particles turn out to be modes (waves, thickenings of regions of space-time, local ways the One is), occurrences will be manifestings of reciprocal dispositionalities of whatever it is that the modes are modes of (see my response to Lam). Manifestations are themselves dispositionally-loaded modes.

Scientists explain why objects behave as they do by identifying properties of objects responsible for this behavior. We can express connections among properties using conditional, if – then locutions. Sometimes we are interested just in the contribution one property makes to he behavior of its possessors. We "abstract" from the possessors' other properties. We can, for instance, consider the behavior of objects just insofar as they are massy, their behavior *qua* massy. But the behavior of a complex object (or mode; I shall omit the qualification henceforth) is determined by interactions among its properties and properties of other objects. Abstraction or partial consideration – "idealisation" – teases out the contribution of individual properties to objects' behavior, but what objects actually do is determined by much more. If – then locutions we make use of to express what we have discovered about objects' properties amount to the characterisation of dispositionalities by reference to (certain of) their manifestations with reciprocal disposition partners. To the extent that these locutions concern properties of the most fundamental things, they are largely exceptionless, resembling Davidson's strict laws. As we focus on more complex objects, our if – thens become increasingly chancy. This is due, in part to the complexity of interactions among complex things. Mostly, however, it is due to our penchant for deploying predicates intended to capture imprecise but salient similarities.

Chapter 10

From being ontologically serious to serious ontology

Michael Esfeld

The paper first argues that if one takes current fundamental physics seriously, one gets to a metaphysics of events and relations in contrast to substances and intrinsic properties. Against that background, the paper discusses Heil's theory of properties as being both categorical and dispositional and his rejection of levels of being. I contrast these views with a Humean metaphysics. My concluding claim is that Heil's account of properties opens up the perspective of a conservative reductionism, which avoids the common reservations about reductionism.

1 Relations vs. intrinsic properties

In this paper, I shall take the liberty to simply pin down a few central issues that arise in constructing a comprehensive metaphysics, basing myself on some of the discussions in the preceding papers. I shall first mention my methodological background of metaphysics grounded on science, then consider Heil's view of properties (sections 2 & 3) and finally explore the perspective of his rejection of the conception of levels of being leading to a conservative reductionism (section 4).

There is a mutual dependence between science and philosophy. One cannot separate metaphysics from science, as is evident for instance from the causal argument for physicalism whose crucial premise is the completeness of physics. But one cannot simply read one's metaphysics off from science either. It is the business of the philosophical interpretation of scientific theories to put forward proposals for ontological commitments that are reasonable consequent upon scientific results.

The history of philosophy is dominated by atomism in the sense of the metaphysical position according to which the world is composed of small, indivisible substances (atoms in a literal sense). These substances are characterised by a few intrinsic properties, they are endurants, existing as a whole for all the time or for a certain time, having no temporal parts, and they are the foundations for change, change being the alteration of accidental properties of these substances. That position fits well with classical mechanics and the classical field theories of the nineteenth century. But it does not fit into the fundamental physical theories of the twentieth century:

– The unification of space and time in *special relativity*, which is maintained in *general relativity*, provides a strong argument for the metaphysics of a block universe (see notably Balashov (2000)): there is a four-dimensional continuum of space-time. Everything that there is simply exists in space-time, occupying a point or a region of space-time; existence is not relative to a time (e.g., it is wrong to maintain that only that what is present exists). The content of the block universe are perdurants – events and processes, the latter having spatial as well as temporal parts. An event is defined by the properties that occur at a space-time point (maybe properties of space-time points themselves, may be properties of fields), a process is a sequence of events. There are no substances that persist as a whole for a certain time (endurants), being the foundations of change. Persisting objects are continuous sequences of events that are similar as regards their properties, forming what is known as a world-line, change is variation in the properties of such events.

– *Quantum theory* provides for a strong argument for a metaphysics of relations instead of intrinsic properties (that metaphysics is put forward under the names of holism and of structural realism; see Esfeld (2004) and the references therein): what is fundamental according to quantum theory are relations of entanglement among quantum systems. As far as the fundamental physical properties are concerned that quantum physics considers, quantum systems do not have these properties separately, but are linked with each other by relations of entanglement; there are no intrinsic properties underlying those relations. Even if there are processes of a dissolution of entanglement (known as state reductions), leading to properties that belong to quantum systems individually, the relations of entanglement are fundamental.

– Turning to space-time itself, there is a strong argument stemming from field theories in favour of the existence of space-time points (see Field (1980), chapter 4). However, *general relativity* provides for a strong argument against the conception of space-time points as substances that are characterised by intrinsic properties (the hole argument; see Earman & Norton (1987)). Instead, the properties of space-time points consist in the metric relations in which these points stand. Thus, the philosophy of space-time fits well into structural realism (see Esfeld & Lam (2006 forthcoming) and Lam (this volume)).

These are piecemeal arguments. There are properties that are neither properties of space-time nor touched by quantum entanglement, most notably mass and charge. Consequently, the last two arguments say nothing against considering those properties as fundamental intrinsic properties. However, regarding properties such as mass and charge as intrinsic is by no means mandatory. More importantly, we lack a unification of quantum theory and general relativity. Nonetheless, whatever may be the future fundamental physical theory that achieves a unified treatment of the phenomena that are currently considered by two different theories, it would be unreasonable to expect that future theory to go back behind the unification of space and time as considered by general relativity or the holism that quantum entanglement manifests. Even if we ignore as yet the content of that future theory, the metaphysical direction seems clear: events instead of enduring substances, and relations instead of intrinsic properties.

2 Powerful vs. Humean properties

The points sketched out in the previous section are to my mind simply commitments that any attempt at a comprehensive contemporary metaphysics should accommodate. It is a pity that many metaphysicians base themselves on common sense instead of paying heed to science. The last two points are at odds with Heil's insistence upon intrinsic properties. However, they do not touch upon Heil's main concern.

The central element of Heil's ontology is his view of each property being both categorical (or qualitative) and dispositional. More precisely, the distinction between "categorical" and "dispositional" is one among predicates, each property being categorical and dispositional in one, making true categorical and dispositional descriptions. That view can be applied to intrinsic properties as well as to relations. If each relation is both categorical and dispositional, it includes the disposition to produce further relations. In the following, I shall therefore take the liberty to use the notion of properties as a generic one, covering both intrinsic properties and relations.

An ontology that regards properties as being both categorical and dispositional is less parsimonious than an ontology that admits only categorical properties. What is today known as Humean metaphysics is the paradigmatic example of a parsimonious ontology of the latter kind. According to David Lewis's thesis of Humean supervenience, for instance, what holds the world together is a network of spatio-temporal relations between points. At those points are fundamental physical properties that are intrinsic and categorical. That's all (Lewis (1986), pp. ix - x). Laws are statements that describe certain salient patterns of regularities in the distribution of these properties. What the laws are supervenes on the distribution of these properties as a whole. The same goes for causation – both on a Humean regularity account as well as on a counterfactual account like the one of Lewis himself (the truthmaker for the counterfactual statements is the distribution of the fundamental physical properties over the whole space-time of the actual world; see Armstrong (2004b), p. 445, and Loewer (forthcoming), section II). Dispositions also supervene on the distribution of the fundamental physical properties in space-time.

Humean metaphysics has to accept the whole distribution of fundamental physical properties in space-time as primitive. Given that distribution, vertical explanations are possible: one can explain how certain configurations of fundamental physical properties make certain higher-level descriptions true. But it is not possible, given the distribution of fundamental physical properties in a certain region of space-time, to account for why there are the fundamental physical properties instantiated in other regions that there are in fact. Given the "big bang" at the origin of the universe, it is not possible to answer the question why the distribution of fundamental physical properties in the universe developed as it did. The only thing that one can do is this one: given the whole distribution of fundamental physical properties in space-time, one can write down the salient patterns of regularities in the distribution of these properties in the form of laws. The laws are merely descriptive, summing up what there is.

Humean metaphysics therefore faces the problem of induction in a metaphysical form: there is nothing in the past distribution of properties that could make true the prediction that the future distribution of properties will be like the past one. Lewis (1994a), section 3, assumes that nature is kind to us, that is, that there will be a few simple salient regularities that apply to the distribution of physical properties throughout the whole universe; but there is nothing in the past distribution of properties that could make such a claim about the whole universe true.

If we switch from a Humean metaphysics of intrinsic, categorical properties to a metaphysics of categorical relations, nothing of substance changes as regards the issues just raised. Again, given the big bang at the origin of the universe, it is not possible to answer the question why the distribution of fundamental physical relations in the universe developed as it did.

This lack of an account is a good motivation to go beyond the sparse ontology of Humean metaphysics and admit dispositions, that is, powers. If the tokens of fundamental physical properties or relations include the power to produce further tokens of fundamental physical properties or relations, then we have an account of why, given the distribution of tokens of fundamental physical properties in a certain region of space-time, there are certain other tokens of fundamental physical properties in other regions. Thus, given the big bang at the origin of the universe, admitting powers at the origin of the universe provides us with metaphysical tools to answer the question why the distribution of fundamental physical properties in the universe developed as it did. In general, if the tokens of the fundamental physical property *A* include the power to produce tokens of the fundamental physical property *B*, then we have an account of why there are sequences of the type *AB* in the universe.

There are two versions of a metaphysics of powerful properties discussed in the current literature:

(I) The one version considers each property to be categorical and dispositional in one. More precisely, to the extent that there is a distinction between the categorical and the dispositional, it is a distinction among predicates or descriptions instead of properties. This version is favoured by Charlie Martin and John Heil among others (see Martin (1997), in particular sections 3 and 12, Heil (2003), chapter 11, as well as Mumford (1998), chapter 9, Mellor (2000), in particular pp. 767 – 768 and Kistler (2005)).

(II) The other version identifies properties with powers (see Shoemaker (1980), Bird (2005), as well as Ellis (2001), in particular chapters 1 and 3; Ellis, however, admits powers as well as categorical properties as two different kinds of properties existing in the world).

Laurent Freland (this volume), section 2, argues that categorical and dispositional predicates exclude one another so that we cannot conceive properties as being both categorical and dispositional without compromising realism. If this argument proves sound, it refutes the first of these versions, but it does not touch the second one.

For the purposes of this paper, the second version is sufficient. The main contrast is the one between a Humean metaphysics and a metaphysics of powerful properties. The difference between the two versions of that latter metaphysics is not great to my mind: the first version does not conceive the distinction between the categorical and the dispositional as an ontological one (so that one cannot even talk in terms of qualitative and dispositional aspects of properties), and the second version does not conceive powers as pure potentialities, but as real, actual properties – and thus as categorical in a certain sense. Furthermore, each power can be considered as qualitative in a certain sense, since it is the power to produce certain specific effects.

According to the ontology of powerful properties, there are necessary connections. If tokens of the property A are or include the power to produce tokens of the property B among other things, then the connection between the A's and the B's is a necessary one. Consequently, if it is a law that all A's are followed by B's, this is so because the A's have and exercise the power to produce B's. The laws of nature thus are metaphysically necessary. In any world in which there are A's, the law that A's produce B's holds.

However, one may wonder whether anything is gained in adding powers to one's ontology. It is not an explanation of why A's are always followed by B's to say that A's are or include the power to produce B's among other things – in the same way as it is not an explanation of why opium makes people fall asleep to say that opium is or includes the power to produce sleep in people among other things. Since we consider fundamental physical properties, there is, of course, not the possibility to go further down in the level of explanations. Is it therefore not simply a mark of intellectual honesty to concede that explanations come to an end once we have reached descriptions in terms of fundamental physical properties and to accept the distribution of the fundamental physical properties over the whole space-time as primitive?

It is correct to point out that adding powers to one's ontology does not lead to a gain in explanation. One either has to accept the whole distribution of fundamental physical properties as primitive or one has to accept powers – such as the power of A's to produce B's – as primitive. The point at issue is a comprehensive and coherent metaphysics. One may voice reservations against admitting powers, since they do not lead to a gain in explanation. But one may also voice reservations against a Humean metaphysics, since one simply has to accept the whole distribution of fundamental physical properties in space-time as primitive, there being no necessary connections. Are there arguments to prefer one of these metaphysical positions to the other one?

3 Two arguments from physics

Let us turn to physics. Both the friends of Humean metaphysics and the friends of powerful properties claim support from physics; Heil himself, however, does not invoke physics. As regards the Humeans, since Russell's famous paper denouncing the notion of causation as production or generation of something (Russell (1912)), they claim that our fundamental physical theories do without the notion of powers or forces. All that our fundamental physical theories state are certain regularities in the distribution of physical properties. There is thus not more to causation than the Humean acknowledges (cf. for instance Redhead (1990), pp. 145 – 147, Loewer (2001), pp. 322 – 324, Field (2003), section 1). However, the friend of powerful properties objects to the Humean that the world of Humean metaphysics is static, whereas physics – notably cosmology – shows that our world is dynamical (e.g. Mumford (1998), p. 214, Ellis (2001), pp. 1 – 2, Molnar (2003), pp. 135 – 137, 178). According to the friend of powers, the admission of powers is mandatory in order to account for the actual world being dynamical. In that respect, one can pursue two arguments stemming from our two current fundamental physical theories. Let us consider these arguments.

(I) What holds the world together? According to Lewis's thesis of Humean supervenience, there are fundamental physical properties instantiated at points that are linked by spatio-temporal relations. In short, what holds the world together are spatio-temporal relations. Humean metaphysics in general presupposes space-time, that is, the network of spatio-temporal relations. These relations are considered to be categorical, and this is seen as proving that the unity of the world can be accounted for in terms of categorical properties only.

However, as we know from general relativity and its application in cosmology, space-time cannot be separated from matter, and it is itself a dynamical entity. Space-time has its origin in the so-called big bang, and it is in continuous expansion. This physical theory of space-time shows first that the metaphysics of powerful properties can be applied to spatio-temporal relations too (cf. Bird (2005), p. 459). Since these relations are dynamical and interact with non-gravitational energy-matter, they can be considered as making true descriptions in terms of powerful properties in the same way as any other fundamental physical property does. More importantly – and also more controversially – one can raise the following question:

what distinguishes a world with a dynamic space-time as described by general relativity from a conceivable world with a Minkowskian flat space-time, that is, a fixed given background network of spatio-temporal relations as some sort of an arena into which physical entities are inserted? One can maintain that a persuasive answer to this question consists in saying that the spatio-temporal relations in a dynamical space-time as described by general relativity include certain powers to produce changes in non-gravitational energy-matter as well as in the metric structure of space-time itself. However, that answer is not mandatory. The Humean can simply accept these changes – like all other changes at the fundamental physical level – as primitive.

(II) The interpretation of quantum physics gives much more often rise to a metaphysical position that admits irreducible dispositions (powers) than does the interpretation of general relativity. Nonetheless, the relations of quantum entanglement are not dispositions as such. They can be considered as categorical. There is an interpretation of quantum physics, going back to Everett (1957), according to which quantum entanglement is universal, encompassing all objects in the world and all their properties. According to that interpretation, the world simply is a huge entangled quantum state, and that's all. That interpretation does not call for the admission of powers. But that interpretation implies that all our other scientific theories, apart from quantum physics thus interpreted, are strictly speaking false: there are no disentangled states out there in the world, hence there are no properties having definite numerical values at all. For instance, the state of Schrödinger's cat remains forever entangled with the state of the atom among others, so that the atom never is in a state of being either integral or decayed and the cat never is in a state of being either alive or dead. To my mind, this is a good reason to reject that interpretation: it is simply not coherent with our other scientific theories, not to mention our common sense knowledge.

The other interpretation of quantum physics – or set of interpretations, of which the one going back to Ghirardi, Rimini & Weber (1986) is the most prominent one – recognises processes of a dissolution of quantum entanglement, known as state reductions, that lead to physical properties possessing definite numerical values. The talk of dispositions or powers in the interpretation of quantum physics is usually linked with that interpretation: the idea is that quantum systems have dispositions or powers to acquire physical properties possessing definite numerical values by means of state reductions. Hence, if one takes a dynamics like the one proposed by Ghirardi, Rimini & Weber (1986) to describe the actual world, the argument is that at least in a world like ours, the relations of quantum entanglement include the power to dissolve themselves (power of state reductions; that power has moreover to be such that there is room for state reductions being probabilistic). (Perhaps this is so in any possible world. For this argument, nothing depends on whether a world of universal quantum entanglement is merely conceivable or also metaphysically possible; the same remark applies to the conceivable world mentioned in the previous argument). However, it is always open to the Humean to simply accept quantum entanglement and the processes of its dissolution as primitive (that is, for instance, simply accept the dynamics that Ghirardi, Rimini & Weber (1986) propose as primitive).

If one endorses a metaphysics of fundamental physical relations being or including powers on the basis of considerations such as the mentioned ones, no commitment to unmanifested powers ensues. As regards these fundamental powers, there is no question of manifestation conditions being outside of them, since there is nothing but quantum entanglement and/or a dynamical space-time to start with. These fundamental powers are quite different from common sense dispositions such as sugar being soluble in water. As regards these latter dispositions, the conditional analysis may be right (see Sparber (this volume), and the references therein). However, as Malzkorn (2000) has shown, the conditional analysis on its own does not settle the issue of the ontology of dispositions.

This section of the paper is inconclusive: we need strong metaphysical arguments why we should prefer a metaphysics of powerful properties to a Humean metaphysics, since the latter is more parsimonious. The arguments stemming from fundamental physics have some persuasive force, but there is no cogent argument from contemporary fundamental physics that favours a metaphysics of powerful properties against a Humean metaphysics (as there are cogent arguments from contemporary physics that favour a metaphysics of events against a metaphysics of substances and a metaphysics of relations against a metaphysics of intrinsic properties). The mentioned arguments come down to exploiting the intuition that there is more to causation than just some regularity pattern or other in the development of the distribution of fundamental physical properties. However, these arguments are unable to provide any reason why that view of causation is right. I think there is an argument for that view of causation, but it relies on biological and mental causation. I shall turn to that argument in the next section.

4 Reduction vs. elimination

Heil's ontology is directed against the view of levels of being. There are no levels of being. Thus, it is inappropriate to talk in terms of a single level of being as well. Taking fundamental physics into account, the view we get to is the following one: there is quantum entanglement, and there are processes of the dissolution of quantum entanglement, resulting in classical physical properties (as described by an appropriate dynamics of quantum systems). Tokens of these properties arrange themselves during cosmic evolution in configurations some of which are more and more complex, making true not only descriptions in terms of fundamental physics, but also descriptions in terms of chemistry, biology, neurobiology, psychology, etc. Thus, there are levels of complexity in the organisation of configurations of fundamental physical properties, and there are levels of description, but no levels of being.

This position is a reductive physicalism: everything that exists is either a fundamental physical token or identical with a configuration of fundamental physical tokens. Modern science provides for a strong argument in favour of reductive physicalism: anything that is in some way or other connected to physical causes and effects can stand in causal relations only if it is identical with fundamental physical tokens or their configurations (the most prominent recent elaboration of that argument and its consequences is Kim (1998) and (2005); for a recent discussion of Kim's position see the papers in Esfeld & Fantini (2005)).

The causal argument for reductive physicalism is independent of the theory of causation that one holds. Even a Humean regularity account or a Lewisian counterfactual account of causation does not open up a way to avoid the reductionist conclusion of that argument by turning systematic overdetermination into a plausible option (see Sparber (2005) who argues against Loewer (2001)). Nonetheless, the metaphysics of causation is relevant when it comes to spelling out the reductionist position to which that argument points. How can one show that, for instance, biological tokens and mental tokens are identical with configurations of physical tokens? That task would be easy if biological and mental properties were defined by their physical composition – as arguably chemical properties are. That task would be impossible to accomplish if biological and mental properties were qualitative intrinsic and categorical properties. In that case, given the causal argument for physicalism, they would not only have no effects whatsoever, but it would also be entirely mysterious how they could arise in cosmic evolution, being caused by physical tokens. Fortunately, there is another conception of biological and mental properties available, namely the functional one. According to that conception, biological and mental properties are notably defined by some characteristic effects that their tokens have. One then discovers configurations of physical tokens that are sufficient to bring about the effects in question, and the causal argument provides a convincing reason for holding that any biological and any mental token is identical with a configuration of physical tokens. Since functional properties are defined in a causal way, the metaphysics of causation is pertinent to spelling out reductive physicalism.

Although the causal argument for reductive physicalism is cogent, reductionism meets with many reservations. In order to win over the philosophers' community – and the public in general – it is crucial to set out that position in such a way that one does not provoke the "nothing but ..." objection ("the mental is nothing but brain states", etc.), giving rise to the impression that something has been left out. Note that identity applies in both directions: if all biological and all mental tokens are identical with configurations of physical tokens, then some configurations of physical tokens are biological or mental tokens. It is hence not true to say that biological and mental tokens are replaced with configurations of physical tokens. This position is an ontological reductionism only for the following reason: everything that there is in the world is a physical token or a configuration of physical tokens; but not everything that there is in the world is a biological or a mental token.

The same applies to descriptions: descriptions that use biological and mental concepts are true in the same way as descriptions that use physical concepts. Both belong to a comprehensive and coherent system of our knowledge. Entities that are identical with configurations of fundamental physical tokens make true higher-level descriptions in the same way as they make true physical descriptions. There is only one relation of truthmaking.

However, we need an account of how one and the same token can make true both a fundamental physical description and higher-level descriptions. If we are to avoid reintroducing levels of being, that account can only be one that shows how any concept that a higher-level description uses can be coordinated with a concept that can be constructed within fundamental physics in such a way that the higher-level concepts are nomologically coextensive with physical concepts (so that we can in principle deduce the higher-level descriptions and theories from the fundamental physical ones). This position then is an epistemological reductionism because it is not possible to construct for any physical concept a higher-level concept that is nomologically coextensive with the physical concept in question. In short, pace Heil (2003), chapter 6, one cannot subscribe to ontological reductionism (identity of all higher-level tokens with configurations of fundamental physical tokens) without subscribing to epistemological reductionism (theory reduction) too.

How can we achieve such nomologically coextensive concepts? According to an idea pursued by Christian Sachse and myself, any higher-level functional concept that a higher-level functional theory F uses can always be made more precise by introducing functional sub-concepts F_1, F_2, F_3, etc. These functional sub-concepts can be constructed in such a way that they are nomologically coextensive with the physical concepts P_1, P_2, P_3, etc. that are constructed within a fundamental physical theory in order describe in physical terms the tokens that make true the functional theory F. However, there is no question here of a semantic way of meaning analysis from the concepts of P to the concepts of F (and *vice versa*). The meaning of these concepts is distinct. The aim is to achieve a nomological coextension of certain concepts constructed within F with certain concepts constructed within P (see Esfeld & Sachse (2006 manuscript) and Sachse (this volume)).

The proposal can be summed up in this way:

(I) Within a comprehensive fundamental physical theory P, we can construct concepts P_1, P_2, P_3, etc. that describe the tokens that come under the concepts of a functional theory F, for any F.

(II) For any F, we can make the concepts of F more precise by constructing functional sub-concepts F_1, F_2, F_3, etc. that are nomologically coextensive with P_1, P_2, P_3, etc.

(III) We can then reduce F to P by inferring F_1, F_2, F_3, etc. from P_1, P_2, P_3, etc., given the nomological coextension, and get to F by simply abstracting from the conceptualisation of side effects that distinguish between F_1, F_2, F_3, etc.

The model we then get to is this one: the entities that there are in the world – the domain "e" on the left hand side of the drawing below – make true descriptions that are related to each other as shown in an idealised way on the right hand side of the drawing:

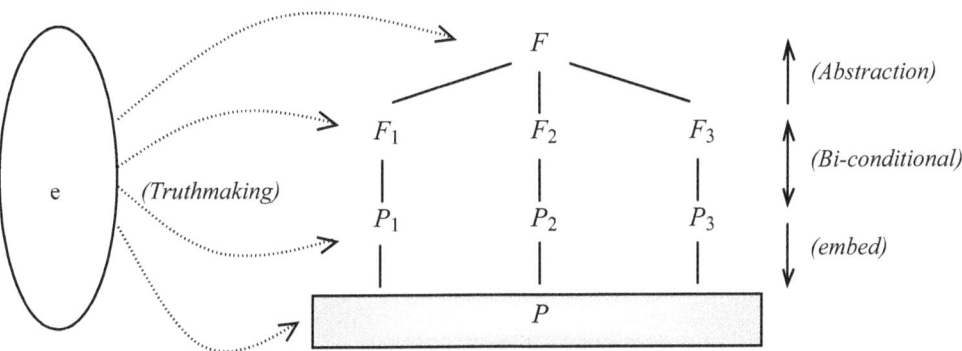

This model is remarkably distinct from the standard reductionist position that goes like this: there are fundamental physical properties instantiated at space-time points. The fundamental physical properties and their configurations make true a fundamental physical description in the first place. Some of these configurations furthermore make true chemical, biological, neurobiological, etc. descriptions. These latter descriptions are entailed by the fundamental physical descriptions. I take Lewis's thesis of Humean supervenience as well as Jackson's *a priori* physicalism to amount to something like this position (cf. Chalmers & Jackson (2001)). There are some passages in Heil (2003) that can be read in that way too (e.g. pp. 41, 45), but this is not Heil's considered position (see chapter 6). This austere reductionist position still is in the grip of the levels of being model: there is only one level of being, the fundamental physical one, making true a privileged level of descriptions, the fundamental physical ones, some of which then imply further, higher-level descriptions. The distinction between this conception and the standard functionalist one is that the functionalist adds higher-level, functional second-order properties corresponding to the higher-level, functional descriptions.

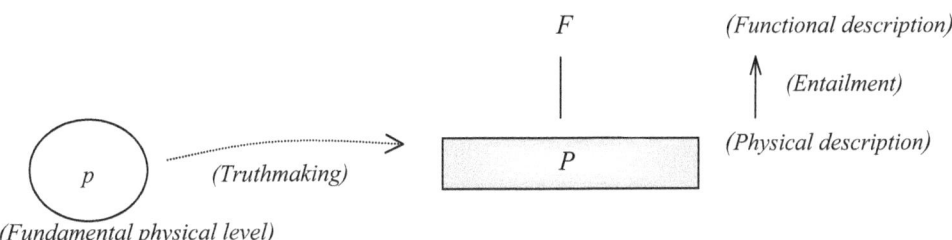

This model gives with some reason rise to reservations about reductionism, for there are only physical entities, and non-physical descriptions are true, but only in a derived, secondary way. The first model, however, does not invite any such worries.

Let us now apply the issue of a Humean metaphysics vs. a metaphysics of powers to these two different ways of spelling out reductionism. Consider the view of causation within Humean metaphysics (I shall confine myself to a Humean regularity view of causation; nothing of substance changes if one switches to a counterfactual account à la Lewis). The fundamental properties are categorical only. Causation is nothing but certain contingent patterns of regularities in the distribution of the fundamental categorical properties. Functional properties, however, cannot be conceived as being categorical only, for what they are consists in the effects that they cause. Humean metaphysics can hence not admit functional properties. We therefore end up with the position that the referents of functional descriptions are configurations of fundamental physical tokens only and that these configurations make true higher-level, functional descriptions in a somewhat secondary way, these descriptions being derived from the fundamental physical descriptions. In brief, a Humean metaphysics is committed to the second model of reductionism that provokes the charge of eliminativism with respect to functional properties such as biological or mental ones: they are not really there, being replaced with physical properties and some contingent regularity patterns in the distribution of physical properties.

By contrast, consider a metaphysics of powerful properties. There is no problem to conceive functional properties as being or including certain powers. Functionalism is often linked with the causal theory of properties (Shoemaker (1980)). If powers go down to the fundamental physical level, there is no problem in maintaining that functional, biological or mental properties exist in the same manner in the world as do fundamental physical properties: some configurations of physical tokens genuinely are biological, or mental tokens. In short, in order to avoid the "nothing but ..." charge against reductionism and be able to maintain a conservative reductionism as outlined in the first drawing above, we have to conceive the dispositional character of properties as applying to all properties including the fundamental physical ones.

That argument can be illustrated by turning to mental causation. Mental causation is experienced in such a way that our intentions produce a good deal of our behaviour in the sense that the existence of the behaviour in question is grounded on the intentions. Humean metaphysics cannot accommodate that experience as being veridical. In Humean metaphysics, the description of a token mental intention refers in each case to – and is made true by – a configuration of fundamental physical tokens. Most of the configurations of fundamental physical tokens that make true a description of the type "intention to raise one's right arm" are contiguous in space and time with configurations of fundamental physical tokens that make true a description of the type "right arm going up". But according to Humean metaphysics, there is nothing in the former configurations that brings about the latter configurations and thus is the ground for their existence. It is simply an entirely contingent matter of fact that configurations of the former type are usually followed by configurations of the latter type.

Russell said in his famous rejection of the law of causality (that is, in short, the idea of the cause having the power to bring about the effect): "A volition "operates" when what it wills takes place; but nothing can operate except a volition." ((1912), p. 11) However, the causal argument for physicalism tells us that if a volition operates, then the volition is identical with a configuration of physical tokens. The causal argument is an argument for the identity of biological, mental, etc. causes with physical causes. It would lose its point if that identity were to deprive the biological, the mental, etc. of its causal force. Thus, in short, if there is mental causation – or biological causation – and if mental, or biological causes are identical with physical causes instead of being eliminated, then the physical causes have to include the power to bring about the effects that define the mental, or the biological causes. Of course, this means only that the physical properties are powerful as well, but not that dispositions in general possess the characteristic features of intentionality.

The argument from functional – notably mental – properties for a metaphysics of causation in terms of powers seems to me to be the most cogent argument for a metaphysics of powerful properties in contrast to a Humean metaphysics. Going for a reductionism that does not provoke the usual reservations has a price, namely to conceive every property as including certain powers. There is nothing from physics that rules out a metaphysics of causation in terms of powers; there are even some considerations from fundamental physics that one can pursue in that sense, although they alone do not lead to a cogent argument for that metaphysics.

There are a lot of open issues here. For instance, it is not at all trivial whether all our mental experience can be conceptualised in terms of entities that are functional, being defined by characteristic effects. Conceiving properties as being categorical and dispositional in one commits us to a functional view of qualia, for it is not possible to separate in that conception a qualitative from a functional-dispositional aspect of properties (cf. Sollberger (this volume)). In short, all the work that remains to be done consists in explaining how functional tokens that are identical with physical tokens make true our beliefs about consciousness, conceptual content, free will, norms, values, etc. Nonetheless, it seems to me that we can gain from Heil's book the perspective of a coherent overall metaphysics of the world and ourselves that is reductionist without eliminating anything.

Commentary

John Heil

Esfeld holds that metaphysics is continuous with physics. This, he adds, does not imply that you can "read off" metaphysical conclusions from empirical theses. But it does mean that metaphysical theses had better not be at odds with our best science.

I agree. Quantum physics provides a nice case study. Most physicists accept the quantum theory as true. The trouble is, we have no very good idea what the world must be like if it is true. Attempts to spell out what quantum theory tells us about the world yield a range of incompatible interpretations, none of which commands anything like universal assent. Lawyers tell us that hard cases make bad law. Quantum physics, in its present state, makes bad metaphysics.

This is not to take an aloof attitude toward physics. On the contrary, it is to go along with the physicists, while recognising that, until we have a clearer conception of what the quantum world must be like, it is a bad idea to use quantum theory as a guide to ontology. Esfeld thinks that physics obliges us to adopt a picture of the world as four-dimensional and as comprising, not substances, but events. I'm doubtful that it tells us this, but I'm willing to listen.

Consider the idea that a substance/attribute ontology of the kind I favour is at odds with what the physicists tell us.[1]

The worry is that my ontology encourages a kind of old-fashioned atomism. As I try to make clear in various places in *From an ontological point of view* (see p. 108, for instance), I have no special attachment to the particles; I am happy to go with Spinoza and dispense with atomism. In so doing, however, we would not be abandoning an ontology of substances and properties. Spinoza's world is a world comprising a single substance, the One. This means that what we ordinarily think of objects – tables, human beings, galaxies – are in fact modes, ways the One is. The One might be space (as Descartes seems to have thought), or space-time, or the quantum field. I am more than happy to move in this direction, but I do not regard such a move as in any way a departure from my original conception.

Notice that it would be a mistake to describe an ontology of the One (as both Esfeld and Harbecke suggest) as an ontology of relations or events, an ontology

---

[1] This point is pressed by Jens Harbecke in his earlier comments.

that abandons "intrinsic properties".[2] It is a conventional substance/attribute ontology with a single substance. Ordinary objects are modes – intrinsic properties – of this substance. To get the picture, think of these objects as wave-like "thickenings" of regions of space-time. Locke, who was partial to the corpuscular picture, thought of ordinary objects as modes, too: fleeting arrangements of corpuscles. So I see the difference between Locke and Spinoza as purely quantitative. The big move is the move from thinking that we can tell from the grammar of a sortal term that, if it denotes anything, it must denote a substance. So far as I can tell, none of the great figures of the Enlightenment accepted this revered tenet of the Picture Theory. Trees and planets turn out to be modes, but no less trees and planets for that.

Esfeld's discussion of Humeanism raises different questions. My thoughts about Humeanism are captured by an old philosophical saw. Consider a world consisting of a flash followed by a bang. Unless you have ingrained Humean preconceptions, you are going to think that there are two possibilities here: (1) the bang merely follows the flash; (2) the flash caused the bang. I am not prepared to give up this conviction in the name of ontological economy.

Esfeld takes seriously the claim that an ontology of powers does not enjoy explanatory advantages over an austere Humeanism. Humeanism provides us with primitive correlations; powers require primitive connections. Humeans, however, are going to be hard pressed to distinguish, as we certainly do distinguish, between accidental and lawlike generalisations. More significantly, I think, powers make it clear why laws of nature do not entail corresponding generalisations. From the fact that water and salt have reciprocal powers that manifest themselves in salt's dissolving in water, it does not follow that all salt dissolves in water, or even that all salt, when placed in water dissolves. Powers can interfere with other powers. Laws of nature need have *no* instances. (For more on laws, see my reply to Padovani.)

Unless we avail ourselves of alternative worlds, Humeanism deprives us of the important insight that objects rarely do all they *could* do. It would be nice to think that there is something about this ball, something about this ball *here and now*, in virtue of which it *would* roll, even if it never does. I say this is a power, and to say that it is a power is not to say that it is not a quality: it is a powerful quality (see my reply to Freland). And I say that this power is explicable in terms of powers of more fundamental things making up the ball. Yes, there will be fundamental powers. But to regard a fundamental fact of this sort as on

---

[2] Far from being an ontology of relations, such an ontology is one in which relations are uniformly internal, hence no addition of being: there is just the One and its intrinsic properties.

a par with a fundamental Humean fact pertaining to every particular thing in this world and in an infinitude of alternative worlds is a stunning example of false economy: pennywise, pound foolish.

Esfeld has much of interest to say about reduction. I describe the position I favour as ontologically, but not analytically or epistemologically reductive. Put very crudely, the idea is that arrangements of the basic things (arrangements of corpuscles or ripplings in the One) serve as truthmakers for claims about the world. These include claims made by physicists, by psychologists, by economists, and claims we make in everyday life. Is this physicalism? I do not regard the mental – physical distinction as a deep one. There are physical truths and mental truths, truths articulated by physicists and by psychologists, but the truthmakers for these are the basic things appropriately arranged. As Esfeld makes clear, we can find asymmetry here, but not in the ontology. You might put it this way: every truthmaker could be given a description in terms of fundamental physics, but not every truthmaker can be given a psychological (or biological) description. Esfeld and I agree: this is in no sense a form of eliminativism.

Esfeld worries that I have left it mysterious how truths of the special sciences or of psychology latch onto the world as they do.

> "How can one show that, for instance, biological tokens and mental tokens are identical with configurations of physical tokens? That task would be easy if biological and mental properties were defined by their physical composition – as arguably chemical properties are." ((this volume), p. 200)

Suppose, as Kim has supposed, that special science concepts could be given functional analyses. This would point us toward configurations of more basic things, those, namely, occupying the right functional role. We could then devise descriptions in the a vocabulary suitable for these configurations. Given the phenomenon of "multiple realisability", there will be many such descriptions. Even so, we could treat each of these complex descriptions as a structured predicate satisfied unmysteriously by configurations of molecules (or whatever). Delving deeper, we could construct finer-grained functional predicates that, if we are on the ball, will line up with the fundamental physical predicates.

Consider solubility. The predicate "is soluble" applies truly to objects in virtue of those objects' possessing different kinds of molecular structure. This has led some philosophers to posit a higher-level property, solubility, corresponding to the predicate, and "multiply realised" by diverse molecular "realisers". Esfeld and I want to eliminate the middle-man and let the predicate "is soluble" be satisfied indifferently by the diverse configurations. But Esfeld worries that this makes it mysterious how "one and the same token can make true both a fundamental level physical description and higher-level descriptions" ((this volume), p. 201). His solution:

> ".. [Any] higher-level functional concept that a higher-level functional theory F uses can always be made more precise by introducing functional sub-concepts F_1, F_2, F_3, etc. These functional sub-concepts can be constructed in such a way that they are nomologically coextensive with the physical concepts P_1, P_2, P_3, etc. that are constructed within a fundamental physical theory in order describe in physical terms the tokens that make true the functional theory F. However, there is no question here of a semantic way of meaning analysis from the concepts of P to the concepts of F (and *vice versa*). The meaning of these concepts is distinct. The aim is to achieve a nomological coextension of certain concepts constructed within F with certain concepts constructed within P (see Esfeld & Sachse (2006 manuscript) and Sachse (this volume))." ((this volume), p. 202)

I allow a "higher-level" predicate, "F", to be satisfied by a range of imperfectly similar complex properties "P_1", "P_2", "P_3". Esfeld's idea is that we can, "working up", so to speak, construct predicates in the vocabulary of fundamental physics for each of these properties ("P_1", "P_2", "P_3") and, "working down", construct predicates "F_1", "F_2", "F_3" so as to achieve alignment. This provides a pipeline from the higher-level "F" to truthmakers that do double-duty as truthmakers for physical descriptions ("P_1", "P_2", "P_3").

I am unclear, however, what "F_1", "F_2", and "F_3" are supposed to add. Their construction relies on our prior apprehension of the extension of our original "F". Perhaps the idea is that the recognition that such predicates *could* be constructed brings with it recognition of the idea that truthmakers for applications of "F" are invariably truthmakers for the application of endless fine-grained physical predicates: "P_1", "P_2", "P_3".

I do not disagree with Esfeld, I just do not see the argument. Think of "F" as providing a description, which, supplemented by nonlinguistic interactions with the world, applies indifferently to P_1, P_2, P_3. Perhaps we could construct coordinated families of predicates here, but. it would seem, this is at most a reflection of the fact that P_1, P_2, P_3 answer to "F".

Undoubtedly I am being obtuse. Perhaps I have been put off by the notion that we need all the intermediate predicates in place to secure reference for higher-level predicates. On reflection, I do not think this is what Esfeld intends, however. The thought, put now in my own words, is that, for any higher-level predicate, "F", we could – or could in principle – look at the truthmakers for "F" and (1) find a description of each of these in the vocabulary of fundamental physics, (2) regard each of these as expressing a way of being F. To this, I have no objection.

Chapter 11

Representationalism and tactile "vision"

Michael Sollberger

In chapter 19 of his book *From an ontological point of view*, John Heil tackles the fundamental issue of representationalism according to which phenomenal content of perceptual experiences can be exhaustively accounted for by representational content. Heil's principal aim consists in showing that representationalism cannot be a coherent philosophical position. Instead of a strict representationalist conception of what perceptual phenomenology amounts to, he puts forward empirical as well as conceptual arguments that are supposed to establish the existence of intrinsic, non-representational qualia. In the present text, I shall discuss and evaluate these arguments by notably emphasising the role and philosophical implications of the empirical purpose. I shall argue that (I) prosthetic vision cannot settle the matter but reveals nonetheless a great deal of instructive findings about perception and that (II) Heil's arguments that are based solely on conceptual considerations, such as the distinction between representation and representational medium, are not conclusive.

1 A first distinction

What is the relation between properties possessed by perceptual experiences and properties possessed by objects experienced?[1] According to Heil, there is a clear-cut difference to be made between them. Suppose you are looking at a tree in front of you. That is, you are undergoing a particular kind of a visual experience of a tree by means of which you see that the tree has a brown trunk, that it is full of green leaves and so on. For simplicity reasons, let us say that all your visual experience is about a tree located in front of you, possessing the properties of having a brown trunk and wearing green leaves. Put differently, your are experiencing something that is shaped and coloured in a particular

---

[1] Throughout the whole text, I shall confine my analysis to perceptual experiences, letting aside other sensory experiences such as bodily sensations. Moreover, when I am talking about properties possessed by perceptual experiences, I always mean properties that are part or could be part of the phenomenology of experience. Neurobiological properties of, say, the central nervous system are therefore not paid attention to.

way. These shape-properties and colour-properties are properties of the object experienced conveyed by your perceptual experience. But what about the properties of your visual experience? It would be very counterintuitive to say that my visual experience has the same properties as the tree. My experience is not likely to be trunk-like shaped or even to be green. Intuitively, my visual experience of the tree does not share any properties with what it is an experience *about*. Admittedly, it is a hard task to spell out in any detail what properties of perceptual experiences really are, but this should not prevent us from assuming a sharp difference between *properties of experiences* and *properties of objects experienced*.

I take this fundamental distinction to be undebatable. There are good intuitive and empirical reasons to believe that my perceptual experience is neither shaped nor colored. Personally, I find it hard to make sense of the very idea that the perceptual state I am in *could* possess categorical properties like shape and color.[2] A possible diagnosis of why Heil thinks the difference intuitively so appealing could lie in the dual character of perceptual experiences: on the one hand, personal descriptions of perceptual experiences can be phenomenological in nature and make thereby an appeal to the felt and qualitative character or, if you want, to the *qualia* of experiences. So conceived, perceptual experiences are conscious states which we are *in*. There is something it is like to be in this particular state and this *what-it-is-likeness* phenomenologically differentiates it from other kinds of conscious perceptual states.[3] On the other hand, we can also focus on what perceptual experiences are about – their about-ness. My visual experience is about the tree with its properties and nothing else. What I want to point out is that these two perspectival aspects of perceptual consciousness involve a sharp difference in properties. Hence, it seems *prima facie* plausible that the properties the what-it-is-likeness and the about-ness of perceptual experiences point to respectively are not to be conflated with each other.

---

[2] Perhaps, some sense-data theorists were inclined to believe that whenever my perceptual experience is about something shaped and coloured, my experience itself has to be shaped and coloured.

[3] Conscious perceptual experiences seem to have some intrinsic qualities by means of which we can individuate and discriminate this particular kind of conscious state from other kinds of conscious states. Listening to a harmonic melody has not the same subjective feel as seeing a painting by Picasso. A gustatory experience of eating potatoes has plausibly nothing to do with feeling a fresh breeze on your skin. These distinct perceptual experiences have some consciously experienced qualities that clearly differ from each other. That's one reason why we can easily discriminate between several kinds of experiential consciousness.

Indeed, someone who is not sympathetic to this distinction might object that I wrongly take the purported what-it-is-likeness to be a genuine form of perceptual consciousness: imagine that you have a visual experience of the tree. How can you know what it is like to be in this conscious perceptual state? The answer, of course, is that you can know this only by introspecting it. But then there is nothing to be found through introspection that resembles shape or colour because introspection is not perceptual in character. Consequently, this qualitative character is trivially described by properties that are not referred to by perceptual means. And so it finally turns out that the diagnosis stressed above is really question begging.

Given that the strength of the counter-argument depends on a specific conception of what introspection is, I do not intend to discuss this argument here. However, as we shall see below, Heil grants that we can become introspectively aware of qualia by undergoing highly unusual experiences. Therefore, he himself should not endorse the counter-argument and should instead subscribe to the analysis according to which one reason for distinguishing between properties of experiences and properties of objects experienced is intimately linked to the dual character of perceptual experience.

2 Representationalism

But, we may ask, what does the qualitative character of perceptual experience – the qualia – really consist in? If qualities of experiences do not resemble qualities of objects experienced, how can we cope with such qualities? At this point, Heil (2003), p. 226, introduces representationalism: "Some philosophers hold that experiences are representational; what we might naturally regard as qualities of the experiences are at bottom *nothing more* than qualities we represent experienced objects as having" (my italics). But Heil thinks that the representationalist account is wrong and doubts "that these [representational] qualities exhaust the qualities of our experience ..." (Heil (2003), p. 226).

Before examining more closely Heil's objection, let us have a look at the proper representationalist claim. Representationalism is a theory about the phenomenal character of experiences. Its core idea can be stated by appeal to supervenience:

(R_W) The phenomenal character of an experience supervenes on its representational content.

Let us call R_W the *weak* thesis of representationalism. All it states is a dependence of phenomenal content on representational content. That is, you cannot alter the phenomenal content of a perceptual experience without *ipso facto* altering its representational content. But crucially, R_W does not yet tell us what experiential qualities of experiences in fact *are*. For this purpose, representationalists[4] adduce the *strong* or *pure* thesis:

(R_S) The phenomenal qualities of an experience are the same as the properties that objects are represented as having in the experience.

Strong representationalism thus affirms that properties of experiences are *identical with* representational properties: phenomenal properties of, say, a visual experience are identical with the "intentional" properties the visual stimulus is represented as exhibiting by the experience. All properties there are to experiential phenomenology are representational in nature, i.e. there is nothing to the what-it-is-likeness of conscious perceptual experiences over and above its representational qualities. In short, there are no intrinsic qualia that are non-representational.[5]

For a better understanding of what R_S and R_W result in, the notion of "representational content" has to be defined. "Representational content" is a term of art for how things are represented to be. Perceptual experience represents the world as being a particular way, that is the representational content of a conscious perceptual state represents things as being thus and so. The content of a perceptual state is how that state represents things as being – what is conveyed by the experience to the subject. My visual experience of the tree – whether I see it veridically or whether I hallucinate it – represents that there is a tree in front of me with a brown trunk and green leaves. These are the properties my experience represents the tree as having.

We are now in a position to see that Heil's first distinction between properties of experiences and properties of objects experienced is neither in conflict with R_W nor with R_S. For representationalism does not claim that my visual experience of the tree is trunk-like shaped or green; this would only be so if

---

[4] See for instance Tye (2002).

[5] A representationalist does not have to deny the existence of intrinsic qualia. For him, qualia can be *essential to* phenomenal experience to the extent that they make a particular kind of experience the kind of experience it actually is. Two experiences differing in qualia are two different kinds of experiences. So interpreted, "intrinsicness" means "essential to". The interpretation of intrinsicness of qualia representationalist are committed to rebutting is the one regarding qualia as *independent* or *monadic* properties of experiences without any relation to other things. Qualia would prove to be non-representational properties only in *this* way. See also Dretske (2000).

qualia were intrinsic and monadic properties of experiences. All it states is that having an experience of a tree is to represent the tree in a particular manner – having a visual experience of the tree means to visually represent the tree. Accordingly, phenomenal experiences can be localised in the central nervous system, but the properties one is aware of in having an experience are not in the central nervous system. In this sense, qualia can be representational or "intentional" properties of experiences.

As we shall see in the following sections, Heil aims at rebutting both R_W and R_S. By attacking R_W, he wants to show that phenomenal content does not supervene on representational content, and by arguing for the falsity of R_S he intends to establish the existence of non-representational qualities of perceptual experiences.

3 The transparency of experience

One main motivation for representationalism is the so-called *transparency of experience*. It is claimed that experience is *transparent* or *diaphanous* inasmuch as we "see through" our experiences straight to the world. The properties we are aware of in perceptual experiences are attributed to the perceived objects: "Look at the tree and try to turn your attention to intrinsic features of your visual experience. I predict you will find that the only features there to turn your attention to will be features of the presented tree, including relation features of the tree 'from here'." (Harman (1990), p. 39) The transparency-thesis can therefore be stated in the following way:

> (T_W) In perception, we do not notice that we are in perceptual states: we normally "see through" our various perceptual states to external objects. What we are aware of in perception are the properties attributed to the experienced objects.

Let us call T_W the *weak* transparency-thesis. Usually, T_W is considered as being too weak for supporting R_S because it does not show that perceptual experience has any other properties except for representational ones. The argument needs to be supplemented with additional premises:

> (T_S) In addition to T_W, two further claims are made: i) if there were additional mental properties to the properties we represent objects of experiences as having, we could know them by introspection but, ii) such properties are never revealed by introspection.

T_S stands for the *strong* transparency-argument, purporting to establish the nothing over and above clause about experience: in perception, there are no additional mental properties to the properties we represent objects as having – properties of experiences are identical with representational properties.

This identity-claim presents a difficulty to Heil. Although subscribing to T_W, he thinks that the diaphanous character of experience ultimately fools the representationalist point of view. The mere fact that we do not usually become aware of intrinsic qualities of our perceptual states does not imply that we cannot, as a matter of principle, become aware of them via some exceptional and unusual circumstances. As a consequence, point ii) of T_S is thought to be erroneous. Incidentally, the acceptance of the intuitive strength of T_W can make us forget that the felt and subjective character of experience must be acknowledged by residual, non-representational properties. Perceptual states we are in are admittedly diaphanous, but this transparency does not make non-existent the intrinsic qualities of experiences: T_S must be false because "having a diaphanous character is not the same as having no character at all" (Heil (2003), p. 226). In order to corroborate his statement, Heil describes the following scenario:

> "Imagine that you have dropped your keys behind the refrigerator. To retrieve them you use a stick to probe in the dark space between the refrigerator and the wall until, passing over clumps of dust, a dried apple core, and a mummified Tim Tam, you feel the keys and rake them out. In this case, you can literally feel the keys through the stick. Your use of the stick is, in Moore's sense, diaphanous. This does not mean, however, that there is no feeling of the stick in your hand as you probe. On the contrary, you *use* these feelings to acquire information about and, if you like, represent the location and character of the car keys. They make up what (following Martin) could be called the material of representation." (Heil (2003), p. 227)

> "In perceiving, we go into qualitatively distinctive sensory states. We (or our brains) use these states to represent how things stand outside us. So used, qualities of our representations become diaphanous; but they do not thereby disappear. Such qualities are not to be identified with qualities being represented." (Heil (2003), p. 227)

This analogy is not straightforward. Let me explain.[6] We should be extremely cautious not to mingle awareness of facts – that X is F – with awareness of

---
[6] The following account borrows from Dretske (2000), p. 456.

properties – the F-ness of X. Importantly, awareness of facts involves use of concepts: as long as I ignore the concept of F-ness, I cannot apply it to any object X. Hence, I cannot be aware of the fact that X is F without knowing when an object X falls under F. On the contrary, I can experience the pure sensory awareness of instantiations of properties – X's F-ness – without employing any concept at all. I may visually experience a tree with a brown trunk in front of me without knowing or possessing the concept of being brown. The same also goes for intrinsic shape properties: I may be visually aware of the shape-property of being a rhombic dodecahedron without being able to apply the concept of being a rhombic dodecahedron to that very object.

Deliberating in this vein, what we really feel by using the stick is some object, i.e. the stick, having some *textural* properties plus *proprioceptive* information about the relative position and movement of our body parts. Motricity and adequate behaviour are essential for gaining information about the keys: we follow the keys' contours and surfaces by being controlled by the incoming tactile data from our grip on the stick. From this *sensorimotor* awareness we *infer* that the end piece of the stick is in contact with a bunch of keys. All we are sensorily aware of then is the tactual feeling of the stick in our hand plus proprioception – i.e. pressure, texture and motricity. As a consequence, the properties we are sensorily aware of are tactile properties of the stick – the stick's F-ness. Hence, the stick-example is already a highly specific one by dint of which we perceive the fact that there is a key behind the refrigerator and not the key's properties. But concepts are *not essential* to perception, because we do not want to deprive babies and animals of genuine perception. This being so, Heil had better offer another analogy which operates without concepts. Otherwise, one might simply object that what the key-analogy attempts to suggest is not valid for usual perception.[7]

Note however that we have to separate the informational level from the phenomenological description. Surely, it is correct to describe the use of the stick as diaphanous, for trained subjects or blind people can acquire so much practical skill and ability in knowing with what kind of object the stick is in contact that they are no longer consciously aware of making any inference. Only in this sense, we may concede that we literally feel the keys through the stick, i.e. that its use is transparent. Nevertheless, as shown by the informational level, we are not in perceptual contact with properties of the keys. Here, we are still making inferences in order to unconsciously deduce a fact on the basis of sensorimotor awareness.

---

[7] At best, the example could be valid for what is sometimes called "epistemic perception".

Consider another example: if we *literally* felt that there were a bunch of keys behind the refrigerator, we would also be permitted to say that we *literally* hear on the phone that someone is unhappy. But this is not what really happens. All we hear are some sounds emitted from the telephone receiver, this is what we are sensorily aware of. In other words, we are aware of acoustic properties – the sensory material – from which we *infer* that the person with whom we are on the telephone is in a bad way. We do not directly hear his, say, unhappiness – with regard to the informational level, we infer that he is unhappy from what is sensorily given to us through this experience. Suppose your telephone partner intends to outsmart you by falsifying his voice. Then, you may *wrongly* think that he is unhappy. But you cannot be wrong as regards the acoustic properties – those representational properties the aural stimulus is represented as exhibiting by the experience – of which you are sensorily conscious. Hence, it is impossible to *literally* hear the unhappiness of your telephone partner. Of course, from a phenomenological point of view, you might testify to the transparency of the voice and sincerely report that you really heard the sadness of your telephone partner. But this is no guarantee of being in perceptual contact with properties referred to by that very experience. As a consequence, phenomenological descriptions on their own cannot reliably tell us whether we are aware of properties or of facts. This question has to be settled by further empirical investigation.

In what sense, then, is Heil's analogy to be read? By saying that the tactile feeling provides the material of representation, he seems to mean that we unconsciously use this sensory information in order to retrieve the keys. Taken one-to-one within the conceptual framework I stated previously, something strange and evidentially false would result, namely that property-awareness is supposed to be unconsciously used for inferring fact-awareness. This is clearly false, as we are sometimes perceptually aware of an object's properties without being fact-aware of that object.[8] This cannot be the story Heil has in mind. If so, we have to find a more flexible and coherent interpretation. Here I suggest a more promising alternative: the qualitative character of perceptual experiences is supposed to be unconsciously used for representing objects of perception. By carrying out this representational usage, these qualities become unconscious and, consequently, transparent. But contrary to what T_S purports, unconscious

---

[8] Obviously, we are unable to become fact-aware of an object without being able to be aware of its properties. But once again we have to emphasise that what we are seeking is a theory of perception at least capable of explaining how we can become perceptually aware of properties.

use of intrinsic qualities of representational sensory states is not tantamount to their non-existence. In the same way as we can focus on the stick's tactile properties, we should in principle also be able to gain introspective access to these experiential qualities.

The first main problem with this idea is the role of attention and transparency of the stick. Whereas we can easily become aware of the stick's tactual properties, it is difficult to see how this should work in usual perception. Keep in mind though that by a simple shift in attention, we can break the stick's transparency away and unveil formerly hidden tactual properties. Even more controversially, we can be aware of both the tactual properties and the fact that there is a bunch of keys at the same time. In usual perception this is not possible. You cannot become aware of the assumed non-representational qualities of experiences by simply shifting your attention. You may turn inwards your focus of attention and introspect your experience but, I predict that you will *prima facie* stumble across nothing but representational properties.[9] In any case, even if we took for granted that there were non-representational qualities of phenomenal experience, we could not identify their existence in the same vein as in the case of the stick's property-awareness. Therefore, the use of the stick seems not to be diaphanous in the same sense as are intrinsic qualities, if any, of representational sensory states.

A second worry concerns the unconscious use of phenomenal content. I take it to be uncontroversial that representational sensory states are effectively used in perception. Incidentally, the use of our central nervous system is clearly a necessary condition for perception. But how do we use it – by appeal to inference? How can the nature of this use be characterised? As long as Heil does

---

[9] When I direct my attention towards my perceptual experience, what I am in fact doing is to go into a higher-level perceptual state – a second-order perspective on my own conscious experience. But this shift in conscious perspective also entails a vivid difference in representational content. The second-order experience I am undergoing inevitably brings with it other properties that are part of its representational content. I submit that these newly added properties are qualities we represent our first-order experience as having. Unlike first-order perceptual experiences, the representational content of second-order perceptual experiences is enriched by the what-it-is-likeness of experiential consciousness. Experienced qualities of the respective experiences have become constitutive of second-order's representational content. Importantly, by undergoing an experience of an experience, I thereby focus my attention on the mode my experience represents things as being. In order to explicate that particular mode, however, I am relying on subjective qualities of my experiential consciousness. Albeit phenomenology strikingly differs from first-order to second-order experiences, the difference in phenomenal content issues from distinct representational contents. An easy shift in attention, as in the stick's case, may thus not be sufficient to get us directly in touch with non-representational qualia.

not clarify this issue more explicitly, his suggestion remains vague. Note also that the stick-example is of no help here: in opposition to the tactile properties of the stick, it is possible that we cannot as a matter of principle become aware of the conjectured intrinsic and non-representational qualia in perception.

Against such a background, we are no longer in a position to assert the existence of qualia on *a priori* grounds alone. It remains an open question whether there are such properties behind the veil of transparency. If phenomenal content were really used for deducing or acquiring representational content, this process could not be phenomenologically explained: my experience of the tree represents to me the tree as having some properties without there being any conscious inference to make – I am *immediately* and *directly* aware of its representational properties. In phenomenological terms, we neither infer X's F-ness nor that X is F in virtue of the qualitative part of perceptual experiences. As a consequence, the link between the what-it-is-likeness and about-ness of perceptual experiences has to be spelled out differently as it is suggested in Heil's analogy.

4   Tactile "vision"

By alluding to an empirical experiment, Heil intends to establish the falsity of R_W as well as of T_S (since R_S implies R_W, he *eo ipso* intends to show that R_S is false too). In a first step, I shall briefly describe what the experiment consists of. In a second step, I shall set out my provisos against Heil's interpretation of the argument. And finally, I shall try to show what alternative philosophical upshot the experiment supports.

4.1   The TVSS device and its empirical results

In a nutshell, a sensory substitution device such as TVSS (Tactile Vision Substitution System) is a prosthetic device which should enable congenitally blind persons to "see". Transforming stimuli characteristic of the sensory modality vision into the other sensory modality touch, TVSS converts the optical image captured by a video camera (the sensor serving as an artificial eye) into an isomorphic tactile image.[10] This tactile image is brought about by a matrix of 400 activators which are arranged in 20 rows and 20 columns of solenoids of one millimeter diameter each. Usually, the matrix – i.e. the stimulator array – is

---

[10] That is, the pattern of tactile stimulation matches and roughly corresponds to the enlarged optical image.

placed either on the subject's back or chest, so that the somatosensory system senses the incoming mechanical energy.

After some training, the congenitally blind persons can detect simple targets and as such are also able to orient themselves. The greater is the training with TVSS the better is the recognition of geometric shapes and ordinary objects. Astonishingly, congenitally blind persons trained with TVSS report a striking phenomenon of *externalisation*: initially, all the subject consciously feels is the tactile contact of the matrix's solenoids on his skin. But after some training, the subject becomes aware of distal objects that are located "out there" in space. That is to say that the subject more and more neglects the successive tactile stimulations on his skin and, instead, becomes aware of stable objects that are at a distance in front of him.[11] Importantly, according to subjects' testimony, the tactile stimulations caused by the matrix can be recalled to awareness at any time and can thus be distinguished from the perception itself. Furthermore, a number of experimental observations confirm that blind persons equipped with TVSS are able to detect perceptive features that are completely new to their experience, such as the interposition of objects, occlusion, moving flames of lighted candles, parallax and many other Gestalt laws.[12] Most impressively, it is even reported that optical illusions – such as the waterfall-effect – can be reproduced by using TVSS devices.[13]

It must be emphasised that these remarkable results can only be achieved by allowing the blind person to actively manipulate the video camera. By making camera-movements from the left to the right, focussing, zooming forward and backward etc., the subject discovers in which way his various sensations correlate with his performed actions. Without any exploratory activity on the part of the subject, the externalisation-process described above does not happen. The establishment of *sensorimotor rules* seems thus necessary for gaining subjective perception of shapes, forms, size etc. of objects in visual space.[14]

---

[11] Note that subjects had no problem transferring the matrix to different skin locations – as from the back to the chest for instance – without affecting recognition skills they previously learned.

[12] Bach-y-Rita (2002), p. 500.

[13] Bach-y-Rita, p. 498. The waterfall-effect consists in the following phenomenon: when you look a couple of time at the water falling continuously down the waterfall and then turn your visual attention towards the unmoved rock at one side of the waterfall, you will have the visual illusion that the rock "flows upstairs".

[14] The talk of sensorimotor rules is to be understood as meaning "a set of rules of interdependence between stimulation and movement". For an elaboration of this idea, cf. Noë & O'Regan (2002) who use the term "sensorimotor contingencies".

4.2 Seeing with the skin?

One philosophically interesting matter to be decided is the following: are persons *seeing with the skin* by using the device? Heil thinks they effectively do:

> "Imagine an agent equipped with an augmented TVSS, one capable of representing all that can be visually represented. I suggest that, despite representational parity, the experience of 'seeing' with a TVSS differs qualitatively from the experience of seeing with the eyes. In both cases, the sensory medium is effectively diaphanous and difficult, even impossible, to describe independently of the objects it is used to represent. Indeed there might be no functional difference between an agent equipped with a TVSS and a sighted agent. ... Nevertheless, I submit that the agents' experiences differ qualitatively." (Heil (2003), p. 228)

This is a tempting interpretation indeed but, in what follows, I shall enumerate four reasons that call Heil's viewpoint into question. But before entering the debate, just one *caveat*: unless subjects trained with TVSS do not give a completely erroneous description of their experiences, I take it for granted that they are, among others, aware of some categorical *visual* properties and not only of facts as in the stick-example. The question at hand is how we could make sense of visual illusions – such as the waterfall-effect, for instance – if not by presupposing that subjects directly are in perceptual contact with visual properties? If I am not mistaken, this discrepancy can be accounted for by an appeal to information processing of the central nervous system – especially the brain's plasticity. The somatosensory cortex might be capable of extracting spatially coded information and visual-motor invariants from the incoming tactile-motor information. What is usually thought to be performed by visual cortices might thus be analysed and treated by other cortical areas as well. However, it seems quite clear that the point at issue is an empirical one and cannot be resolved by *a priori* reasoning alone.

(I) In order to make perceptual judgements, subjects using TVSS are typically relying on visual *means* (interposition, occlusion etc.) but not on visual phenomenology. They refer to *cues* in identification and object recognition.[15] For sure, there is clearly a *spatial function* of TVSS, but spatial function is not sufficient for visual phenomenology. Non-visual senses of

---

[15] Cf. Guarniero (1974). We find these cues in monocular vision, such as familiar size and interposition of objects.

other creatures may be spatial in the same manner – like the lateral line of fishes – without being accompanied by visual phenomenology.[16]

(II) What about the agents' possibility to shift his attention to the tactile irritations on his skin? It may be assumed that the phenomenology of TVSS is a *new kind* of phenomenology, one that is described by subjects partly by visual and partly by tactile means. Its phenomenal content is derived from spatial as well as tactile content. In addition, both vision and touch can give us sensory access to spatial content, although spatial content in vision differs from spatial content in touch. Why not claim that the spatial content of TVSS is visual and not tactile? We may then insist upon visual phenomenology of TVSS as regards its spatial content. Its tactile content, however, does not evaporate; it prohibits the overall phenomenology of TVSS to be exclusively visual.

(III) Not being a matter of all or nothing, we might talk about a *quasi-visual phenomenology* of TVSS.[17] Vision involves lots of different aspects and TVSS may provide us with some but not all of them. This, after all, incorporates just the idea that "seeing" with the skin and seeing with the eyes have *common sensibles*. Since depth cues and their sensorimotor rules are a part of the features exclusive to the visual domain, there probably is a big share of seeing by gaining access to these traits.[18] Among other Gestalt laws and heuristics of the visual system, familiar size and interposition are visual invariants both in TVSS and vision and are therefore very similar to each other. On the contrary, stereovision is completely absent in TVSS. But what about stereo blind or one-eyed persons? It goes without saying that we are ready to attribute vision to them. Does this signify that blind persons using TVSS do see in the same way? Not necessarily. Visual invariants we seemingly encounter both in vision and TVSS are not related, respectively, to the same sensorimotor rules. Supposing that these senso-

---

[16] The lateral line is a sensory organ consisting of fluid filled sacs with hair-like sensory apparatus that are open to the water through a series of pores (creating a line along the side of the fish). Sensing water currents and pressure, the lateral line is capable of localising the source of underwater vibrations.

[17] This thesis is also empirically supported. After training, the regional cerebral blood flow changes and shows a significant occipital increase in the blind persons (in neurobiology, occipital cortex regions are thought to be mainly concerned with processing of visually coded information).

[18] By sensorimotor rules, I mean rules applied to neurophysiological cycles and circuits that connect sensory data with other sensory data and with motricity (behavior). For instance, when we see a tiger (visual data) we usually get anxious (emotional data) and take flight (motricity).

rimotor rules play a role in contributing to the particularities of different modalities, the phenomenology of visual invariants will not be experienced identically in TVSS and vision.[19]

(IV) Heil points to the *functional equivalence* between an agent equipped with TVSS and a normal sighted agent. I take this to be illusory, as we are not to confuse visual-motor rules with sensorimotor rules *tout court*. Both agents might be functionally indistinguishable *with respect to* the spatial content of their perceptual experience (cf. point II). But this only concerns visual-motor rules and not sensorimotor rules. The representational content of TVSS experiences conveys spatial as well as tactile information. This kind of tactile information being absent in normal vision, the overall sensorimotor rules then change from TVSS to vision and with it the agents' functional dispositions.

4.3 What TVSS really tells us

The precedent considerations yield a clear denial of the idea that TVSS could provide a counter-example against R_W and T_S. I tried to frame two main criticisms: first, as said by Heil, "seeing" with the skin is not like seeing with the eyes; second, contrary to what Heil suggests, representational content in TVSS cannot be the same as in normal vision *in principle*. Consequently, we cannot become introspectively aware of non-representational qualia by undergoing TVSS experiences in the way Heil envisages. Representationalists may thus simply reply that what-it-is-like to "see" with TVSS does not equate what-it-is-like to see with the eyes in virtue of the fact that the respective representational contents of the two experiences are not at all the same. After having said what TVSS does not imply, let us now have a look at what it can positively tell.

To my mind, what is plainly called into question by TVSS findings is every philosophical account according to which perception rests upon *passively* received information. As presented in section 4.1, the subject must be able to *causally interact* with his environment, otherwise the experience remains wholly tactile. By executing this exploratory activity, he seeks and constructs rules of lawful relations between his behaviour and subsequent sen-

---

[19] The underlying idea is that different modalities such as vision, audition, degustation etc. owe their particular phenomenal character in part to the specificities of their respective sensorimotor rules. Against such a background, we cannot really isolate vision from motricity and from other senses. Systematic correlations and interactions between them are always to be expected.

sations. Only in this way the subject becomes aware of the emergence of structured percepts containing, among others, categorical visual properties. Sensation and active exploration (motricity/behaviour) cannot be dissociated from each other in order to get TVSS's quasi-visual phenomenology. This points to the essential part of *sensorimotor rules* in perception: perception and action go hand in hand.[20] The perceptual content of structured percepts is determined by the agents' interaction with the environment, i.e. by the sensorimotor rules. In consequence, given that perceptual states are the representational states we are in, representational content of perceptual experiences is fixed by sensorimotor rules: representational content supervenes on sensorimotor rules. And, if we further assume the validity of R_W, we can infer that phenomenal content of experiences supervenes on sensorimotor rules. Note, however, that this is not to say that the phenomenal character of perceptual experiences is identical with or nothing over and above the sensorimotor rules. These rules only determine the felt character of perceptual experiences – no identity-thesis whatsoever is stated.

Furthermore, these findings support *externalism* with respect to perceptual content.[21] Roughly, this kind of externalism claims that causal relations with the environment in part *determine* perceptual content. This evidently is the case in TVSS, provided that "perceptual content" means "what is conveyed to you by the experience". Causally interacting with our environment is necessary for structured percepts along with quasi-visual phenomenology to come into existence. The striking difference in TVSS's perceptual content – vibration on the skin vs. distal objects in space – is thus due to changing causal relations with the environment. Hence, in order to account for perceptual content, we always

---

[20] Instead of demanding that action has to be actually accomplished we might talk of dispositions to act in an adequate way. A further point that has to be raised is whether the subject's exploratory activity must really be executed actively. Perhaps, and this might be a viable metaphysical possibility, passive movement on its own may be sufficient for establishing sensorimotor rules. We may imagine a subject passively sitting on a chair moving through the landscape; as I see it, TVSS does not *a priori* exclude the possibility that such a subject cannot acquire the relevant sensorimotor rules and thereby get the TVSS's quasi-visual phenomenology. Against such as background, it might be more appropriate to highlight the essential part of *movement* in perception than that of action.

[21] Note that Heil's *internalistic* contention is about content of thoughts and not about content of perceptual states. See (Heil (2003), § 18). Additionally, note that this sort of externalism I am referring to does not claim an ontol-ogical dependence of perceptual content on ontologically independent objects – all it talks about is causal dependence. After all, empirical experiments are clearly inapt to yield some argument for or against ontological externalism.

have to consider the causal activities we exert in connection with our environment – these activities partly *determine* what perceptual content consists of.

5 Representation and representational medium

Arguing against R_S, Heil insists on distinguishing representation and representational medium: imagine having the film *The legend of Zorro* on DVD as well as on VHS. Though being assembled from different materials, DVD and VHS are *representational media* in which the optical patterns of *The legend of Zorro* are embedded. In both cases, these media are used to represent the same objects and their properties. That is to say that we can have a great variety of representational media having the same representational content. But properties represented by the DVD and VHS – say hero Zorro who is saving his beautiful wife – are not identical with properties of the DVD and VHS *qua* representational media. There is a key difference between properties of the representational medium and properties of what it represents.

> "Representation requires a representational medium; the use of a representation requires the use of this medium. You can create a representation using oil paints and canvas, or water colours on paper, but you cannot manufacture a pure representation. When we use a representation as representation, we typically ignore this medium (the medium becomes diaphanous). ... If conscious experiences are representational, then, they cannot be wholly representational. They must have qualities not reducible to represented qualities. These account for at least some of the character of conscious experiences, their what-it-is-likeness." (Heil (2003), p. 231)

There are compelling reasons that this argument is sound. For it is quite fair to assume that perceptual experiences at least partly supervene on physiological states of our overall central nervous system and particularly on brain-states. If so, the central nervous system with its anatomy and physiological functioning figures as the representational medium by means of which we represent our environment. This medium is characterised by neurobiological properties. The crucial idea, then, is that these neurobiological properties, on their own, contribute to the phenomenal character of perceptual experiences: "The what-it-is-likeness of conscious experience stems from the nature of the representational medium and (as the representationalists' contend) what is represented" (Heil

(2003), p. 229). Via a slight modification of R_W we arrive at what I take to be Heil's alternative account:

(C_{Heil}) The phenomenal character of an experience supervenes on its representational content *plus* the nature of the representational medium.[22]

From now on, intrinsic properties of the medium have to be taken into consideration. For instance, think of spooky ghosts-entities whose make-up has nothing to do with ours. According to C_{Heil}, these beings will probably not have the same phenomenal content as we do, even though, it is assumed, we both share the same representational content.[23] I take this outcome to be plausible.

However, the argument is a conceptual one. All it shows is that we cannot easily conceive of *pure* representations that could be thoroughly characterised in terms of representational properties. Our concept of "representation" always requires a medium in virtue of which the representational function can be carried out. But does this suffice for C_{Heil}? As we saw, there is no other evidence in favour of C_{Heil}, be it empirical or conceptual. If the existence of intrinsic, non-representational properties of perceptual experiences stood and fell with this argument, Heil would be skating on thin ice.

Moreover, his own ontological framework could be advanced against C_{Heil}. In the light of Heil's denial of the Picture Theory of language (p. 5) and of a corollary of it, namely principle Φ,[24] it seems as though he should grant that the conceptual difference he is relying on between representational properties and properties of the representational medium is only a difference in description but not in entities. Like in his example with the Necker cube (p. 120), what we are actually dealing with are two different epistemic ways of describing ontologically identical properties. The talk about intrinsic-categorical qualia on the one hand and extrinsic-representational properties on the other is comparable with two perspectives which both refer to the same property. If this is

---

[22] In order to have a more elaborated idea of what C_{Heil} amounts to, we would have to know what is exactly meant by the representational medium's "nature". As a first approximation, we may think of the medium's intrinsic make-up together with the functional role it plays in the relevant context.

[23] We assume in addition that these spooky ghost-entities can represent the same things as we do. This point should be granted because, as we saw above with DVD and VHS, different representational media can represent the same things.

[24] (Φ) "When a predicate applies truly to an object, it does so in virtue of designating a property possessed by that object and by every object to which the predicate truly applies (or would apply)." (p. 26)

correct, then C_{Heil} falls short of Heil's own ontology and, in the end, he should subscribe to R_S.

There is still another proposal representationalists might make contra C_{Heil}: all they have to point to is an asymmetry in the above analogy. They could, for instance, underscore the role of *consciousness* or *activity* in human representation: in opposition to canvas, oil paints, DVD and VHS, human cognisers are conscious beings who actively represent their environment. Hence, undergoing a perceptual experience and thereby representing things might not obey the same *conceptual* constraints as DVD's and the like. Further, they could simply deny that representational media such as DVD's are diaphanous in the same way as perception: representational media prove diaphanous only temporarily, namely inasmuch as we are accustomed to direct our attention to their representational function. But this contingent matter is due only to habit and thus shows nothing essential about representational media. Perception however, is essentially diaphanous and so in the end, the analogy fails.[25]

---

[25] I was claiming in chapter 4.2 that blind people can get in direct perceptual contact with visual properties thanks to TVSS. But since we can become aware of tactile sensations on the skin as well as of distal objects in space, does this prove that perception is not essentially diaphanous? I do not think that TVSS is a case where we can lift the veil of transparency and thereby become aware of non-representational qualia. From a phenomenological point of view, the tactile sensation on the skin has nothing to do with the perception of distal objects. Rather, we are aware of two different perceptual occurrences. Therefore, a shift in attention from visual perception to haptic perception and *vice versa* does not reveal non-representational qualia of perceptual consciousness. Consequently, as described by Heil, perceiving visual properties with the help of TVSS is diaphanous without constituting a counter-argument against the thesis that perception is essentially diaphanous.

Commentary

John Heil

Sollberger makes a number of interesting points, but I am not convinced that the various positions he attacks are ones that I defend or would want to defend. As a rule in philosophy, it is wise to be wary of criticisms that begin with reformulations of the position under attack the proceed to show that these lead to absurdity. Under the circumstances, it occurs to me that the most sensible way to respond to Sollberger is to say clearly what I had in mind in discussing qualities of experience. It remains to be seen whether the points I intended to make are susceptible to Sollberger's criticisms.

First, it is important to note that my qualms about the adequacy of representationalist accounts of conscious experience were never meant as decisive refutations, much less as a basis for an alternative theory of conscious experience. On my view perceptual experiences of the world around us are mutual manifestations of features of our perceptual system and features of incoming stimuli. This, I think, is perfectly consistent with any number of accounts of perception and perceptual experience.

Second, I have argued at some length elsewhere that the senses are best individuated by reference to the nature of the stimuli from which they are used to extract information as to how things stand distally (see Heil (1983), chapter 1, Heil (forthcoming)). Vision, for instance, is concerned with the extraction of information from structured ambient light; audition concerns information extraction from impact waves in the medium in which the perceiver is embedded.

Sollberger is sceptical that it is right to associate vision with a TVSS. But if it works, a TVSS supplies information carried in structured light, and it is natural to associate vision with light. How would you decide whether an Alpha Centaurian had eyes? Well, one possibility is that you would try to discover whether the creature had a light-sensitive organ that it used to negotiate its environment. Unlike sonar, eyes don't work, or work as well, in the dark; unlike touch, eyes don't enable us to see around opaque barriers. I say the TVSS affords primitive vision. If you disagree, the ball is in your court: how ought we to individuate the senses?

So I take a TVSS to provide a feeble kind of prosthetic vision. Agents using a TVSS are initially aware of goings on at the interface of the device and their skin. But they quickly learn to use the device to extract information about their environment from ambient light. Sollberger thinks that information extraction requires action on the part of the perceiver. Speaking as someone who studied under and admired J. J. Gibson, I am happy to agree. Indeed, this is something on which I would want to insist. None of this has much to do with qualities of conscious perceptual experiences, however.

A third point worth noting is that I argue at some length in *From an ontological point of view* that properties of concrete objects quite generally are both qualitative and dispositional. Properties are powerful qualities. Whatever you might think of this doctrine, it implies that *anything*, any concrete object, with properties has qualities. The thought that qualities (or "intrinsic qualities" – are there *extrinsic* qualities?) are peculiarly mental is an old idea going back to Renaissance science, which regarded the world as a colourless, silent, antiseptic expanse of particles in motion. This shifts qualities from the world to the mind; all well and good for the physicists, but hard to square with a conception of the mind rooted in the natural world. If minds have qualities, then these had better not be alien to the world physics tells us is out there.

What I find puzzling about attempts to reduce qualities of experience to qualities experienced things are represented as possessing, is that this seems clearly to leave out consideration of the representational medium and *its* qualities. You will have to admit that it is hard to see how you could have a representation without a *medium* of representation. This medium, simply by virtue of having properties, has qualities of its own. A photograph has qualities describable quite independently of whatever it is a photograph of. Of course it might be natural to describe a photograph by describing what it is a photograph of, but that is another matter.

Sollberger seems to think that it is an argument against this point to say that, in considering the photograph's qualities, we are considering qualities we represent it to have. Yes we are. But these qualities can be just as real as those of objects the photograph depicts.

My invocation of the TVSS in *From an ontological point of view* (chapter 19) was meant as a way of bringing home this point about the importance of representational media. Anyone who concedes that a TVSS, or an enhanced, science fiction version of a TVSS affords prosthetic vision would surely concede that the way objects are experienced via a TVSS differs from the way they are experienced via normal vision. Sollberger spends a good deal of time pointing out how use of a real TVSS falls far short of vision. I agree. It seems possible to imagine two creatures, however, one with limited monochromatic vision, and one whose visual system is the biological counterpart of a dramatically enhanced TVSS. I say (1) there is no reason these creatures could not find themselves in representationally equivalent perceptual states, but (2) there is some reason to think that the qualities of their experiences will differ. This is not a deep argument, it is an appeal to your capacity to imagine what it would be like to encounter the world with a very different kind of visual system.

Chapter 12

Intentionality is not only a mark of the cognitive

Marc Aurel Hunziker

The paper firstly provides a sceptic look at Heil's point of view of intentionality and diagnoses a lack of clarity. Heil does not clearly side with one of the prominent views about the subject of intentionality and seems to waver between a naturalistic position (intentionality is a common feature of all kind of dispositions) and a position that is likely to be a traditional one (intentionality is a feature of the mental only). In a second step the paper tries to shed light on Heil's view by considering different positions about intentionality and dispositions. Finally, the paper sets out a moderate alternative view of intentionality that claims that there are unconscious representational states. This position clearly avoids including radical naturalistic claims and is likely to be compatible with Heil's intended depiction of intentionality.

1 Heil on intentionality

Since Franz Brentano, intentionality is generally taken to be an important mark of the mental. The capacity to represent or to be-about was considered by Brentano to characterise mental states only (cf. Jacob (2003)). Philosophers who develop theories about intentionality normally either side with Brentano's dictum or argue against it by claiming that intentionality is something which is afforded already by purely physical entities. At first glance, Heil seems to side with Brentano's view. His definition is meagre but clearly defines intentionality as a feature of a cognitive mental state: "Intentionality is the capacity for representational thought." (Heil (2003), p. 208) This view is supported by the remark that the self-concept of intelligent agents and intentionality are conceptually entangled. In a second step, Heil analyses dispositions and emphasises that dispositions project or are directed towards their possible manifestations. Dispositions can even be directed towards their non-existent manifestations and therefore possess the "mark of the intentional", the intentional state's being about a non-existent manifestation (Heil's example is this one: a salt crystal drifting in a universe that lacks water would still be water soluble). The directedness exhibited by ordinary dispositions seems to be sufficient to claim that dispositions afford "natural intentionality" (Heil's inverted commas). Heil's clearly indicated aim is to make sense of the intentionality of intelligent agents by making use of the "natural intentionality" afforded by dispositions. Thoughts about x analysed as an internal manifestation of the disposition to react with the entity x in a certain way, e.g. to utter sentences containing the name "x", should, according to Heil, allow us to understand the directedness of intentional states. Generally speaking, the directedness of thoughts and other mental states lies in the dispositionality of agents.

Heil's exposition of the phenomenon of intentionality is vague and certainly needs some further explications. It is unclear whether we should understand Heil's conception as naturalistic (intentionality is clearly a feature of the physical) or traditional (intentionality is only a mark of the mental). Given the first case, we could understand the talk of "natural intentionality" either as the commitment to intentionality being a widespread feature of nature (every entity that possesses dispositions has intentional states) or we could understand that talk as referring to a feature that only complex entities equipped with dispositions exhibit, such as animals. The claim then is that intentionality is not a feature of conscious mental states only. While the first reading is in conflict with Heil's above mentioned definition of intentionality, the second reading stands in a sharp contrast to the view that dispositions afford "natural intentionality". These unclear points catapult the chapter about intentionality into nebulous fields, the statements are unclear and in the worst case contradictory.

The most relevant question is what "natural intentionality" means. Is this only a metaphor to express certain similarities between mental states and dispositions (therefore the inverted commas) or does Heil support the view that, in Molnar's words, "something *very much like* intentionality is a pervasive and ineliminable feature of the physical world" (Molnar (2003) p. 61, his italics)? Should we understand "natural intentionality" in the sense that it is the kind of intentionality which is found in inanimate entities such as electrons and salt crystals? Does this kind of primitive intentionality provide the starting point for an evolution of intentionality towards the kind we find in intelligent agents? If this were the case, could we think of it, in Martin's words, as being important "for a gradualist and naturalistic depiction of the evolving of the mental from the non-mental" (Martin (1996) p. 191)?

2 The marks of intentionality and intentionality as a feature of the non-mental

In Martin and Pfeifer (1986) and Place (1996) we can find five features of intentionality, while Molnar (2003) mentions only four and Bird (forthcoming), chapter 6, expands the set of features to six. Summing up, one can say that the most salient features of intentionality are the following five ones:

(I) *Directedness*:

An intentional state is directed to something beyond itself, to the intentional object.

(II) *The possible inexistence of the object towards which an intentional state is directed*:

The existence of the object towards which an intentional state is directed is never guaranteed.

(III) *Indeterminacy*:

Intentional objects are vague in the sense that in the paradigmatic case of thought the object is not thought of as an object of e.g. a particular height, whereas actual objects are never vague or indeterminate.

(IV) *Intensionality/"referential opacity"*:

If two substantival expressions designate the same object, the truth value of a sentence that contains one of these expressions is not preserved if the one substantival expression is substituted for the other one within an intensional context.

(V) *Chisholm's permissible falsity of an embedded declarative sentence*:

Neither the truth nor the falsity of a proposition is implied by the use of an embedded declarative sentence in order to ascribe an intentional state to someone or something.

In their 1986 analysis, *Intentionality and the non-psychological*, Martin and Pfeifer demonstrate that the salient features of intentionality all fail to distinguish intentional mental states from non-intentional dispositional physical states. In a less opaque study in 1996, *Intentionality as the mark of the dispositional*, Place subsequently follows this analysis and considered intentionality to be the mark of the dispositional. Place concluded that Brentano got it wrong and that "intentionality is a technical term whose meaning is fixed by the criteria which philosophers have proposed for its use ... and that intentionality is the mark, not of the mental, but of the dispositional" (Place (1996), p. 92). Place further developed his approach and drew a distinction between the marks of intentionality and intensionality. The latter is, Place thought, a feature of locutions and sentences whereas intentionality applies to states and events (cf. Bird (forthcoming), chapter 6). An intensional object or context denotes the grammatical object of a verb. This allows for the distinction between intensional and extensional contexts. The intentional object denotes the object towards which an intentional state is directed. According to this definition, we should understand the first three of the mentioned features as marks of an intentional state, while the latter two apply to intensional sentences only. Place considers the first three marks to be "aspects of a single principle, the principle whereby an intentional state is directed [in our case: mark I] towards the coming about of a state of affairs which not only need not, but does not yet exist [mark II], and whose precise form will remain indeterminate [mark III] until it does which it will may never do" (Place (1996), p. 105). Directedness is therefore a sufficient condition for intentionality.

In Place's view, dispositions are states such that the entity that possesses the dispositions is orientated towards the coming about of a possible future state which does not yet exist and which may never exist, but which, if it exists and thus becomes determinate, will constitute a manifestation of that disposition (cf. Place (1996), p. 105). This analysis establishes a conceptually necessary connection between dispositions and intentional states.

Since Place does not accept an ontology which conceives properties as being categorical and dispositional in one and therefore stands in opposition to Heil, I think we should leave him here. Nonetheless, it is important to notice the similarities between Heil's and Place's positions. Heil seems to accept the conclusion that dispositions are directed towards their manifestation and he considers that directness to be sufficient for "natural intentionality". This reading would entitle us to remove the inverted commas and to conclude that intentionality is a widespread feature of the world.

Another approach by Molnar (2003) tries to show that something very much like intentionality is a salient feature of the physical world. Molnar distinguishes *mental intentionality* (MI) from *physical intentionality* (PI) and warns of the overestimation of the analogy between these two kinds of intentionality, because they are not exactly similar (cf. Molnar (2003), p. 68). Molnar states that the directedness of intentionality is often explained by the ability of items being able to point to something beyond themselves only by somehow including or containing *a representation* of the entity to which they point (cf. Molnar (2003), p. 71). Representative items are mainly explained as parts of a symbolic system that refer to, or describe, something beyond themselves. This view maintains that intentionality can only be explained and understood on the basis of a theory of meaning as aboutness and therefore puts forward an argument against (PI) because physical dispositions have no intelligible content that represents their manifestations. Generally speaking, the projectibility, the directedness, of physical dispositions could not be explained in semantic terms according to this point of view. Molnar's line of argumentation mainly aims at the destruction of the thesis that intentionality can only be explained and understood from within a theory of meaning. He argues for the existence of a certain kind of states or properties that are (I) mental, (II) not semantic (therefore not representational), but (III) intentional and therefore enable one in analogy to (MI) to ascribe intentionality to physical states.

The paradigmatic example is pain, which we regard, for the sake of the argument (let us forget about hardcore cognitivists' claims), as a mental state. Pain undoubtedly fits into most of the features of intentionality mentioned. Pains are *directed* in the sense that they are felt at a location and are individuated by their location. Furthermore, phantom limb pain occurs at *non-existent locations*. Sometimes one cannot locate pain at a *determinate* location, it may be fuzzily bounded (one my feel pain "below" the knee, "near" the elbow). *Opaque contexts* are created by ascriptions of pain-at-a-location. Compare the following examples: if a CD is in a computer and the computer is in the office, then there is a CD in the office. If pain is in one's finger and the finger in one's mouth, then there is pain in one's mouth. Since there is no reason to assume that there is a multiple understanding of "in", the differences in the example arise from differences in the two contexts of use of the word – the one transparent and the other one opaque (cf. Molnar (2003), p. 75).

Are pains meaningful? Since there is no aspect or element distinguishable within the sensation of pain that refers to, or describes, the location in which pain is felt, in the way in which an auditory image is involved in the hearing of a sound that may be taken as representing the sound as it was emitted, Molnar does not find any representational content in pain. Pains do not mean their location and do not represent something as hurting but the subject experiencing pain gets information about the location of pain due to the transparent character of the experience. Molnar therefore concludes that pain is directed towards its intentional object without representing it.

All this leads Molnar to the suggestion that there are two kinds of (MI) which correspond roughly to the traditional division of the mind into the rational and the sentient. While the intentionality of the rational mind is analysable in terms of semantic content, the intentionality of the sentient mind is not. Bodily sensations afford non-symbolic information-conveying relations to some of their non-accidental companions (i.e. their causes, in the case of pain bodily damage or disturbance), but not to the locations that are their intentional object. Since the directedness of sensations to their intentional object cannot be understood in terms of meaning at all, Molnar concludes that we cannot distinguish between sensations and purely physical dispositions.

Heil seems to be very close to Molnar's analysis. On the one hand, natural intentionality in inverted commas could be understood as (PI) which is not exactly similar to (MI). On the other hand, Heil never speaks of dispositions representing something; he only mentions the projectibility or the directedness of dispositions. Although there are these similarities between Heil and Molnar, this cannot be the whole story of Heil's approach to intentionality. According to Heil, intentionality is grounded in the dispositionality of agents. This points rather to an understanding of the intentionality of intelligent agents which is gradually developed from the intentionality that we find already on a very basic level of simple physical dispositions. How should we otherwise understand the claim that we should make use of the "natural intentionality" which is afforded by dispositions to make sense of the intentionality of intelligent agents?

Another approach by Martin and Pfeifer (1986) considered the lack of distinction between purely physical and mental dispositions to be a serious threat to the typical notion of intentionality and a "quick road to panpsychism". Subsequently, they offered an alternative analysis which should prevent us from falling into animism. The key to the problem is to note the fact that some intentional states possess representations which are directed to a unique particular thing and not to everything else which "happens to be just like it" (Martin and Pfeifer (1986), p. 551). The same cannot be said for causal dispositions and capacities because they are *for* things or states of affairs of *a kind*. If Alphöhi wants *his* Alphorn, he is interested only in exactly *that* Alphorn and not just anything like it. Every copy or replica might satisfy Alphöhi because recognitional capacities do not enable subjects to differentiate between similar things, but his *wanting* would not be satisfied that way. In case of realisations of causal dispositions it does not matter if there is *this* or another object or a state of affairs *exactly* like it.

This attempt clearly needs some further reflections on how representations are incorporated in intentional states such as that they are directed towards a particular individual and on how it could be that the realisation conditions are satisfied by the particular individual. A first outline is given by Martin and Pfeifer (p. 552) and focuses on the subject's perceptual abilities underlying a certain intentional mental state. Another important part plays the self which emerges from perceptual experiences. Therefore, representations are incorporated in intentional mental states through experience and possess a projective character through traces of perceptual memory. Most importantly, specific experiential input that tends to activate certain specific intentional states, and specific experiential output which these states tend to activate are constitutional for the kind of the intentional state.

The whole story aims at the role of intelligent agents with perceptual capacities. Since Martin and Pfeifer were adherents of Brentano's exclusivity claim, they refused to accept the conclusions of their own analysis. Martin further developed his account (cf. Martin (1996), pp. 187 – 191 for the whole passage) and defended his view of finding directedness in everything against Armstrong who charged him of anthropomorphism. This seems to be a highly remarkable shift towards physical intentionality. Martin defines directedness and selectiveness, even to what is absent or non-existent, as *intrinsic* features of dispositionality of the properties of all, even simplest non-mental, entities. This internal projectibility to "any-of-a-kind-that-may-come-along" is further satisfied within the entity itself by its dispositional states and clearly does not require that the dispositional states themselves have anything X-like as their typical cause. In his own words it "would be outlandish to go against nature itself and to deprive the directedness of mental dispositions of such a natural narrow (inside to outside) function". In my opinion, we could understand this as a first ray of light on an evolutionary approach to intentionality. Indeed, inspired by neurophysiological research on sub-cortical structures which normally unconsciously process stimuli but induce reactions that are similar to some conscious mental states, Martin points towards the evolving of the mental from the non-mental and, therefore, to a gradual development of intentionality.

Martin's later approach seems to be the most close to Heil's understanding of intentionality. The importance of the conceptual entanglement of the self and intentionality in Heil's approach is exceptionally mirrored in Martin's thesis, which offers also the possibility to use the natural intentionality of dispositions in order to explain intentionality of minds.

3   A fundamental critic

Bird ((forthcoming), chapter 6) tackles the different attempts which try to establish an understanding of intentionality which suits for non-mental entities and is relevant to the explanation of the intentionality of minds. In my view, the main point of the assault is the claim that intentionality is a non-compositional property. Let us first look at the vocabulary of the argument (Bird's terminology and examples):

Compositional:

A property P of an entity X is compositional if the possession of P by X depends on the possession of P by the parts of X. E.g.: in classical physics mass is compositional in a simple additive way: the mass of an object is equal to the sum of the masses of its parts.

Non-compositional:

A property is non-compositional if it is not compositional and so is either semi-compositional or acompositional. Emergent properties are generally non-compositional, but non-compositional properties need not be emergent. E.g.: let $D<a,b>$ be the direction of the line joining the centres of objects a and b, then D is not a compositional property of the ordered pair $<a,b>$, although it is not emergent either.

Semi-compositional:

A property P of object X is semi-compositional iff:

(i) for some set S of (non-overlapping) proper parts of X, P is compositional relative to S.

(ii) or some set S^* of (non-overlapping) proper parts of X
   (a) P is not compositional relative to S^*
   (b) The possession of P by X supervenes on facts about S^*
   (c) There is no set S^{**} of (non-overlapping) proper parts of X that are themselves parts of the members of S^* such that P is compositional relative to S^{**}.

Acompositional:

Properties that are neither compositional nor semi-compositional.

According to Bird, intentionality is either semi-compositional or acompositional. Under a modular point of view it might be regarded as semi-compositional. In this case the intentionality of the whole would depend in a certain way on the intentionality of the modules. Despite this view, Bird thinks that intentionality in general is never built up out of the intentionality of smaller physical parts of its physical realiser. If x thinks about Napoleon this is not a consequence of x's neurons individually having intentionality directed towards Napoleon or generally being directed towards something else. Bird claims that this is true for every approach to intentionality. The *causal* account describes thoughts by its causes. Thoughts and any mental states are non-compositional properties and the causal relation that is supposed to explain the thought's intentionality would be between the cause of the thought and at least a neuronal network, not between the cause and individual neurons. The *representational* account explains the thought's being about x because it contains some form of representation of x. The property of being a representation, either a mental or otherwise, is a non-compositional one. A pictorial representation of x is of x because it uniquely resembles it. It is important to notice that it is the picture as a whole that uniquely resembles x and not its parts. We may say that some parts of the picture resemble some parts of x, but they may also resemble numerous other parts of y's and z's. The *evolutionary* account explains the intentionality of minds because their structures have evolved in response to certain kinds of selection pressure. Since the structures that have evolved are large-scale structures, not their smallest parts, Bird stresses here too that an evolutionary account makes intentionality also non-compositional. Generally speaking, since intentionality is non-compositional, Bird concludes, the fact that all dispositions are directed towards their manifestation is irrelevant for the explanation of the intentionality of minds.

Bird's analysis of the intentional as a non-compositional property seems to be a serious threat to Place's, Molnar's and Martin's and therefore Heil's approach to intentionality. Even if we ascribe intentionality to subatomic particles, we could, from this point of view, not derive the intentionality of intelligent agents from their constituents, such as single neurons and highly developed brain structures. Especially Heil's claim that we should make sense of the intentionality of agents by using the "natural intentionality" of dispositions seems threatened.

4 An application: the amygdala, unconscious and concious representation

Bird's criticism is probably right with regard to Place's radical analysis which reinterprets intentionality as a, until now, mis-applied term. Place did not intend to contribute to the explanation of mental intentionality. In Molnar's case it is possibly not effective because he drew a distinct line between mental and physical intentionality and never intended to make sense of the former with the latter. While Heil's approach is more threatened by Bird because of its fuzziness, Martin's case is more complicated. Martin opted for the thesis of a gradual development of intentionality but never claimed that an evolutionary story alone would explain the phenomenon that we find in minds of intelligent agents. In contrast to Bird, Molnar and Martin offer an at least plausible story of how we should conceive of intentionality in non-cognitive systems. Although Molnar's pain-example clearly shows that a painful state is a non-representational one, I present here an example (a similar line of argumentation is provided by Cunningham (1998)) which suggests that we find intentionality in biological systems which are able to represent their surroundings. The clue is to deny that intentionality is a feature solely of the cognitive.

Neuroanatomy considers sub-cortical brain structures as evolutionary older than cortical structures. Stimuli exclusively processed in the former normally remain unconscious while such processed in the latter penetrate sooner or later to consciousness. Higher developed organisms such as apes, finbacks and homo sapiens differ from less developed creatures essentially in the amount of convolutions of the neo-cortex. A sophisticated ability to conscious experience and of reacting to the environment is thus related to the extension of cerebral corticalisation. Fundamental physiological features of organisms and behaviour which appears earlier in the steps of evolution are mediated by sub-cortical structures. An interesting structure of the mammalian brain, which lies on the medial surface of both of the brain's temporal lobe's, is called the amygdala. It receives sensory input which codes information about the environment from sub-cortical and cortical structures as well. The amygdala can activate the parasympathetic nervous system, influence the secretion of stress hormones, and induce a startle reflex (please note that this is an absolutely incomplete list of the various features of the amygdala, but it is sufficient for the purpose of this paper). This almond shaped brain structure is famous for its mediator role in emotion, especially fear and anxiety.

Although theorising about emotions is a dangerous mine-field, consider yourself being in a state of fear. Hiking in Southern Switzerland you would discover a snake in front of you. Suddenly after your perception of the snake you would feel fear because you have certain beliefs about snakes which include the view that snakes are generally poisonous and therefore dangerous for you. You would certainly be afraid *of* it. In other words, undergoing an intentional state you would represent your surrounding mentally. This short description gives us a rudimentary summary of a cognitive approach to emotions which locates the intentional character of an emotion in its constituent beliefs (cf. Cunningham (1998) p. 450). In other words, the dispositionality of thoughts, i.e. in this case to think *of* snakes as dangerous reptiles, would have caused your fear. Taking into account Martin's claim of a gradually developed intentionality during evolution, and considering the fact that avoidance, or fight or flight reactions are evolutionary old behaviours, it should be possible to find a similar disposition on the sub-cortical level which would induce a non-cognitive state in the organism.

Research on fear conditioning carried out by Joseph LeDoux (cf. LeDoux (2000)) suggests precisely such an account. Investigating how it is possible to condition rats through auditory stimuli, LeDoux was especially interested in the underlying brain structures of the eventual conditioning. He discovered that some parts of the rat's neo-cortex which process auditory stimuli and are normally associated with cognition were not needed in conditioning trials with simple stimuli. On the other hand, the amygdala and the thalamus, two sub-cortical brain nuclei, were necessary for fear response. Since neuronal circuits and pathways are similar in all mammals we can be sure in believing that this finding applies also to humans. As already mentioned, the amygdala is involved in mediating fear responses. It receives sensory afferences via two ways. The thalamus distributes incoming sensory data incredibly fast directly to the amygdala and twice times slower to the cortex. LeDoux called the first way the "quick and dirty" route because it conveys only a rough representation of the stimuli experienced. In LeDoux' theory the amygdala plays the role of processing the affective significance of a stimulus. Mammalian brains have the incredible capacity to learn and remember the emotional significance of stimuli and events and with increasing experience to alternate the valuation of stimuli if necessary.

Again, imagine yourself hiking in lovely Switzerland and bumping into a "something" which would cause you immediately to shrink back without recognising the "something" as a snake. A couple of seconds after your retreat, the same rudimentary representation which was already processed by your amygdala would be further computed by the cortex for a detailed interpretation of the frightening "something" and would lead you to the recognition of the "something" as a snake. Your amygdala induced, without you being aware, a flight reaction which prevented you from getting in touch with an unlovely, vicious reptile. Thus, the physiological changes in your body would not be initiated by a conscious mental state but by a disposition of your central nervous system. This initial reaction would either be supported or inhibited by the cognitive state which comes short after your physiological reaction. Generally speaking, an unconscious representation on a sub-cortical level would have led to an affective evaluation of the stimulus in relation to you, the organism.

This whole story of LeDoux's discovery perfectly fits into the pattern of intentionality developed by Martin.

Firstly, the brain circuits do not neutrally process the incoming stimuli. Rather, they are rated in reference to their relative effects on the organism, the representational medium.

Secondly, we can say that a rudimentary representation leads to a specific fear reaction in the case in which fear is perceptually induced (cf. Cunningham (1998)). This representation contains information about sensory modalities that are being stimulated as well as information about some features of the object being sensed. There must therefore be a certain disposition in the amygdala which urges the organism to certain reactions with respect not only to an object but also to a certain affective value.

Thirdly, sub-cortical induced fear is obviously evolutionary. The advantage of quick reactions in possibly dangerous situations is crucial to survival. Since the cognitive has evolved from the non-cognitive and we find intentionality on this level, we can infer that there was a gradual development from the intentional of the non-cognitive to the intentional of the cognitive.

Fourthly, at least in the case of humans we can assume that there is an interaction between these two levels of representation. The rough representation which unconsciously induces a flight reaction has certainly effects on the emerging conscious representation through the increased arousal of the organism. Furthermore, long-term-potentiation as an adaptive mechanism on the cellular level causes changes in the dispositional features of the amygdala. Its altered dispositional set undoubtedly influences the dispositions of the mental. If you firstly shrink back in front of Damien Hirst's artworks and then get used to the view of a pickled tiger shark in the sense that there is an adaptation to it on the cellular level, your mental dispositions alter because you do not undergo noticeable changes in arousal anymore.

A few more and clarifying words should be said about the ability of organisms for unconscious, non-cognitive representation. It is important to notice that it is not a certain particular region or part of the body which represents something; rather it is a certain particular state of the whole organism which is representing under the direction of a central unit, such as the brain or parts of the brain. In the case mentioned, a certain external condition x which stands in a certain relation to the organism (presence of a dangerous entity which is potentially harmful to the organism) is represented by a certain internal state z of the organism. This state z is poised to induce a certain reaction of the organism which guarantees the survival of the organism in an environment containing stimulus x. It is clear that the state z could also occur without being caused by the external stimulus x. This opens the case for misrepresentations. If state z represents condition x and this state occurs in the presence of a black garden hose, it clearly misrepresents the actual external condition if garden hoses are not harmful for the organism. In analogy, we could look at the famous frog snapping at flying black balls. In the normal case in the presence of flies, a certain internal state z which represents the condition x (presence of a nutritious entity which is potentially valuable for the organism) induces the organism to snap at flies (a reaction which increases its probability of survival). If state z induces the frog to snap at flying black balls, state z misrepresents an actual external condition as being condition x.

I think that this form of misrepresentation suits the second mark of intentionality, the possible inexistence of the intentional object which is nowhere in the literature clearly defined (cf. Cunningham (1998)). In the case of the hiker or the frog, state z represents a non-existent condition x and therefore misrepresents another actual condition. Note that this understanding of intentionality only tries to pick out the evolutionary root of this phenomenon and does not claim that intentionality is a feature of non-living entities. Clearly, it is not able to give an account of what is needed to get from non-mental to mental intentionality but, nonetheless, it is at least able to deconstruct Brentano's view.

5 Conclusion

There is much conceptual confusion about the notion of intentionality. Place's radical re-interpretation does not contribute to the explanation of the phenomenon. Molnar's approach convincingly shows that non-representational states of beings meet the salient features of intentionality while Martin provides a plausible base for an evolutionary understanding of the development of intentionality. Heil's approach to intentionality is unclear because it seems to pick out features of the different approaches mentioned. It is not clear how we should make use of "natural intentionality" in order to make sense of intentionality. Probably it is best to understand Heil's "natural intentionality" as Molnar's physical intentionality and interpret it as a necessary but not sufficient condition for the intentionality of minds. Bird's killer argument tries to deny this possibility. Since it is highly unlikely that intentionality just plops into the human mind at our level of evolution and Bird does not offer any other plausible alternative, the burden of proof is surely not on the side of the proponents of physical intentionality. Physical intentionality should possibly be regarded as a first trail to unravel the mystery of mental intentionality. However, I strongly believe that the snake example clearly shows that it is wrong to ascribe intentionality only to cognitive mental states. In contrast to Molnar I also claim to have shown that there are unconscious representational states.

Commentary
John Heil

Hunziker thinks I waver on Brentano's characterisation of the intentionality as "the mark of the mental". Part of what I try to argue in *From an ontological point of view* is that the mental – physical distinction is not a deep distinction. There is but one world variously described or considered. If ways the world is serve as truthmakers for descriptions, then the truthmaker for every true description could be given a description in the language of basic physics (see Esfeld's discussion and my reply, above). This is supervenience.[1]

I do not identify intentionality with dispositionality. George Molnar, echoing John Burnheim and C. B. Martin, has recently described dispositionality as "natural intentionality". I understand this designation as suggestive, not definitional. Intentionality is rooted in our dispositional makeup, but an object can have endless dispositional characteristics without thereby being capable of intentionality.

Intentionality is projective: intentional states are of or for this or that. In coming to terms with intentionality, dispositionality looks promising because dispositions are *for* particular kinds of manifestation with particular kinds of reciprocal dispositional partner that might or might not exist. What makes a given thought a thought about *tomatoes*? One possibility is that the thought has a causal history bound up with tomatoes. This would mean that Swampman lacks thoughts about much of anything. But only a philosopher with a theory would say that.

This falls well short of a theory of intentionality. Hunziker describes my reflections on intentionality as "vague", "nebulous", "unclear", and "in the worst case contradictory". I doubt that any position could be all of these, but, in any case, I reject the idea that only a theory derived from uncontroversial premises and in which every substantive term receives an explicit definition is philosophically respectable. To my knowledge there is no clear, worked-out account of how it is that causal relations are supposed to fix reference. Nevertheless many philosophers have been impressed with this idea and pushed ahead with it, even when it leads, as Swampman nicely illustrates, to apparently counter-intuitive results. Think of my discussion as a suggestion that dispositionality might replace causality in our thoughts about intentionality and reference.

---

[1] Thus conceived, mental-physical supervenience is not an under-specified dependence relation between families of properties, but a constraint on the application of predicates.

Let me briefly comment on the phrase "natural intentionality". Could there be any other kind? Some philosophers have thought that intentionality depends on linguistic or social factors. But what are these? Do speech and action stand, somehow, outside the natural domain? Suppose it turned out that intentional states required linguistic or social grounding. Would this make them any less natural? Or does "natural" mean "nonlinguistic, non-social"? If it does, where exactly do language and society stand with respect to the natural order?

A final remark. Hunziker argues at length that intentionality need not be "cognitive". (I could be catty and point out that he nowhere provides a precise definition of "cognitive".) I see no reason to disagree (assuming a suitably narrow understanding of "cognitive"). It seems natural, in fact, to think of various bodily systems as representing bodily states and acting on these representations. Much has been written recently about the "brain in the gut", for instance. I am happy to think that the gut, or the thermoregulatory system have intentional elements that, though vital, have nothing much to do with what we ordinarily regard as cognition.

Bibliography

Armstrong, David (1968), *A materialist theory of the mind*, London: Routledge and Kegan Paul.

Armstrong David (1978), *A theory of universals*, Cambridge: Cambridge University Press.

Armstrong, David (1985), *What is a law of nature*, Cambridge: Cambridge University Press.

Armstrong, David (1997), *A world of states of affairs*, Cambridge: Cambridge University Press.

Armstrong, David (2004a), *Truth and truthmakers*, Cambridge: Cambridge University Press.

Armstrong, David (2004b), 'Going through the open door again: counterfactual versus singularist theories of causation'. In: Collins, John, Hall, Ned, Paul, LA (eds.), *Causation and counterfactuals*, Cambridge (Massachusetts): MIT Press: 445 – 457.

Bach-y-Rita, Paul (2002), 'Sensory substitution and qualia'. In: Noë, Alva, Thompson, Evan, *Vision and mind*, Cambridge: MIT Press.

Balashov, Yuri (2000), 'Enduring and perduring objects in Minkowski space-time', *Philosophical Studies*, 99: 129 – 166.

Beebee, Helen, Dodd, Julian (eds.) (2005), *Truthmakers. The contemporary debate*, Oxford: Oxford University Press.

Benacerraf, Paul (1965), 'What numbers could not be', *Philosophical Review*, 74: 47 – 73.

Benacerraf, Paul (1973), 'Mathematical truth', *Journal of Philosophy*, 70: 61 – 79.

Bigelow, John (1988), *The reality of numbers: a physicalist's philosophy of mathematics*. Oxford: Clarendon Press.

Bigelow, John, Ellis, Brian, Lierse, Caroline (1992), 'The world as one of a kind: natural necessity and laws of nature', *British Journal for the Philosophy of Science*, 43: 371 – 388.

Bird, Alexander (1998), 'Dispositions and antidotes', *The Philosophical Quarterly*, 48: 227 – 234.

Bird, Alexander (2005), 'Laws and essences', *Ratio*, 18: 437 – 461.

Bird, Alexander (2006 forthcoming), 'Potency and modality', *Synthese*.

Bird, Alexander (forthcoming), *Law and property*, at http://eis.bris.ac.uk/~plajb/research/Law_and_Property.pdf

Bishop, Robert (2006), 'The hidden premiss in the causal argument for physicalism', *Analysis*, 66: 44 – 52.

Black, Robert (2000), 'Against quidditism', *Australasian Journal of Philosophy*, 78, 78 – 104.

Block, Ned (1980), 'What is functionalism?'. In: Ned Block (ed.), *Readings in philosophy of psychology*, London: Methuen, 171 – 184.

Bontly, Thomas (2002), 'The supervenience argument generalizes', *Philosophical Studies*, 109: 75 – 96.

Brandom, Robert (2000), *Articulating reasons. An introduction to inferentialism*, Harvard (Massachusetts) and London: Harvard University Press.

Campbell, Keith (1976), *Metaphysics: an introduction*, Encino, Calif: Dickenson Publishing Co.

Cao, Tyan Yu (2003), 'Can we dissolve physical entities into mathematical structure?', *Synthese*, 136: 51 – 71.

Capitan, William, Merrill, Daniel (eds.) (1967), *Art, mind, and religion*, Pittsburgh: University of Pittsburgh Press.

Carnap, Rudolf (1936), 'Testability and meaning', *Philosophy of Science*, 3: 419 – 471.

Carnap, Rudolf (1937), 'Testability and meaning – continued', *Philosophy of Science*, 4: 1 – 40.

Cartwright, Nancy (1983), *How the laws of physics lie*, Oxford: Clarendon Press.

Cartwright, Nancy (1999), *The dappled world. A study of the boundaries of science*, Cambridge: Cambridge University Press.

Chakravartty, Anjan (2003), 'The structuralist conception of objects', *Philosophy of Science*, 70: 867 – 878.

Chalmers, David, Jackson, Frank (2001), 'Conceptual analysis and reductive explanation', *Philosophical Review*, 110: 315 – 360.

Cohen, Ted (1990), 'There are no ties at first base', *Yale Review*, 79: 314 – 322.

Cross, Troy (2005), 'What is a disposition?', *Synthese*, 144: 321 – 341.

Cunningham, Suzanne (1998), 'Two faces of intentionality', *Philosophy of Science*, 64: 445 – 460.

Dipert, Randall (1997), 'The mathematical structure of the world: the world as a graph', *Journal of Philosophy*, 94: 329 – 358.

Dorato, Mauro (2000), 'Substantivalism, relationism, and structural space-time realism', *Foundations of Physics*, 30: 1605 – 1628.

Dorato, Mauro (2005), *The software of the universe. An introduction to the history and philosophy of laws of nature*, Aldershot: Ashgate.

Dretske, Fred (1977), 'Laws of nature', *Philosophy of Science*, 44: 248 – 268.

Dretske, Fred (2000), 'Reply to Lopes', *Philosophy and Phenomenological Research*, 60/2: 455 – 459.

Earman, John (1993), 'In defense of laws: reflections on Bas van Fraassen's Laws and symmetry', *Philosophy and Phenomenological Research*, 53 (2): 413 – 419.

Earman, John, Norton, John (1987), 'What price spacetime substantivalism? The hole argument', *British Journal for the Philosophy of Science*, 38: 515 – 525.

Ellis, Brian, (1999), 'Response to David Armstrong'. In : Sankey, Howard (ed.), *Causation and law of nature*, Dordrecht, Kluwer.

Ellis, Brian (2001), *Scientific essentialism*, Cambridge: Cambridge University Press.

Ellis, Brian (2002), *The philosophy of nature, A guide to new essentialism*, Chesham: Acumen Publishing.

Engel, Pascal, (2002), *Truth*, Chesham: Acumen.

Esfeld, Michael (2004), 'Quantum entanglement and a metaphysics of relations', *Studies in History and Philosophy of Modern Physics*, 35B: 625 – 641.

Esfeld, Michael (2005), 'Le pragmatisme en sémantique et en épistémologie contemporaines', *Philosophia Scientiae*, 9: 31 – 48.

Esfeld, Michael, Fantini, Bernardino (eds.) (2005), *Causation in biomedical sciences*. Special issue of *History and Philosophy of the Life Sciences*, 27.3 – 4.

Esfeld, Michael, Lam, Vincent (2006 forthcoming), 'Moderate structural realism about space-time', *Synthese*.

Esfeld, Michael, Sachse, Christian (2006 mauscript), 'Reduction through functional sub-types'.

Everett, Hugh (1957), '"Relative state" formulation of quantum mechanics', *Reviews of Modern Physics*, 29: 454 – 462. Reprinted in DeWitt, Bryce, Graham, Neill (eds.) (1973), *The many-worlds interpretation of quantum mechanics*, Princeton: Princeton University Press: 141 – 149.

Fetzer, James (1977), 'A world of dispositions', *Synthese*, 34: 397 – 421. Reprinted in Tuomela (1978), 163 – 187.

Field, Hartry (1980), *Science without numbers. A defence of nominalism*, Oxford: Blackwell.

Field, Hartry (2003), 'Causation in a physical world'. In: Loux, Michael, Zimmerman, Dean (eds.), *The Oxford handbook of metaphysics*, Oxford: Oxford University Press.

Fodor, Jerry (1968), *Psychological explanation: An introduction to the philosophy of psychology*, New York: Random House.

Fodor, Jerry (1974), 'Special sciences (or the disunity of science as working hypothesis)', *Synthese*, 28: 97 – 115.

Fodor, Jerry (1997), 'Special sciences – still autonomous after all these years', *Philosophical Perspectives 1, Mind, Causation, and World*: 143 – 162.

Francescotti, Robert (1999), 'How to define intrinsic properties', *Noûs*, 33(4): 590 – 609.

French, Steven, Ladyman, James (2003), 'Remodelling structural realism: quantum physics and the metaphysics of structure', *Synthese*, 136: 31 – 56.

Ghirardi, Giancarlo, Rimini, Alberto, Weber, Tullio (1986), 'Unified dynamics for microscopic and macroscopic systems', *Physical Review*, D34: 470 – 491.

Guarniero, G. (1974), 'Experience of tactile vision', *Perception*, 3: 101 – 104.

Gundersen, Lars (2002), 'In defence of the conditional account of dispositions', *Synthese*, 130: 389 – 411.

Guttenplan, Samuel (ed.) (1994), *A companion to the philosophy of mind*, Oxford: Basil Blackwell.

Harman, Gilbert (1990), 'The intrinsic quality of experience', *Philosophical Perspectives*, 4: 31 – 52.

Heil, John (1999), 'Multiple realizability', *American Philosophical Quarterly*, 36(3): 189 – 208.

Heil, John (2003), *From an ontological point of view*, Oxford: Oxford University Press.

Heil, John (2003b), 'Multiply realized properties'. In: Walter, Sven, Heckmann, Dieter (eds.), *Physicalism and mental causation. The metaphysics of mind and action*, Exeter: Imprint Academic.

Heil, John, Mele, Alfred (eds.) (1993), *Mental causation*, Oxford: Clarendon Press.

Heil, John, Robb, David (2003), 'Mental properties', *American Philosophical Quarterly*, 40(3): 175 – 196.

Hoefer, Carl (1996), 'The metaphysics of space-time substantivalism', *Journal of Philosophy*, 93: 5 – 27.

Hooker, Clifford (1981), 'Towards a general theory of reduction. Part I: Historical and scientific setting. Part II: Identity in reduction. Part III: Cross-categorial reduction', *Dialogue*, 20: 38 – 60; 201– 236; 496 – 529.

Horgan, Terry (1982), 'Supervenience and microphysics', *Pacific Philosophical Quarterly*, 63: 29 – 43.

Horwich, Paul (1998), *Truth*, 2nd edition, Oxford: Oxford University Press.

Jacob, Pierre (2003), 'Intentionality', *The Stanford Encyclopedia of Philosophy*, Fall 2003 Edition, Zalta, Edward (ed.) at http://plato.stanford.edu/archives/fall2003/entries/intentionality

Kim, Jaegwon (1984), 'Concepts of supervenience', *Philosophy and Phenomenological Research*, 65: 153 – 176.

Kim, Jaegwon (1992), 'Multiple realization and the metaphysics of reduction', *Philosophy and Phenomenological Research*, 52: 1 – 26.

Kim, Jaegwon (1993a), 'The nonreductivist's troubles with mental causation'. In: Heil, John, Mele, Alfred (eds.) (1993): 189 – 210. Reprinted in Kim (1993b): 336 – 357.

Kim, Jaegwon (1993b), *Supervenience and mind: selected philosophical essays*, Cambridge: Cambridge University Press.

Kim, Jaegwon (1998), *Mind in a physical world: an essay on the mind-body problem and mental causation*, Cambridge, Massachusetts: MIT Press.

Kim Jaegwon (2002), 'The layered model: metaphysical considerations', *Philosophical Explorations*, Volume V (I): 2 – 20.

Kim Jaegwon (2003), 'Blocking causal drainage and other maintenance chores with mental causation', *Philosophy and Phenomenological Research*, 67: 151 – 176.

Kim, Jaegwon (2005), *Physicalism, or something near enough*. Princeton: Princeton University Press.

Kistler, Max (2005), 'L'efficacité causale des propriétés dispositionnelles macroscopiques'. In: Gnassounou, Bruno, Kistler, Max (eds.), *Causes, pouvoir, dispositions en philosophie. Le retour des vertus dormitives*, Paris: PUF: 115 – 154.

Künne, Wolfgang (2003), *Conceptions of truth*, Oxford: Oxford University Press.

Ladyman, James (1998), 'What is structural realism?', *Studies in History and Philosophy of Modern Science*, 29: 409 – 424.

Langton, Rae, Lewis, David (1998), 'Defining "intrinsic"', *Philosophy and Phenomenological Research*, 58(2): 333 – 345.

LeDoux, Joseph (2000), 'Emotion circuits in the brain', *Annual Review of Neuroscience*, 23: 155 – 184.

Lenay, Charles et al. (2003), 'Sensory substitution: limits and perspectives'. In: Hatwell, Yvette et al., *Touching for knowing, cognitive psychology of haptic manual perception*, Amsterdam/Philadelphia: John Benjamins Publishing Company.

Lewis, David (1966), 'An argument for the identity theory', *Journal of Philosophy*, 63: 17 – 25.

Lewis, David (1986), *Philosophical papers. Volume 2*, Oxford: Oxford University Press.

Lewis, David (1994a), 'Humean supervenience debugged', *Mind*, 103: 473 – 490.

Lewis, David (1994b), 'Reduction of mind'. In: Guttenplan, Samuel (ed.), *A companion to the philosophy of mind* Oxford: Basil Blackwell.

Lewis, David (1997), 'Finkish dispositions', *The Philosophical Quarterly*, 47: 143 – 158.

Lewis David (1999), *Papers in metaphysics and epistemology*, Cambridge: Cambridge University Press.

Lewis, David (2004), 'Causation as influence'. In: Collins, John, Hall, Ned, Paul, L.A. (eds.), *Causation and counterfactuals*, Cambridge (Massachusetts): MIT Press: 75 – 106.

Locke, John (16901978), *An essay concerning human understanding*, Nidditch, Peter (ed.), Oxford: Clarendon Press.

Loewer, Barry (2001), 'Review of Jaegwon Kim, Mind in a physical World. An essay on the mind-body problem and mental causation, Cambridge (Massachusetts): MIT Press 1998', *Journal of Philosophy*, 98: 315 – 324.

Loewer, Barry (forthcoming), 'Counterfactuals and the second law'. In: Price, Huw (ed.), *Causation and counterfactuals*, Oxford: Oxford University Press.

Lynch, Michael (1998), *Truth in context. An essay on pluralism and objectivity*, Cambridge, Massachusetts, London: MIT press.

Mackie, John (1977), 'Dispositions, grounds and causes', *Synthese*, 34, 361 – 369. Reprinted in Tuomela (1978), 99 – 107.

Malzkorn, Wolfgang (2000), 'Realism, functionalism and the conditional analysis of dispositions', *The Philosophical Quarterly*, 50: 452 – 469.

Martin, Charles (1994), 'Dispositions and conditionals', *The Philosophical Quarterly*, 44: 1 – 8.

Martin, Charles (1996), 'Final replies to Place and Armstrong'. In: Crane, Tim (ed.), (1996), *Dispositions. A debate*, London: Routledge.

Martin, Charles (1997), 'On the need for properties: the road to Pythagoreanism and back', *Synthese*, 112, 193 – 231.

Martin, Charles, Pfeifer, Karl (1986), 'Intentionality and the non-psychological', *Philosophy and Phenomenological Research*, 46, 531 – 554.

Mellor, Hugh (1974), 'In defense of dispositions', *The Philosophical Review*, 83: 157 – 181.

Mellor, Hugh (2000), 'The semantics and ontology of dispositions', *Mind*, 109: 757 – 780.

Milne, Peter (2005), 'Not every truth has a truthmaker', *Analysis*, 65: 221 – 224.

Molnar, George (2003), *Powers: a study in metaphysics*, Oxford: Oxford University Press.

Mulligan, Kevin, Simons, Peter, Smith, Barry (1984), 'Truth-makers', *Philosophy and Phenomenological Research*, 44: 287 – 321.

Mumford, Stephen (1998), *Dispositions*, Oxford: Clarendon Press.

Mumford, Stephen (1999), 'Intentionality and the physical: a new theory of disposition ascription', *The Philosophical Quarterly*, 49, 215 – 225.

Mumford, Stephen (2000), 'Review of The dappled world', *Philosophy*, 75: 613 – 616.

Mumford, Stephen (2004a), 'L'état des lois'. In: Monnoyer, Jean-Maurice (ed.), *La structure du monde: objets, propriétés, états de choses*, Paris: Vrin.

Mumford, Stephen (2004b), *Laws in nature*, London: Routledge.

Neale, Stephen (1995), 'The philosophical relevance of Gödel's slingshot', *Mind*, 104: 761 – 825.

Neale Stephen (2001), *Facing facts*, Oxford: Oxford University Press.

Noë, Alva, O'Regan, Kevin (2002), 'On the brain-basis of visual consciousness: a sensorimotor account'. In: Noë, Alva, Thompson, Evan, *Vision and mind*, Cambridge: MIT Press.

Oppenheim, Paul, Putnam, Hilary (1958), 'The unity of science as a working hypothesis'. In: Feigl, Herbert, Scriven, Michael, Grover, Maxwell (eds.), *Concepts, theories and the mind-body problem, Minnesota Studies in the Philosophy of Science, volume 2*, Minneapolis: University of Minnesota Press: 3 – 35.

Place, Ullin (1956), 'Is consciousness a brain process?', *British Journal of Psychology*, 47: 44 – 50.

Place, Ullin (1996), 'Intentionality as the mark of the dispositional', *Dialectica*, 50: 91 – 120.

Pineda, David (2002), 'The causal exclusion puzzle', *European Journal of Philosophy*, 10.1: 26 – 42.

Prior, Elisabeth, Pargetter, Robert, Jackson, Frank (1982), 'Three theses about dispositions', *American Philosophical Quarterly*, 19: 251 – 257.

Psillos, Stathis (2005), 'What do powers do when they are not manifested?', *Philosophy and Phenomenological Research*. Available at http://www.phs.uoa.gr/~psillos/Publications.htm

Psillos, Stathis (2006), 'Cartwright's realist toil: from entities to capacities'. In: Bovens, Luc, Hartmann, Stephan (eds.), *Nancy Cartwright's philosophy of science*, London: Routledge.

Putnam, Hilary (1967), 'Psychological predicates'. In: Capitan, William, Merrill, Daniel, *Art, mind, and religion*. Reprinted as 'The nature of mental states'. In: Putnam (1975).

Putnam, Hilary (1975), *Mind, language and reality: Philosophical Papers*, volume 2, Cambridge: Cambridge University Press.

Putnam, Hilary (1981), *Reason, truth and history*, Cambridge: Cambridge University Press.

Redhead, Michael (1990), 'Explanation'. In: Knowles, Dudley (ed.), *Explanation and its limits*, Cambridge: Cambridge University Press: 135 – 154.

Reichenbach, Hans (1938), *Experience and prediction*, Chicago: University of Chicago Press.

Rosenberg, Alexander (1994). *Instrumental biology or the disunity of science*, Chicago: University of Chicago Press.

Rovelli, Carlo (1997), 'Halfway through the woods: contemporary research on space and time'. In: Earman, John, Norton, John (eds.), *The cosmos of science: essays of exploration*, Pittsburgh: University of Pittsburgh Press.

Russell, Bertrand (1912), 'On the notion of cause', *Proceedings of the Aristotelian Society*, 13: 1 – 26.

Sachse, Christian (2005), 'Reduction of biological properties by means of functional sub-types', *History and Philosophy of the Life Sciences*, 27: 427 – 441.

Saunders, Simon (2003), 'Physics and Leibniz' principles'. In: Brading, Katherine, Castellani, Elena (eds.), *Symmetries in physics: philosophical reflections*, Cambridge: Cambridge University Press, 289 – 307.

Searle, John (1992), *The rediscovery of the mind*, Cambridge (Massachusetts): MIT Press.

Searle, John (1995), *The construction of social reality*, Harmondsworth: The Penguin Press.

Shoemaker, Sydney (1980), 'Causality and properties'. In: van Inwagen, Peter (ed.), *Time and cause*, Dordrecht: Reidel: 109 – 135. Reprinted in Sydney Shoemaker (1984), *Identity, cause, and mind. Philosophical essays*, Cambridge: Cambridge University Press: 206 – 233.

Shoemaker, Sydney (1998), 'Causal and metaphysical necessity', *Pacific Philosophical Quarterly*, 79: 59 – 77.

Smart, John (1959), 'Sensations and brain processes', *Philosophical Review*, 68: 141 – 156.

Sparber, Georg (2005), 'Counterfactual overdetermination vs. the causal exclusion problem', *History and Philosophy of the Life Sciences*, 27: 479 – 490.

Stachel, John (1993), 'The meaning of general covariance. The hole story'. In: Earman, John et al. (eds.), *Philosophical problems of the internal and external worlds. Essays on the philosophy of Adolf Gruenbaum*, Pittsburgh: University of Pittsburgh Press: 129 – 160.

Tooley, Michael (1977), 'The nature of laws', *Canadian Journal of Philosophy*, 7: 667 – 698.

Tuomela, Raimo (ed.) (1978), *Dispositions*, Synthese Library, 113. Dordrecht & Boston: Reidel.

Tye, Michael (2002), 'Representationalism and the transparency of experience', *Noûs*, 36: 137 – 151.

Vallentyne, Peter (1997), 'Intrinsic properties defined', *Philosophical Studies*, 88: 209 – 219.

van Fraassen, Bas (1989), *Laws and symmetry*, Oxford: Clarendon Press.

Wasserman, Ryan, Manley, David (manuscript), 'On linking dispositions with conditionals', at http://myweb.facstaff.wwu.edu/wasserr/research.html

White, B.W. et al. (1970), 'Seeing with the skin', *Perception and Psychophysics*, 7 – 23.

Wittgenstein, Ludwig (1921/1961), *Tractatus Logico-Philosophicus*, Pears, David, McGuinness, Brian, trans., London: Routledge.

Wittgenstein, Ludwig (1953/1968), *Philosophical Investigations*, Anscombe, Elisabeth, trans., Oxford: Basil Blackwell.

Index

abstraction, 159, 163, 165, 171, 181, 190
analysis
   best system, 132, 174
   causal, 150–154
   conditional, 12, 123, 126–128, 130, 131, 133, 135, 140, 141, 150–153, 178, 190, 199
   counterfactual, *see* conditional
   functional, 153
   philosophical, 56
   semantic, 133
animism, 240
anthropomorphism, 241
anti-realism, 144, 147, 151, 152, 155, 159–163, 166, 167
anti-reductionism, 91, 99, 110
antidotes, 131, 152
Aristotle, 155
Armstrong, David M., 19, 21–23, 30, 32–35, 37, 39, 43, 114, 125, 132, 136, 147, 149, 151, 153, 155, 158, 159, 165, 166, 170, 173, 176–178, 180, 181, 189, 194, 241
atomism, 191, 207

Bach-y-Rita, Paul, 223
Balashov, Yuri, 192
Barcan, Ruth, 149
Beebee, Helen, 33
Benacerraf, Paul, 26
big bang, 194, 195, 197

Bigelow, John, 22, 173, 177
Bird, Alexander, 127, 128, 143, 144, 146–149, 152, 155, 159, 195, 237, 238, 242–244, 248
Black, Robert, 147
Block, Ned, 17, 153
Bontly, Thomas, 69
Brandom, Robert, 39
Brentano, Franz, 235, 237, 241, 247, 249
Burgess, Anthony, 127
Burnheim, John, 249

Campbell, Keith, 113, 155
Cao, Tyan Yu, 112
capacities, 66, 140, 175, 180–186, 190, 235, 240
Carnap, Rudolf, 133
Cartwright, Nancy, 13, 173, 175, 180, 182–186
causal exclusion argument, 51, 54, 56, 125
causation, 12, 37, 52, 70, 153, 164, 194, 200, 204
   biological, 200, 205
   higher-level, 20, 34, 37, 70
   mental, 77, 78, 200, 204, 205
   powerful, 123–137
Chakravartty, Anjan, 112
Chalmers, Alan, 180
Chalmers, David, 32, 35, 203
Chisholm, Roderick, 237
Church, Alonzo, 34

Cohen, Ted, 27
conditionals, *see* counterfactuals
consciousness, 206, 230, 244
    experiential, 214, 221
    perceptual, 214, 215, 230
counterfactuals, 121, 126–128, 130–137, 140, 141, 144, 150–152, 194, 200, 204
Cross, Troy, 127, 129
Cunningham, Susanne, 244–247

Davidson, Donald, 190
deduction
    inter-theoretic, 91–107
Descartes, René, 15, 16, 88, 122, 207
Dipert, Randall, 115, 116, 122
dispositions, *see* dispositional properties
Dodd, Julian, 33
Dorato, Mauro, 115, 118
Dretske, Fred, 173, 216, 218

Earman, John, 118, 174, 192
Einstein, Albert, 118
Eleatic Principle, 51, 52, 157
eliminativism, 12, 44, 47, 55–58, 61, 66–68, 75, 76, 84, 85, 88, 106, 126, 130, 133, 134, 152, 166, 200–206, 209
Ellis, Brian, 149, 151, 155, 160, 173, 177, 195, 197
emergence, 42, 227, 241, 242
empiricism
    logical, 11, 39
Engel, Pascal, 34, 35
Enlightenment, 15, 16, 169, 208
epiphenomenalism, 52, 68
Everett, Hugh, 198

explanation, 31, 37, 81, 85, 137, 148, 150, 151, 196
    biological, 96, 97
    homogeneous, 96–99, 103–105, 107
    physical, 94–99, 102, 103, 105, 182
    vertical, 194
externalism, 227

Fantini, Bernardino, 200
Fetzer, James, 160, 162
Field, Hartry, 192, 197
finkish dispositions, 12, 126–133, 140, 141, 152
Fodor, Jerry, 16, 53, 54, 93
Francescotti, Robert, 83
French, Steven, 112
functionalism, 12, 17, 19, 49–52, 54, 68, 144, 152, 153, 167, 170, 203, 204

Ghirardi, Giancarlo, 198, 199
Gibson, James J., 232
God, 88, 126, 127, 130, 132, 178, 189, 190
Gödel, Kurt, 34
Guarniero, G., 224
Gundersen, Lars B., 127, 128, 131, 133, 136, 137

Harman, Gilbert, 217
Heil, John, 195
Hirst, Damien, 246
Hoefer, Carl, 118
holism, 192, 193
Hooker, Clifford A., 103
Horgan, Terry, 83
Horwich, Paul, 32

Hume, David, 12, 45, 132, 134, 135, 137, 139, 140, 173, 174, 191, 193–195, 197–200, 203–205, 208, 209

idealisation, *see* abstraction
identity principle, 124, 146, 147, 156, 157, 159, 163
identity thesis, 12, 123, 125, 143, 149, 152–157, 162, 165, 166, 170, 171
inference ticket, 30, 38, 39, 41
intentionality, 13, 151, 235–250
    mental, 238, 244, 247, 248
    natural, 13, 236, 238, 240, 241, 243, 248–250
    physical, 238, 241, 244, 248
    primitive, 236

Jackson, Frank, 170, 203
Jacob, Pierre, 235

Kant, Immanuel, 161, 162
Kim, Jaegwon, 12, 19, 51–54, 69, 70, 95, 99, 200, 209
Kistler, Max, 195
Kubrick, Stanley, 127
Künne, Paul, 33, 35

Ladyman, James, 111, 112
Langton, Rae, 83
laws, 12, 13, 37, 53, 85, 86, 125, 130, 132–135, 137, 147, 157, 165, 166, 170, 173–187, 189, 190, 194, 196, 208
    ceteris paribus, 134, 179, 183, 184
    basic, *see* fundamental
    causal, 53
    contingent, 132, 157, 175, 177, 178, 189
    exceptionless, 182, 183, 190
    fundamental, 37, 182, 183
    Gestalt, 223, 225
    necessary, 143, 146, 177, 178
    physical, 182, 183
    strict, *see* exceptionless
    uninstantiated, 134
    unmanifested, 130
    vertical, 52, 53
LeDoux, Joseph, 245, 246
Leibniz, Gottfried W., 15, 118, 190, 260
levels
    of abstraction, 61
    of being, 11, 12, 21, 30, 31, 33, 37, 44, 47–70, 77, 78, 116, 143, 158, 191, 200, 201, 203
    of complexity, 31, 55, 76, 78, 84, 200
    of description, 31, 48, 55, 200
    of explanation, 31, 196
    of organisation, 31
    of representation, 246
Lewis, David, 12, 19, 24, 30, 45, 83, 127, 130, 132, 133, 136, 137, 139, 140, 146, 147, 149, 169, 174, 194, 197, 200, 203, 204
Lierse, Caroline, 173, 177
linguisticism, 18, 27, 89
Locke, John, 15, 16, 23, 88, 114, 122, 159, 162, 169, 171, 176, 208
Loewer, Barry, 194, 197, 200
Lorentz, Hendrik, 118
Ludovico method, 128, 130, 131
Lynch, Michael, 161, 162

Mackie, John L., 144, 147
Malzkorn, Wolfgang, 126, 127, 133, 152, 199
Manley, David, 127, 137
Martin, Charles B., 12, 18, 29, 31, 32, 126–129, 131, 132, 140, 148, 151, 153, 156, 166, 169, 175, 180, 195, 218, 236, 237, 240, 241, 243–246, 248, 249
materialism, 17
Meinong, Alexius, 147, 149
Mellor, Hugh D., 131–133, 135, 195
metaphysics, 11, 12, 26, 191, 192, 196, 197, 199, 206, 207
   Humean, 12, 45, 132–137, 139, 140, 191, 193–195, 197, 199, 204, 205, 208
   of a block universe, 192
   of causation, 200, 201, 205
   of dispositions, *see* of powers
   of events, 191
   of intrinsic properties, 192
   of laws, 174, 185
   of mind and cognition, 11
   of nature, 113, 116, 118, 119
   of powers, 12, 195, 204
   of properties, 116, 117
     categorical, 199
     dispositional, 199
   of relations, 111, 112, 114–117, 119, 120, 191, 192, 199
     categorical, 194, 199
     dispositional, 199
   pluralistic, 53, 155, 161
Mill, John S., 174
Milne, Peter, 30
Minkovski, Hermann, 198

Molnar, George, 149, 151, 154–156, 158, 160, 162, 197, 236–240, 243, 244, 248, 249
Moore, George E., 218
Mulligan, Kevin, 33
multiple realisation, 12, 16–19, 44, 47, 53, 54, 61, 64, 68, 70, 91, 93, 96–99, 107, 153, 170, 209, 210
Mumford, Stephen, 143, 144, 147, 148, 150–154, 159–162, 164, 167, 174, 183, 185, 186, 195, 197

Neale, Stephen, 34
Noë, Alva, 223
nomological machine, 184–186
Norton, John, 118, 192

objects, 19, 21, 22, 33, 36, 39, 42, 48–51, 56–72, 75–89, 109, 112–115, 117, 118, 120–122, 124–126, 130, 131, 136, 139–141, 147, 150, 154, 165, 171, 172, 175–178, 180, 181, 183–187, 189, 190, 192, 198, 207–209, 213–220, 223, 224, 227–229, 232, 237, 242, 246, 249
   as bundles of properties, 79, 111, 113, 176
   as modes, 87, 208
   as substances, 68
   as substrata, 68
   bare, 36
   basic, *see* fundamental
   complex, 21, 76, 77, 80–84, 86–88, 190
   concrete, 169, 232
   distal, 223, 227, 230

fundamental, 69, 78, 79, 81–83, 87, 113, 114
higher-level, 59, 68
intentional, 237–240, 247
physical, 36, 38, 39
simple, 69
Occam's razor, 113
ontological seriousness, 11, 12, 15, 18, 19, 24–27, 47, 112, 119, 175, 191
ontology, 13, 15, 18, 21, 25–27, 40, 44, 48, 56, 69, 75, 76, 78, 80, 85, 86, 88, 109, 111, 112, 116, 119, 120, 122, 151, 154, 159, 160, 162, 176, 180–182, 186, 187, 191–209, 230, 238
and epistemology, 89, 122, 141, 176, 186
dualistic, 155, 160
eliminativist, 77
layered, 48, 51, 54, 55, 58
monistic, 48, 53, 56, 68, 76, 166
O'Reagan, Kevin, 223
overdetermination, 37, 52, 68, 152, 200

panpsychism, 151, 240
Pargetter, Robert, 170
parsimony, 27, 75, 76, 84, 113, 114, 145, 193, 194, 199
partial consideration, *see* abstraction
parts
spatial, 69, 192
temporal, 191, 192
Pfeifer, Karl, 237, 240, 241
phenomenalism, 30, 37, 39, 40
physicalism, 201, 205, 209
a priori, 203
reductive, 12, 191, 200, 201
physics, 12, 49, 55–58, 64, 68, 92–98, 101, 102, 105–107, 113, 118, 121, 122, 133, 174, 182, 183, 197, 199, 205, 207, 232, 242
basic, *see* fundamental
completeness of, 51, 68, 91, 93–95, 98, 105, 182, 191
fundamental, 17, 50, 51, 58, 71, 91, 109, 112, 115, 122, 183, 191, 200, 201, 205, 209–211, 249
general relativity, 114, 115, 118, 120, 192, 193, 197, 198
quantum, 18, 25, 93, 114, 121, 192, 193, 198, 207
special relativity, 192
Picasso, Pablo, 214
Picture Theory, 18, 30, 47, 48, 50, 55–58, 71, 76, 77, 79, 81, 86, 87, 116, 117, 119, 122, 126, 144–149, 152, 154, 155, 158, 160, 163, 165, 167, 175, 176, 208, 229
Pineda, David, 64
Place, Ullin T., 16, 151, 237, 238, 243, 244, 247
positivism, 39, 40
predicates, 18, 19, 32, 33, 38, 44, 48–50, 53, 55, 57–62, 64–68, 70, 72, 73, 88, 109, 110, 116, 130, 132, 134, 135, 160, 161, 190, 209–211, 229, 249
and properties, 11, 18, 30, 44, 48, 57, 71, 87, 109, 122, 126, 131, 145, 160, 193
basic, *see* fundamental

categorical, 195
dispositional, 195
functional, 209
fundamental, 44, 57, 72
higher-level, 19, 51, 56, 60, 64, 65, 68, 71, 72, 77, 210, 211
higher-order, 49, 54, 57
homogeneous, 70
indeterminate, 152
mental, 20, 109
multiply applying, 61
physical, 109, 110, 209, 210
psychological, 19
relational, 146
single, 16, 49, 50, 58
Prior, Elisabeth, 170
projectability, 53, 54
properties, 11–13, 17–21, 44, 48–53, 55–62, 64–69, 71, 75–88, 109–113, 116, 121–127, 130, 131, 134–137, 139, 144–148, 150–153, 155–166, 169–172, 175, 177–181, 183, 185, 189–192, 194, 198, 204, 206, 207, 213–217, 219–222, 224, 228–230, 232, 241, 243, 249
   and predicates, *see* predicates and properties
   as particulars, 75, 76, 79, 80, 82, 87, 175
   as powers, 117, 121, 147, 153, 155, 159, 172
   as qualities, 172, 176, 232
   as universals, 27, 75, 76, 78, 79, 125, 149, 176, 181, 189
   basic, *see* fundamental
   biological, 75, 78, 200, 201, 204, 209
   bundles of, 75, 79, 111, 176
   categorical, 11, 12, 75–77, 123, 124, 136, 139, 143, 149, 155–158, 161, 163, 165, 169, 170, 173, 174, 177, 180, 183, 186, 191, 193–197, 201, 204, 205, 214, 224, 227, 232, 238
   chemical, 200, 209
   complex, 12, 65, 75–78, 80–86, 88, 210
   compositional, 242
   conditional, 15
   disjunctive, 15, 54
   dispositional, 11, 12, 67, 76, 77, 83, 111, 116, 123–127, 130, 132, 133, 135, 136, 139–141, 143, 156–161, 163, 169, 170, 173, 174, 177, 180, 183, 186, 191, 193, 195–197, 204, 205, 232, 238
   emergent, 242
   extrinsic, 83, 84, 144, 146, 148, 149, 165, 229
   first-order, 11, 181
   functional, 54, 201, 204, 205
   fundamental, 59, 62, 64, 66, 67, 75, 76, 78, 80, 81, 83, 85, 86, 133, 134, 193, 204
   genuine, 53, 67, 77, 82, 83
   hierarchies of, 21, 30, 31
   higher-level, 17–20, 37, 49, 51–53, 58, 60, 75–78, 81, 83–85, 125, 152, 170, 181, 183, 209
   higher-order, 49, 52
   homogeneous, 49–51
   Humean, 193–200
   immaterial, 17
   intentional, 216, 217, 239

intrinsic, 12, 22, 67, 83, 84, 111, 113–115, 117–122, 125, 132, 133, 144, 146–150, 155–157, 159–161, 165, 177, 182, 191–194, 201, 208, 217, 219, 229
  lower-level, 49, 52, 53
  mental, 17, 75, 77, 78, 83, 85, 200, 201, 204, 205, 209, 217, 218, 239
  modal, 80, 181
  multiply based, 54
  multiply realised, 17, 54, 61, 85
  neurobiological, 213, 228
  non-compositional, 242, 243
  non-representational, 216, 218
  of experiences, 214–216, 218
  of objects experienced, 214–216
  phenomenal, 216
  physical, 17, 49, 51, 52, 60, 67, 77, 109, 110, 194, 198, 200, 204
    fundamental, 12, 52, 76, 135, 192, 194–197, 199, 200, 203, 204
    micro-, 78
  powerful, *see* dispositional
  qualitative, *see* categorical
  realising, 16–17, 54, 185
  relational, 113, 117, 162, 191–193
  representational, 216–218, 220–222, 229
  second-order, 11, 158, 203
  secondary, 162
  semi-compositional, 242
  sparse, 85, 145
propositions, 11, 15, 22–24, 31, 32, 34, 35, 44, 237

Psillos, Stathis, 149, 184, 185
Putnam, Hilary, 16, 23, 162

qualia, 13, 77, 214–217, 222
  functional, 206
  intrinsic, 216, 229
  non-representational, 213, 216, 221, 222, 226, 230
  representational, 13, 217
quidditism, 146, 158
quiddity, 155, 159
Quine, Willard V.O., 11

Ramsey sentence, 133
Ramsey, Franck P., 133, 174
realism, 13, 19, 71, 72, 91, 92, 106, 144, 150, 154, 155, 159, 160, 162, 163, 166, 167, 174, 187, 195
  anti-, 171
  as mind independence, 159, 167
  dispositional, 143–167, 169
  modal, 173, 175, 178, 181–182, 186
  nomological, 174
  pure, 55, 56, 68
  qualitative, 163, 166
  relational, 146, 165
  relativistic, 160–162, 167
  scientific, 49
  space-time, 118
  structural, 12, 111–114, 118–120, 192, 193
Redhead, Michael, 197
reductionism, 12, 55, 68, 165, 166, 191, 200–206, 209
  conservative, 13, 55, 107, 191, 204
  eliminativist, 13

epistemological, 12, 91–107, 202
ontological, 11–13, 55, 68, 91, 92, 95, 105, 106, 201, 202
Reichenbach, Hans, 39, 40
relations
    as constitutive, 113–115, 117, 121, 148, 155
    as fundamental, 111, 195, 199
    as nessecitation, 177
    as properties, 113
    categorical, 155, 194
    causal, 19, 20, 30, 134, 137, 139, 147, 200, 227, 249
    counterfactual, 133
    dispositions as, 111, 125
    first-order, 132
    fundamental, 114, 115
    higher-level, 20
    inter-level, 37, 52, 56
    lawlike, 54, 136, 180, 226
    material, 114
    metric, 192
    natural, 146
    necessary, 133, 135
    of entanglement, 192, 198
    of necessitation, 22
    physical, 195, 199
    pure, 12, 111, 116, 121, 122
    second-order, 181, 189
    similarity, 54, 58, 59, 61, 62, 68, 70
    spatio-temporal, 114, 118, 119, 194, 197, 198
    without relata, 112
representationalism, 213, 215–222, 230
    strong, 216
    weak, 216

Rimini, Alberto, 198, 199
Robb, David, 77, 83
Rosenberg, Alexander, 100
Rovelli, Carlo, 115
Russell, Bertrand, 197, 205
Ryle, Gilbert, 30, 37, 38, 40, 41, 144, 151

Saunders, Simon, 118
schemes
    conceptual, 13, 160, 161, 163–165
    dispositional, *see* conceptual
    disquotational, 32, 33
    qualitative, *see* conceptual
    reductive, 59
    relativistic, 160
Schrödinger, Erwin, 198
science, 19, 88, 89, 121, 173, 176, 182, 183, 189, 191, 200
    empirical, 79, 85, 112, 179
    physical, *see* physics
    social, 85
    special, 17, 18, 20, 21, 44, 47, 72, 77, 78, 80, 81, 85, 86, 88, 91–107, 122, 133, 209
Searle, John, 35
Shoemaker, Sidney, 146, 156, 173, 176–178, 180, 181, 204
Shoemaker, Sydney, 179, 195
similarity, 19, 48, 54, 55, 58–68, 70–73, 85, 86, 128, 130, 135, 190, 192
    as internal relation, 71
    imperfect, 59, 61–63, 65, 71, 72, 210
    objective, 71
    partial, 59, 61

perfect, 58, 59, 61, 62, 71, 72
primitive, 58, 59, 85, 135
qualitative, 135
Simons, Peter, 33
Slingshot argument, 34
Smart, John J.C., 16
Smith, Barry, 33
space-time, 16, 35, 79, 87, 114, 115, 117–120, 132, 135, 190, 192–199, 203, 207, 208
Spinoza, Baruch, 16, 26, 88, 114, 115, 122, 169, 171, 207, 208
Stachel, John, 118
states
    categorical, 153
    conscious, 214, 241, 246
    dispositional, 241
    functional, 152, 153
    fundamental, 63, 64
    higher-level, 64, 68, 221
    intentional, 149, 151, 235–238, 240, 241, 245, 249, 250
    molecular, 63
    neurological, 18, 19, 37, 77, 201, 228
    non-representational, 248
    of affairs, 21–23, 33, 35, 39, 43, 147, 238, 240
    of mind, 16, 17, 19, 59, 77, 235–237, 239, 243, 244, 248
    perceptual, 214–218, 227, 233
    physical, 77, 160, 228, 237, 239
    quantum, 198
    representational, 13, 221, 227, 235, 248
sub-concepts, 93, 99, 101, 103–107, 202, 210
substances, *see* objects

substantivalism, 114, 115, 118
supervenience, 22, 31, 52, 70, 81, 132, 149, 165, 178, 194, 197, 203, 215, 217, 227–229, 242, 249
Swampman, 249
Swinburne, Richard, 155, 157, 165

Tarski, Alfred, 43
Tooley, Michael, 173
totality fact, 32, 35
truthmaking, 11, 12, 16, 21–23, 29–31, 33–37, 39, 42–45, 48, 49, 201
    and entailment, 31, 32, 35
    principle, 30, 38, 40, 41, 43, 44, 132, 144, 148, 149, 154, 161
Tuomela, Raimo, 147, 160
TVSS, 222–227, 230–233
Tye, Michael, 216

universals, *see* properties as universals

Vallentyne, Peter, 83
van Fraassen, Bas, 134, 174

Wasserman, Ryan, 127, 137
Weber, Tullio, 198, 199
Wittgenstein, Ludwig, 19, 23, 72

Notes on contributors

John Heil is professor of philosophy at Washington University, St. Louis (Missouri), and Monash University, Melbourne. His main areas of research are metaphysics and the philosophy of mind.
http://www.artsci.wustl.edu/~philos/people.php?lookup=heil.html
jh@wustl.edu

Michael Esfeld is professor of epistemology and philosophy of science at the University of Lausanne. His main areas of research are the metaphysics of science, in particular the philosophy of physics, and the philosophy of mind.
http://www2.unil.ch/philo/Pages/epistemologie/bio_cv_esfeld/Home_esfeld.html
Michael-Andreas.Esfeld@unil.ch

Laurent Freland is working on a PhD Thesis on the ontology of dispositions at the University of Geneva in the PhD programme of the Centre romand for logic, history & philosophy of science.
laurent.freland@tele2.fr

Simon Friederich is studying physics and philosophy at the University of Göttingen and at the Swiss Federal Institute of Technology in Lausanne.
simmarich@web.de

Jens Harbecke did a Master in Philosophy at King's College, London, and is now working on a PhD thesis on the metaphysics of causation, events and properties at the University of Lausanne in the PhD programme of the Centre romand for logic, history & philosophy of science.
http://www2.unil.ch/philo/Pages/epistemologie/home_harbecke.html
Jens.Harbecke@unil.ch

Vera Hoffmann is working on a PhD thesis on the metaphysics of causation at the University of Tübingen. She is visiting fellow of the Centre romand for logic, history & philosophy of science.
http://www.uni-tuebingen.de/selbstbewusstsein/hlink.html
vera.hoffmann@uni-tuebingen.de

Marc Aurel Hunziker is studying philosophy and neurobiology at the University of Fribourg and will start a PhD thesis on free will at the University of Lausanne in the PhD programme of the Centre romand for logic, history & philosophy of science.

marcaurel@mails.ch

Vincent Lam studied mathematics and physics at the Swiss Federal Institute of Technology in Lausanne and is now working on a PhD thesis on the philosophy of space-time at the University of Lausanne in the PhD programme of the Centre romand for logic, history & philosophy of science.

http://www2.unil.ch/philo/Pages/epistemologie/Home_lam.html
Vincent.Lam@unil.ch

Flavia Padovani is working on a PhD thesis on probability and causality in the young Reichenbach at the University of Geneva in the PhD programme of the Centre romand for logic, history & philosophy of science.

flavia.padovani@lettres.unige.ch

Christian Sachse studied philosophy and biology at the University of Cologne and is now writing a PhD thesis on reductionism at the University of Lausanne in the PhD programme of the Centre romand for logic, history & philosophy of science.

http://www2.unil.ch/philo/Pages/epistemologie/home_sachse.html
Christian.Sachse@unil.ch

Michael Sollberger is studying philosophy and neurobiology at the University of Fribourg and will start a PhD thesis on representationalism at the University of Lausanne in the PhD programme of the Centre romand for logic, history & philosophy of science.

http://www.unifr.ch/philo/modern-contemporary/sollberger
michael.sollberger@unifr.ch

Georg Sparber is working on a PhD thesis on the metaphysics of dispositions, laws and causation at the University of Lausanne in the PhD programme of the Centre romand for logic, history & philosophy of science.

http://www2.unil.ch/philo/Pages/epistemologie/home_sparber.html
Georg.Sparber@unil.ch

Giovanni Tuzet wrote his PhD Thesis on Peirce at the University of Paris XII. He teaches philosophy of law at the Bocconi University of Milan and is postdoctoral fellow of the Centre romand for logic, history & philosophy of science.

giovanni.tuzet@unibocconi.it

Metaphysical Research

Edited by Uwe Meixner • Johanna Seibt • Barry Smith • Daniel von Wachter

Band 1
Klaus Petrus (Ed.)
On Human Persons
ISBN 3-937202-31-5
Paperback, 214 pp., EUR 26,00

Band 2
André Zdunek
Ontologie, Wahrheit und Kausalität
Ontologische Theorien der Kausalität vor dem Hintergrund der Verteidigung von Ontologie als Kategorienlehre
ISBN 3-937202-35-8
Hardcover, 276 Seiten EUR 45,00

Band 3
Gerhard Schönrich (Hrsg.)
Institutionen und ihre Ontologie
ISBN 3-937202-75-7
Hardcover, 332 Seiten, EUR 49,00

Band 4
Richard Swinburne
Gibt es einen Gott?
Aus dem engl. übersetzt von Carl Thormann
ISBN 3-937202-91-9
ontos taschenbuch, 158 Seiten, EUR 14,90

Band 5
William P. Alston
Gott wahrnehmen
Die Erkenntnistheorie religiöser Erfahrung
Übersetzt von Björn Bordon und Hendrik Udvari
ISBN 3-937202-66-8
Paperback, 385 Seiten, EUR 39,00

ontos verlag

Frankfurt I Paris I Ebikon I Lancaster I New Brunswick

P.O. Box 15 41
63133 Heusenstamm bei Frankfurt
www.ontosverlag.com
info@ontosverlag.com

www.ingramcontent.com/pod-product-compliance
Lightning Source LLC
Chambersburg PA
CBHW040741300426
44111CB00027B/2998